Meridians feminism, race, transn___

VOLUME 23 · NUMBER 2 · OCTOBER 2024

SPECIAL ISSUE
Counterpoints

EDITOR'S INTRODUCTION
Ginetta E. B. Candelario · 297

IN THE TRENCHES
Feminist Development Justice as Emancipatory Praxis:
Recognizing the Knowledge of Social Movements "From Below"
Nasha Mohamed, Sutapa Chattopadhyay, and Levi Gahman · 306

COUNTERPOINT
Consumption as Changemaking and Producers as Artists:
Theorizing Alt-Profit Corporations from a Transnational
Feminist Perspective
Debjani Chakravarty and Christine Standish · 332

ESSAY
The Unforgetting of Claribel Alegría: Reckoning with Capitalist
Catastrophe in El Salvador
Guadalupe Escobar · 360

RESPONSE
Response to Kuokkanen: On Structural Violence, Bad Faith, and Strategic
Ignorance in Norwegian Wind Power Development
Henrikke Sæthre Ellingsen · 384

ESSAY
"Enhancing Human Dignity Here and Around the World": The Black
Sorority as International Uplift Movement
Aisha A. Upton Azzam · 392

COUNTERPOINT
De-naming: Unraveling the Sex-Skin and Gender-Mask Technologies
in the Colonial Naming Structure
Chia-Hsu Jessica Chang · 417

IN THE TRENCHES

Colectiva Feminista en Construcción: Building a Transnational
Feminist Pedagogy
Aurora Santiago Ortiz · 439

ESSAY

Coming Out for Community, Coming Out for the Cause: Queer Arab
American Activism in the 1990s
Umayyah Cable · 465

INTERVIEW

Within and Outside the Black-Maghrebi Binary: A Conversation
with Maha Abdelhamid
Shreya Parikh · 490

MEMOIR

According to the Record
Lisa E. Wright · 510

POETRY

Catalog of Writings Left by Chinese Railroad Laborers
of the CPRR and "唔需 (No Need)"
Caroline M. Mar · 523

POETRY

Maric★★★
Ming Li (Ari) Wu · 525

ESSAY

Beyond Black Girlhood: An Underground Railroad to Nowhere
Chamara Moore · 528

ELIZABETH ALEXANDER CREATIVE WRITING AWARD 2024 WINNER FOR PROSE

The Ice Seller of Hell
Maryam Ala Amjadi · 548

ARTIST STATEMENT

For Those of Us Who Live at the Shoreline
La Vaughn Belle · 566

ERRATA

Erratum
Dia Da Costa · 568

Erratum
Elena Ruiz · 568

Ginetta E. B. Candelario

Editor's Introduction

[*Meridians*] will provide a critical forum for conversations between feminists of color, enabling women to build bridges between one another's work, to forge links across different generations, and to make connections among our institutional and social locations.
—Smith-Wesleyan Editorial Group, vol. 1, no. 1, fall 2000

The time has come to end systems of governance that are beholden to principles of capitalism, rooted in Western thought, driven by neoliberal logics, and that continue to exploit and oppress women and negatively racialized communities.
—Nasha Mohamed, Sutapa Chattopadhyay, and Levi Gahman

In the introduction to the first *Meridians* issue, published in the fall of 2000, readers were informed by the Smith-Wesleyan founding editorial collective that what they called "Counterpoints" would be one of several regularly recurring features in future issues. They conceptualized this feature thus:

Counterpoints initiates a self-conscious examination of the analytical and political vocabulary of the fields in which feminists work. Our first conversation with five members of our founding advisory board examines the meanings that the terms of the journal's subtitle have for them, particularly as geography and generation transform the meanings of race and feminism. Future symposia may interrogate other key words, now emerging or already established in various discourses, as well as elaborate on the history and contemporary usefulness of particular terms in making theory and doing

MERIDIANS · feminism, race, transnationalism   23:2 October 2024
DOI: 10.1215/15366936-11367024 © 2024 Smith College

politics. If such a public forum fosters productive disagreement or even con-
troversy, *Meridians* will have advanced its goal of enlarging the public arena
for conversations among women of color. (Smith-Wesleyan Editorial Group
2000: xii)

As I read through the contents of the present issue, I realized that every
piece indeed offers "a self-conscious examination of the analytical and
political vocabulary" of the wide-ranging disciplinary, discursive, temporal, archival, activist, and geographic fields the authors engage. In addition, each piece illustrates exemplary deployment of both conventional
and innovative qualitative methods, as well as conventional and idiosyn-
cratic archives, subjects, and texts. Thus, although only some of the pieces
are explicitly labeled "Counterpoint" features, together they also form a
"combination of two or more melodies into a harmony in which each keeps
its own identity."[1] The result is that this issue offers a *Meridians* community
chorus of authors who are committed to lending their polyphonic intersectional feminist voices to the cause of restorative and redistributive
justice.

We open the issue with "Feminist Development Justice as Emancipatory
Praxis: Recognizing the Knowledge of Social Movements 'From Below'" by
Nasha Mohamed, Sutapa Chattopadhyay, and Levi Gahman. This "In the
Trenches" piece presents the principles of "feminist development justice"
articulated by grassroots social movements of the Global South "that are
decidedly anti-capitalist, anti-imperialist, and anti-patriarchal" counterpoints to "'modern' development programs [that] are inextricably linked to
the enduring colonial order of the . . . global (capitalist) economy." These
principles have been at the center of the global organizing efforts of Asian
Pacific Forum on Women, Law, and Development (APWLD), an independent transnational feminist organization born of the 1985 Third World
Forum on Women held in Nairobi, Kenya. For nearly forty years, the
APWLD has initiated multiple organizing campaigns that build the local
capacity of "systematically marginalized groups, in particular women,
across a range of Asia-Pacific geographies" to "effect justice, promote
equality, and defend human rights" from below, that is, at the grassroots
and community level. To that end, the APWLD has magnified the voices of
women from the "Majority World" who demand "an economy that puts the
dignity of people at its heart and represents a call to arms for feminist
people-centered economies in which local communities have sovereignty

and decision-making power over the means of production/distribution" (Mohamed, Chattopadhyay, and Gahman, this issue).

In "Consumption as Changemaking and Producers as Artists: Theorizing Alt-Profit Corporations from a Transnational Feminist Perspective," the sociologists Debjani Chakravarty and Christine Standish document how transnational corporations have attempted to co-opt precisely the kind of critical socio-economic-justice projects that would center the needs of craftswomen and artisanal makers from the "Majority World." Chakravarty and Standish's "Counterpoint" coins the term *alt-profit* and undertakes a critical analysis of the "McDonalized" rhetorical strategies deployed by twelve Global North–based transnational corporations. These alt-profit-driven companies market "compassionate consumption" as altruistic support for women from the Global South who support themselves, their families, and their communities through small-scale production, while deflecting attention away from the inherently exploitative nature of production-consumption relations in a hierarchically organized geopolitical landscape. For example, the authors note that the consumers pictured on these companies' websites are largely white, middle-class to upper-middle-class women from the Global North who exemplify Western femininity, while the producers are largely "nonwhite women . . . dressed in local or 'traditional' attire" and pictured in groups. These visual strategies exemplify and reify the implicitly naturalized and depoliticized racial and classed nature of gendered compassionate consumption purveyed by the alt-profit companies that Chakravarty and Standish study. They argue that alt-profit-based companies "create and contribute to neoliberal ideologies of individual responsibility and economic efficiency of free trade without holding social structures (governmental, economic, epistemological, and technological, to name a few) accountable."

Reckoning with the legacies of the social harm wrought by the interrelated forces of global capitalism, imperialism, and patriarchy is the focus of "The Unforgetting of Claribel Alegría: Reckoning with Capitalist Catastrophe in El Salvador" by Guadalupe Escobar. Escobar's piece is a counterpointal literary analysis of two of Alegría's texts, a *testimonio* and a novel, which according to Escobar expose "the entanglements of state terror and foreign interests" in racialized and gendered capitalist globalization processes through a critique of local coffee production regimes and the intimate apparel industry in the latter half of the twentieth century. Alegría's texts also "illuminate rationales for radicalism" and for Salvadoran peasant and Indigenous women's extensive participation in revolutionary struggles. Moreover, Escobar argues that the novel *Ashes of Izalco* and the testimonio *They Won't Take Me Alive* act "as narrative acts of 'unforgetting'" that enable "confronting traumatic histories, uncovering international economic conditions, and rethinking memory practices" more broadly.

The challenges of remaining critically attuned to the bad-faith strategies of capitalists pursuing their interests is addressed in Henrikke Ellingsen's "Response to Kuokkanen: On Structural Violence, Bad Faith, and Strategic Ignorance in Norwegian Wind Power Development." This "Response" to Ruana Kuokkanen's essay—"Are Reindeer the New Buffalo? Climate Change, the Green Shift, and Manifest Destiny in Sápmi"—which was published in our "BIPOC Europe" special issue (vol. 22, no. 1, spring 2023), is a first for *Meridians*. I decided to publish it because, in keeping with this issue's "Counterpoint" theme, Ellingsen acknowledges the validity of Kuokkanen's critique and took this opportunity to reflect on and critically look at what kind of colonial narrative she contributed to by using certain terms that were not in line with her intentions and moreover contributed to the colonial narrative she herself is critical of. Likewise, Aisha Upton Azzam's analysis of the Black sorority movement's international activism in "Enhancing Human Dignity Here and Around the World" shows "how such activism may have also implicitly employed the very neoliberal, neocolonial, and patriarchal ideals and practices the BSM explicitly stated they wished to resist and overturn."

The "always already" present impossibility of escape from paradigmatic dehumanization for those who accept the terms and terminology of the colonizers is carefully unspooled in "De-naming: Unraveling the Sex-Skin and Gender-Mask Technologies in the Colonial Naming Structure." Chia-Hsu Jessica Chang begins this piece by taking up "Sylvia Wynter's interpretation of Frantz Fanon's" theorization of the "'white mask' as a cultural technology" of racialization, along with María Lugones's theorization of the coloniality of gender, to elucidate how "sex and gender [operate] as two cultural technologies that co-constitute a structure *isomorphic* to the colored-skin/white-mask structure." She then "examines how the colonizer's cultural technologies and the colonial naming structure impact the gender politics of third-world state feminists" by considering the case of Taiwan. In that context, state feminists' agendas, discourse, and ideologies about domestic and sex workers exemplify the irredeemably dehumanizing premise of modernity's terms and techniques. Chia-Hsu argues that truly liberatory feminism pursues a "*de-naming* process to resist dehumanizing labels. . . . The 'de' in 'de-naming' seeks decoloniality that uproots colonial meanings that sentence us to symbolic death."

Aurora Santiago Ortiz's "Colectiva Feminista en Construcción: Building a Transnational Feminist Pedagogy" documents a Black Puerto Rican feminist political organization's decade of transnational activism against sexism, racism, and homophobia on the island using strategies that undertake the sort of "de-naming" that Chia-Hsu posits is central to decoloniality. La Cole, as the Colectiva Feminista is known to its members, utilizes creative strategies to educate elected/appointed officials and the general public about its decolonial agenda's aims and desired outcomes, and to decolonize their own practice and thinking. This pedagogical agenda is rooted in the insights into the complex nature of oppression and exploitation, as well as successful liberation strategies, offered by radical traditions of social justice in the Americas such as the Black Panthers, the Young Lords, the Combahee River Collective, Krenshaw's theorization of intersectionality, the Ejército Zapatista de Liberación Nacional, and the Movement for Black Lives, in addition to Marxist and decolonial feminisms. Santiago Ortiz utilizes feminist participatory action methods to document how La Cole deploys a "double pedagogy [that] operates on two levels: internally, as part of its members' political education and development, and externally, by reshaping Puerto Rico's public sphere." Through creative strategies such as changing the lyrics of popular songs and ditties that often normalize misogynist and racist violence to promote the group's position on issues such as reproductive justice, transphobia, and feminicide during more conventional protest actions, La Cole subverts cultural norms using culturally appropriate vehicles.

The polyvocality historically required to effectively demand recognition and rights within the multiple identity-based communities we belong to when we do/cannot conform to their norms is clear in "Coming Out for Community, Coming Out for the Cause: Queer Arab American Activism in the 1990s" by Umayyah Cable. This essay analyzes Palestinian American lesbian activist Huda Jadallah's tripartite project of building a queer Arab American community, contesting Arab American homophobia, and addressing anti-Arab racism within queer communities as a counterpoint to hegemonic notions of "outness." Cable's rendering of Jadallah's activism is a "dual outing process" that counters the colonialist nature of the "outness paradigm" and its attendant reification of hegemonic gender, class, ethno-racial and sexual identities, while also "strategically utiliz[ing] outness to subvert the politics of cultural authenticity . . . which . . . constructs gender and sexual transgressions as a threat to Arab American identity." Utilizing qualitative methods such as open-ended interviewing, archival research, discourse analysis, and visual analysis, Cable offers an innovative contribution to multiple historiographies: Arab American, queer of color, lesbian feminist, and social movements, to name but a few.

Similarly, in our Interview feature, "Within and outside the Black-Maghrebi Binary: A Conversation with Maha Abdelhamid," sociologist Shreya Parikh's interlocutor explains how her work addresses anti-Muslim and anti-Black racism in France, Tunisia, and the Tunisian diaspora in France. According to Parikh, Dr. Abdelhamid's experience as a Black Muslim Tunisian feminist scholar engaged in anti-racist activism in both Tunisia and France not only informs her work as a scholar, social worker, filmmaker, and organizer but also highlights how anti-Blackness operates in Global South contexts such as North Africa/the Maghreb and its diaspora, where "Arab and Muslim . . . [is] antonymous to the category of Black." Thus, as is often the case with those of us who do not embody the "typical type" held to be representative of our multiple identities, Abdelhamid has distanced herself from both Black and Maghrebi feminist groups that see and respond to her as Other. This "disturbing and discomforting" pattern leads Abdelhamid to critique the lack of "intersectionality in the work of the marginalized feminist groups in France," while also constructing a Black political identity rooted in the salience of her embodied experience of anti-Blackness across geographies, communities, and languages.

Along the same lines, if in an entirely different place and time, "According to the Record," Lisa E. Wright's memoir, offers a microhistory that illustrates broader historical patterns in Black women's experiences of and attitudes toward giving birth under shifting Jim Crow medical regimes. Wright's extended analysis of a single document—her grandmother's 1938 West Virginia birth certificate—illuminates how seemingly mundane particulars, such as who exactly attended her great-grandmother's labor and delivery—a Black midwife or a white male medical doctor—make visible the racial, gender, and class structures that determine life-and-death outcomes for Black women and their families. As Wright's account makes clear, although many decades and well-established legislation separated her own positive labor and delivery experiences and those of her great-grandmother and grandmother, Black women's labor and delivery experiences continue to be of higher risk of death and/or injury for both mother and child because of systemic racism.

Going further back in time, poet Caroline M. Mar's "Catalogue of Writings Left by Chinese Railroad Laborers of the CPRR" offers another innovative intervention/correction to the state's official record. Mar's poem draws attention to the fact that there is little, if any, documentation of the experiences of the thousands of Chinese men who not only built the Central Pacific Railroad in the mid-nineteenth century, but lent their engineering and technical expertise to the task of blasting and bridge building alike. In addition to the inevitable injuries ranging from commonplace to incapacitating to deadly, these workers were also subject to equally destructive Sinophobic violence. Mar utterly effectively uses square brackets that enclose blank space where presumably words should be, but are not. According to grammarist.com, there are seven rules for the use of square brackets:

1. Use brackets to clarify nouns and pronouns in a quote that are unclear . . .
2. Use brackets to translate a foreign word or phrase in a quote . . .
3. Use brackets to indicate the change of the first letter of quoted material from uppercase to lowercase or vice versa . . .
4. Use brackets surrounding the Latin term *sic*, meaning "thus" or "so," to indicate an error or unusual word usage in a quote. This indicates the original writer included the error . . .
5. Use brackets to indicate when you change a quote to emphasize a specific portion of the passage . . .
6. Use brackets to censor any inappropriate materials found in the original text . . .
7. Use brackets inside parentheses to replace parentheses inside parentheses . . .[2]

Each of the appropriate uses that these rules set out indicates the many ways that Chinese railroad laborers were subjected to racist violence that ran the gamut from discursive, psychological, symbolic, structural, and physical. To add insult to injury, they were also subsequently subjected to archival, historiographic, and epistemic violence in that their stories were systematically distorted, erased, discarded, or overlooked.

Like Mar's, Ming Li (Ari) Wu's poem "Maric***" uses punctuation innovatively to signal the significance of that which is not uttered yet is conveyed clearly. Wu's title signals the overlap between their Puerto Rican childhood names and the Spanish-language homophobic slur that is equal parts dissonant and dissociative when mouthed in their mother tongue. Wu's (counter)pointed play on words signals how their "non-binary mouth" offers a refuge, a solace, an anchor, and ultimately, a euphonious response to the contradictions they embody. They are at home in, of, and with themselves, much like the figure in our cover art by La Vaughn Belle. According to the artist, For Those of Us Who Live at the Shoreline is inspired by Audre Lorde's poem, "A Litany for Survival" and beautifully "explores the relationship between the body, landscape, history, and memory."

In a similar vein, Chamara Moore's "Beyond Black Girlhood: An Underground Railroad to Nowhere" argues that Cora, a protagonist of Colson Whitehead's award-winning novel The Underground Railroad, is a character whose story illustrates "the ways Speculative fiction allows Black writers to inject narratives regarding allegories of freedom and liberation into more traditional genres like the Bildungsroman." Unlike the white/Eurocentric subjects typical of Bildungsroman, Moore argues that because Cora makes herself into her own means to freedom—the underground railroad's railway—Whitehead's novel interrogates what "coming of age" means for Black girls who are "historically barred from both the categories of 'girlhood' and human."

Finally, we close the issue with this year's Elizabeth Alexander Creative Writing Award winner for prose, "The Ice Seller of Hell" by Maryam Ala Amjadi. This short story centers the perspectives of an Iranian college student as she navigates not only the desecularization of her society but also austerity measures adopted by the government in response to the US-led economic sanctions, and the gendered impact of their combined consequences. The Creative Writing Advisory Board described this story as "striking and shocking and so utterly relatable all at the same time" and a "masterful balance of the spectacular and the mundane." Amjadi's skill as a storyteller lies in her ability to flesh out her protagonist's particular perspective while subtly offering a clear picture of the life-and-death stakes for young, intellectually engaged women navigating a historically cosmopolitan society currently operating under a sectarian regime. The day she narrates allows us to accompany her through co-ed university classrooms and campus fields; upscale bohemian cafes and flirtations with potential "sex sans courtship" crushes; hideaways in the park suitable for a smoke break and "the labyrinthine pages" of a twelfth-century Persian romance; crowded public transportation and the neighborhood store rationing women's sanitary products; and finally, the sanctuary of her own bedroom and naked body. In sum, "The Ice Seller of Hell" offers especially poignant insight into the context of Jina Mahsa Amini's death as a result of the beatings she was subjected to while in the custody of Iran's Gasht-e Ershad (morality police) in September of 2022, and of the women-led protests against the regime she inspired. They came together across ethnicity, religion, and language under one slogan chanted in Azeria, Balochi, Persian, and its original Kurdish: "Jin, Jiyan, Azadî." Women, Life, Freedom.[3]

Notes

1   Merriam-Webster.com Dictionary, s.v. "counterpoint," https://www.merriam -webster.com/dictionary/counterpoint (accessed March 17, 2024).

2   Danielle Macleod, "When to Use Square Brackets [. . .]—With Examples," *Grammarist*, https://grammarist.com/punctuation/square-brackets/ (accessed March 5, 2024).

3   "Death of Jina Mahsa Amini, Iranian Citizen," Britannica online, https://www .britannica.com/biography/death-of-Jina-Mahsa-Amini (accessed March 18, 2024); Adam Zeidan, "Woman, Life, Freedom," *Britannica* online, https:// britannica.com/topic/Woman-Life-Freedom (accessed March 18, 2024).

Work Cited

Smith-Wesleyan Editorial Group. 2000. Introduction to *Meridians* 1, no. 1: ix–xv. https://doi.org/10.1215/15366936-1.1.ix.

Nasha Mohamed, Sutapa Chattopadhyay, and Levi Gahman

Feminist Development Justice as Emancipatory Praxis
Recognizing the Knowledge of Social Movements "From Below"

Abstract: This article offers a comprehensive overview of feminist development justice, a transformative framework designed to reduce global inequalities that is being advanced by the Asia Pacific Forum on Women, Law, and Development (APWLD). The piece aims to unsettle and expand mainstream development studies literature, which critical scholars argue remains plagued by Eurocentrism and ongoing colonial modes of knowledge production. Additionally, it advocates for more recognition and citation of the grassroots analysis and frontline praxis of progressive social movements in the Global South that are guided by emancipatory politics and feminist ethics. We begin with a synopsis of development studies' lack of attention to the enduring consequences of race, colonial power, and imperialism, as well as highlight arguments being made about the radical potential yet qualified merit of knowledges generated by social movements. We then present readers with the concept of feminist development justice, the justice-based pillars on which the framework rests, and the political work of the APWLD. The article ends with a succinct conclusion on what is at stake vis-à-vis extractivism and the seemingly intractable "development" challenges at hand and how grassroots social movements can be rich sources to draw from regarding liberatory change and building better worlds.

MERIDIANS · feminism, race, transnationalism   23:2 October 2024
DOI: 10.1215/15366936-11266444 © 2024 Smith College

Introduction

The Dilemmas of "Development"

In paying heed to recent calls being made for scholars of development studies to be more attentive to the ongoing influences of race and imperialism in their scholarship (Patel 2020; Rutzibwa 2019)—yet in still avowing that gender and power relations remain as influential as ever vis-à-vis orthodox development agendas and their aftermaths (Dutta 2021; LeBaron and Gore 2020)—this article offers a comprehensive overview of "feminist development justice." First and foremost, feminist development justice is a transformative framework being advanced by Majority World women and grassroots organizers from the Global South, specifically, the Asia Pacific Forum on Women, Law, and Development (APWLD). The remit of feminist development justice aims to reckon with the historical-structural injustices and casualties committed in the name of "development" and economic "growth."

Notably, as argued by numerous transnational and postcolonial feminists (Ashiagbor 2021; Seppälä 2016; Yazzie 2018), exploitation, environmental degradation, and social harms committed in the name of "modern" development programs are inextricably linked to the enduring colonial order of the world and global (capitalist) economy in particular. In this same vein, research within the realm of critical and alternative approaches to development reveals these injustices disproportionately affect negatively racialized communities and women (Le Tran et al. 2020; Muñoz and Villarreal 2019). It is indeed obvious that more critical awareness of—and strident interventions into—the problems, dilemmas, and crimes of development are needed, both intellectually and practically.

Accordingly, and in finding generative merit in collective action and praxis-based approaches to social change amid the injurious outcomes of colonial modernity and neoliberal development, this article introduces readers to the APWLD's feminist development justice framework. In so doing, we, like other critical scholars (De Jong, Icaza, and Rutazibwa 2019; Fadaee 2017), contend that researchers working in development studies have much to learn from the knowledge(s) being produced by autonomous social movements in the Global South regarding resistance, emancipatory politics, and how to most effectively go about resolving the planet's most pressing "global challenges" (Motta and Nilsen 2011). Here, we must openly note we are referring to grassroots social movements composed primarily of rank-and-file community members who are beholden to progressive if not radical politics and feminist ethics, as pluralistic and often multidimensional the terms *progressive, feminist,* and *radical* all may be.

On the points of transparency and positionality, we should note we are not direct contributors to the APWLD, which is due to reasons that are geographical (not political). Even though we are not formally a part of the activist network due to distance, we are three community- and movement-engaged researchers (one born in South Asia now in North America, one from the West Indies, and one currently based in the circum-Caribbean) who share the APWLD's convictions and have been inspired by their members' grounded work. In short, we feel their notion of feminist development justice should be trafficked to all corners of both academia and the globe. This is due in part to the fact that there are numerous scholars across academia, particularly the Global North, who write quite elegantly about the violence of capital, borders, and the state, and who will accept invitations to speak to politicians and on professional panels about the suffering of "Others" as experts. Regrettably, there are far fewer who are engaged in frontline praxis that are accountable to, coauthoring with, and putting their research agenda in the service of grassroots movements. We feel the APWLD's efforts exemplify a valuable approach to addressing such disparities.

With respect to the structure of the article, first we begin by illustrating the academic literature we aim to contribute to; that is, both longstanding and emergent scholarly conversations arguing that mainstream development studies need to: 1) be *further* stretched and expanded to incorporate more forceful scrutiny of the links among capital, coloniality, race, imperialism, and the state; and 2) make room for—not to mention cite and explicitly reference—the crucial insights and pivotal roles of grassroots (feminist) social movements vis-à-vis struggles for justice and freedom. Next, we briefly describe the work of the APWLD while providing a detailed overview of their notion of feminist development justice. Following this, we offer an extended summary of the five "foundational shifts" that serve as the pillars and framework of feminist development justices by drawing from research findings, empirical data, and literature produced by the APWLD. Last, we end the article with a conclusion that reiterates our main thesis and call to action.

Social Movements "From Below"

A multitude of critical theorists and researchers working in fields ranging from political economy to postcolonialism have suggested that "development" continues to be a neocolonial Trojan horse and remains an enduring practice of heteropatriarchal capitalism (Mohanty 2003; Ossome 2021). Under the guise of "modernity" and a pretense of "progress," land and resources are being grabbed, human rights—especially those of women and negatively racialized groups—are being abandoned, and the unequal distribution of wealth and power remains mystified and shielded from critical exposure and meaningful intervention (Biccum 2005; Shiva 2016). This is due in part to the exploitation and aggression of "development" being discursively packaged as "growth" and job-generating "economic stimulus." For many, development represents an ongoing legacy of imperial belligerence that gets a free pass because it masquerades as well-intentioned "foreign aid" and "business as usual." Whatever the moniker, it is patently obvious that when it comes to "development" under global capitalism—race, gender, and colonial power still matter, undoubtedly (Patel 2020; Wilson 2012). This is particularly the case for communities "from below."

From below, for context, is a polysemic term that recognizes the political agency of people and places that have been targeted for exploitation, domination, or exclusion—both historically and in the present day. It is often taken up by and applicable to groups who are oppressed or have been systemically marginalized because of either their social identities (e.g., race, gender, class, religion, [dis]ability) or geographies (e.g., "Third World," "lesser-developed countries")—sometimes both. For example, most activists we see toppling the statues of enslavers—or rural peasants and Indigenous people we read about who are defending the environment—are organizing, often under threat, "from below." Amid this reality, it is vital to realize that development, along with its attendant injustices, sits in places. Different cultural settings, geopolitical situations, and socio-historical contexts all play major parts in development in terms of where and on whom it lands, as well as where emancipatory critiques of and concrete responses to it are emerging. Here, the role and knowledges offered by social movements "from below" and "beyond the core" cannot be overstated (Nilsen, Pleyers, and Cox 2017).

A word of caution is in order regarding our broader call to respect and cite the knowledges of social movements. Globally, social movements, for better or worse, are as numerous as they are diverse, which means that their pluralistic politics and goals are by no means uniform. Movements fall along an ideological spectrum that can range from anti-imperialist liberation armies engaging in combat, to ultranationalist political elites promulgating authoritarian populism, to pacifist mutual-aid collectives advocating for community well-being or migrant rights. The aims and aspirations of movements vary as much as their tactics and strategies do, not to mention their contradictions, and no social movement is infallible or beyond critique. With this caveat in mind, we qualify our proposal to pay heed to the acumen and ideas of grassroots movements in the Global South by noting that the movements we have in mind are those committed to emancipatory politics that are decidedly anticapitalist, anti-imperialist, and anti-patriarchal. On this point, there is neither a perfect movement to point to as a blueprint nor is there a conceptual silver bullet that will serve as a panacea, but there are several to draw inspiration from, hence our appeal to the APWLD's framework of feminist development justice.

Feminist Development Justice

The Asia Pacific Forum on Women, Law, and Development (APWLD) is an independent transnational organization led by women "from below" seeking to stop the exploitation and injustice that occurs because of development (Pederson 2019). For over three decades, the APWLD, which was formed in Nairobi, Kenya, in 1985 at the Third World Forum on Women, has created a database containing activist and social movement resources retrieved from nearly two hundred fifty-member groups from almost thirty countries across the Asia-Pacific (Familara 2014). The organization's primary aim is now oriented toward advancing women's human rights and "development justice" through feminist participatory action research (APWLD 2019a; Godden et al. 2020). In short, the women of the APWLD refuse to accept development as "business as usual" and realize that if left unchallenged and unchanged the survival of both humanity and the planet is at stake. While the discourses and worldviews surrounding prevailing definitions and ideas about "human rights" remain critiqued as products of liberal-colonial modernity (Mohanty 2003), defending the human rights of others, nevertheless, is paramount. Hence, the APWLD (2014) have committed to grassroots mobilizing, anti-racist feminist activism, and praxis-driven social change.

A detailed evaluation must be made prior to taking steps toward structural transformation, and for this reason, the APWLD has provided the international community with evidence demonstrating how a patriarchal world is leading to its own demise (APWLD 2020c). Their *Development Justice* 2.0 overview notes that only 26 people, most of whom are men, own the same amount of wealth as the world's poorest 3.5 billion people, the majority of whom are women (APWLD 2019a). Moreover, though wealthy "developed" nations claim to be "helping" and assisting "lesser developed" countries, critical analysis suggests otherwise. In 2012, according to the APWLD (2019a), developing countries received nearly US$1.5 trillion in investments and aid but lost over US$3 trillion due to unregulated corporate greed. Being pushed to the brink of global climate catastrophe is but one upshot. It is reported that only one hundred corporations are responsible for over 70 percent of global carbon emissions, yet the people who are suffering from the repercussions of emissions are contributing substantially less to them (Griffin 2017). For example, the Pacific Islands are experiencing rising sea levels, which are leaving countless civilians homeless. The situation is so dire that research warns of irreversible damage to the planet if large-scale immediate action is not taken on the global level (Matthews and Solomon 2013).

If irreparable damage to the planet is not reason enough to challenge capitalist states, confront neoliberal trade, and reorganize economies, the APWLD (2020a) demonstrates that human rights infringements, governmental corruption, and war are being exacerbated by corporate profit accumulation that is being pushed as "economic development." For many, this is a life-or-death issue. According to Front Line Defenders (2020), more than three hundred human rights and land defense activists were murdered in 2019. As Frantz Fanon (1963) intimated over half a century ago, the hoarding of resources and squandering of wealth solely to prove that one imperialist country is more powerful than another are equivalent to reckless saber rattling that will culminate in nothing other than mutually assured destruction. Contrariwise, the APWLD defines development success as upholding dignity and promoting basic human rights in which every individual is entitled to accessible education, a life with neither slavery nor torture, and freedom of speech and bodily autonomy, among other rights (Taguiwalo and Chakma 2019).

Development injustices are not going unnoticed. Communities across the Majority World are resisting discriminatory and exploitative orthodox models of neoliberal development (APWLD 2014). In fact, countless people are now demanding development justice, which, according to the APWLD (Pederson 2019), "is a model that places the poor, the marginalized, and the planet at the heart of development. It aims to reduce inequalities between countries, within countries, and between men and women and others using five foundational shifts." The APWLD (2019a) goes on to state regarding corporatized-capitalist development:

> This model of development has completely failed the majority of the Earth. It has channeled wealth from working people to the rich, and from developing countries to wealthy countries. It has contributed to the warming of our Earth, caused the displacement of millions of people, lowered real wages, increased labor migration and caused finance, environment, food and energy crises which continue to devastate the lives of women in the Global South. The world urgently needs a new model of development, a model that asserts the right to development for all peoples over private profit.

For the APWLD, five foundational shifts are necessary to successfully bring development justice to fruition, which include forms of justice that are: redistributive, economic, social and gender, environmental and climate, and accountable to peoples. These five shifts will be expanded on in subsequent sections.

In short, male-dominated institutions, heteropatriarchal states, and liberal-capitalist logics continue to fail societies due to their power-fixated and profit-driven policies (Mies 1988). For the APWLD, this signals an urgent need for radical women with anti-racist, anti-classist, and anti-imperialist politics to take hold of the reins and guide international and local agendas toward more sustainable and just futures (Lutvey et al. 2015), futures that are marked neither by discrimination, marginalization, and violence nor by the false promises of "social responsibility" by politicians and corporations who fail to deliver. In turn, the feminist activists of the APWLD are fighting against the oppressive institutions of militarism, patriarchy, and neoliberalism—and they are doing so via a commitment to development justice and its five pillars of justice, which we will now detail.

Redistributive Justice

Redistributive justice aims to at once correct the "economic imbalance between the Global North and South" (Gurumurthy and Chami 2019: 23) and transform existing development models as a way of redressing "inequalities of wealth, power, and resources" (Familara 2014: 380). It further aspires to rectify current systemic processes that dispossess developing countries as a means of returning assets to the communities and countries from which they came—away from corporations and elites.

Under redistributive justice, concentrated power and wealth in the hands of the minority are returned to the masses. In addition, adhering to principles of redistributive justice ensures that the revenue generated by workers is dispersed back to the people (i.e., workers) who actually created the profit in the first place (APWLD 2020c). Meaning, economic decisions are not left up to governments beholden to (i.e., bought and sold by) corporate power at the expense of the well-being of others (Chakma 2016). The APWLD asserts that the people—as a collective—are entitled to equally cocreate and participate in their own democratic governance systems, decision-making processes, and economic institutions—and that anything less would be fundamentally authoritarian, not to mention perpetuate patriarchal dominance (Napier-Moore et al. 2017).

Global inequality, too, can be partially addressed via taxation policies by governments that prioritize the common good through communalist-socialist principles. As the APWLD (2019a) explains, "Just an extra 0.5% tax on the world's richest could educate 262 million children and provide healthcare for 3.3 million people. Cutting 10% of annual investments in the defense sector could end poverty and hunger in 15 years." Redistributive justice can be achieved by overturning legislation and policies that transfer wealth and resources from the "poor" to the wealthy and private capital. One such example took place in Chhattisgarh, India (Kujur 2008), where Tata Steel sought to take land from ten villages, but nearly two thousand farmers united, resisted, and fought back for close to a decade. Ultimately, the government consented to the farmers' demands and struggle, which forced Tata Steel to withdraw. Another example are the communities in Jakarta who were fighting for potable water and given one of the highest water tariffs in Southeast Asia for decades (Douglass 2010). They were resisting privatization through a class-action lawsuit until the Supreme Court recognized the privatization of water as a violation of community rights. This is just one of the countless instances demonstrating how the political agency and collective action of people "from below"—regardless of status and credentials—can hold the powers that be accountable.

As the longstanding feminist maxim goes, the personal is indeed the political. The stories, lived experiences, agency, and subaltern voices of people in the Majority World matter, despite the fact that mainstream development indicators and far too much of academia gloss over them (Spivak 1988). For example, in an attempt to improve universal public services for decent work and living wages, Erwiana Sulistyaningsih (2019), an

APWLD member, describes her experience as one of the many Indonesian women who are suffering under the exploitative working conditions generated under neoliberalism. Erwiana was among the less fortunate residing in a village in East Java whose parents were not able to access education. Her mother left their family to become a domestic worker in Brunei and her father was a landless subsistence farmer. She reported that none of the villagers could have afforded to attend university, and universal access to education remains a challenge in rural areas.

When Erwiana migrated to Jakarta at age seventeen, she found a job as a waitress where she was overworked and underpaid. It became impossible to afford living costs in Jakarta, so she left after two years and joined three hundred other women and girls in an eight-month training to become migrant domestic workers. This, however, was a manipulative scheme that took advantage of noncredentialed women by sending them to work in hostile households, sometimes without pay, where they frequently experienced abuse, confinement, or malnourishment. The "job providing" firm Erwiana worked for forced the migrant laborers to sign contracts stating they would repay approximately US$2000 in monthly installments for the "training." Without money to pay back the balance, Erwiana was trapped in debt bondage and the agency refused to assist her until she repaid them in full. In detailing the extortion, Erwiana (Sulistyaningsih 2019) states,

> Domestic workers like me are all over the region, caring for children and the elderly, doing the invisible work that isn't counted in the GDP. We are not poor; we are *made* poor. We can stop exploiting the millions of migrant workers. If I had access to education and jobs that meet decent work and living wage standards, my life would be different. I would not have to migrate to Jakarta or to Hong Kong. If either country had provided universal healthcare to workers like me, I would not be in this situation and could live a life with dignity.

This is only one of countless cases in which a capitalist-patriarchal state both abandoned and exploited a working woman. Under neoliberal schemes like these, women are often forced to migrate in search of better jobs—for better futures—but at every border they cross, if they are even able to cross, they find themselves subjugated because capitalist logics place little to no value on their lives or the socially reproductive labor they disproportionately perform (Bhattacharya 2017). Across the Majority World, it is not uncommon for women and daughters to forgo attending school because they regularly become family providers. An economy that supports women and girls, as well as *revalues* and refrains from privatizing social reproduction—that is, an economy that funds health care, education, childcare, nutritious food provision, and so on—is urgently needed (Barry and Gahman 2020). Erwiana, in speaking not only to the everyday realities women like her face, went further to recommend that states should reduce military spending and that "good governance means establishing policies and practices that restore the power of communities and people to determine how resources and state budgets get used" (APWLD 2019a).

Economic Justice

The APWLD suggests that one indicator of economic justice is when economies are put at the service of the people, rather than when people are put in the service of the economy. This means people and workers democratically define and decide what their work is, where it will be used, and how the fruits of it will be shared and distributed. Economic justice recognizes and values the labor of workers and affords them a decent income, a living wage, and the freedom to join unions and organize (Gurumurthy and Chami 2019). Some argue that economic justice will create a more productive economy given that people who feel empowered and find their work meaningful are more likely to be engaged and efficient. Regardless, creating jobs that make the best of peoples' talents and accommodate their desires will effect a healthier and safer society.

On this front, the women of APWLD have already begun to confront supranational capitalist organizations (e.g., International Monetary Fund, World Bank, World Trade Organization [WTO]) that continue to seek to transfer wealth from the poor to the rich, further subjugate the working classes, and prevent marginalized communities from defining and guiding development. For evidence of the APWLD's track record, we can look at a press release they issued against the WTO in 2013, which states that hundreds of women from different countries in the Asia-Pacific region gathered at Bajra Sandhi Field in the Renon neighborhood of Denpasar, Bali, for the Feminist Carnival Action against the WTO. Here, women farmers, domestic workers, and migrant workers collectively mobilized and chanted in unison: "Women resist WTO! Economic Justice Now!" (APWLD 2013). The feminist mobilization called for the total rejection of the WTO and the undemocratic free trade regimes it buttresses. A statement released by the APWLD, alongside dozens of other community service organizations and advocacy groups, encapsulates their sentiment toward neoliberal globalization and patriarchal capitalism: "We are opposing the WTO because it channels wealth and power away from poor women and gives it to foreign governments, corporations and domestic elites. WTO triggers land grabbing, forced evictions, exploitative labor migration, reduces food sovereignty and robs women of their livelihoods." This is an explicit demand for an economy that puts the dignity of people at its heart and represents a call to arms for feminist people-centered economies in which local communities have sovereignty and decision-making power over the means of production/distribution. According to the APWLD, which later went on to develop a program called Women Interrogating Trade and Corporate Hegemony (WITCH), a key aim in the fight against androcentric corporatism focuses on

> building the capacity of women's rights organizations to understand the impact of trade and investments rules on women's human rights; and increase the power of feminist movements to interrogate and halt the growing power of corporations. The program works with APWLD members and other social movements to demand spaces and political decisions for trade and investment frameworks that promote, protect and fulfil human rights and promote Development Justice.

The goal of the WITCH initiative is to push for trade and investment agreements in the region that adhere to human rights obligations and incorporate the voice and demands of Asian-Pacific women committed to development justice (APWLD 2018). They protest policies that promote neoliberal development aggression, privatization, deregulation, and austerity, which have always had disparate negative impacts on the poor (Ruspini 2020). In evidencing this, the syndicate notes that women constitute nearly three-quarters of the world's working and abject poor, the vast majority of whom are bearing the brunt of neoliberal austerity policies. Capitalist trade agreements consolidate power and funnel resources to the ruling classes—resources that oftentimes are extracted from ecosystems where peasant, Indigenous, or cash-poor communities reside (Chattopadhyay 2012)—meaning, influence and wealth are expropriated from working people and placed in the hands of wealthy elites, former imperial countries, and/or transnational businesses. Corporations and wealthy nations (e.g., in the West, Global North, Minority World) with majority sway in and the backing of institutions like the IMF, World Bank, and WTO then enforce policies that erode protections of the environment, reduce labor laws, strip intellectual property rights, and widen the digital divide (Gurumurthy and Chami 2019). Here, the APWLD (2017) asserts,

> While being promoted as a means for sustainable development, trade agreements promote disenfranchisement, erode social protections for health care and education and drive the migration of poor people under conditions of great personal and financial risk. Trade agreements also facilitate environmental destruction in the search for profit, making poor people even more vulnerable when disasters strike.

The APWLD is also engaged in a No RCEP campaign, which opposes a mega-free trade agreement called the Regional Comprehensive Economic Partnership (RCEP) (Shejni 2019). Due to its geographic location and given that it includes fifteen countries in South and Southeast Asia, RCEP affects nearly one-third of the world's population and represents nearly 30 percent of the global GDP. A major criticism of the agreement is the sweeping detrimental impacts it poses to ecosystems, local agricultural systems, work visas, labor protections, subsistence communities, and intellectual property rights across the region. In directly confronting the neoliberal agreement, the APWLD (2017) notes, "The trade agreement seeks supremacy of corporations over the lives of people. Our No RCEP campaign highlights the contradictions of government's global commitments to sustainable development while entering into binding agreements that prioritize corporate profit."

The APWLD is at the forefront of strengthening and building cross-movement collaborations for equitable direct trade and economic justice. They have arranged capacity-building programs and developed tools and resources to enable grassroots women's movements to effectively engage with and understand trade deals and investment plans, along with the attendant harmful impacts neoliberal policies have on human rights and local communities. The APWLD's efforts in advancing economic justice have also led them to develop resources comprising evidence, data, and political consciousness–raising literature that detail how human rights are adversely affected by "free trade" and corporate investment strategies, as well as how demanding development justice can prevent and mitigate exploitation.

Social and Gender Justice
The Asia-Pacific contains two-thirds of the world's "poorest" people, with women constituting the majority (APWLD 2019a). Regional governments

and policymakers have historically failed to understand that women are forced to bear the deleterious consequences of orthodox development policies, which typically benefit a wealthy, oft male-dominated minority (Sheill et al. 2019). It is not uncommon for women from a host of demographics, inter alia rural, Indigenous, migrant, low caste, or working class, to be exposed to marginalization and human rights violations when neoliberal policies are enacted (Wattimena 2018). Various studies also evidence how economic liberalization has exacerbated climate change, environmental degradation, institutionalized discrimination, increased militarization, escalations of fundamentalism, and dispossession (Lutvey et al. 2015). Numerous women across the region depend on the land and the resources it provides for their survival. When they are displaced or their access to land is restricted, families are at risk and placed under duress.

Sexual and reproductive injustices, alongside gender-based violence, also persist. Women are targets for harassment or assault both at home and in the workplace (Woo et al. 2010). Under a capitalist economic system, heteropatriarchal governments habitually fail to protect women's rights in the workplace while also enabling misogynist social relations at large. Because women are incongruently excluded from policymaking processes, they face institutionalized discrimination, and the abuses they suffer can go unresolved and dismissed. In many cases, marginalized women have no access to proper legal aid, forcing them to remain in inimical situations (Sheill et al. 2019). This occurs in conjunction with transnational corporations and capitalist states accumulating more profit from the un(der)paid and unnoticed socially reproductive labor women disproportionately perform (Bhattacharya 2017).

According to the International Trade Union Confederation 2019 Index (Lamubol 2019), the Asia-Pacific is the second worst region globally apropos mistreating workers. Revealingly, in 2018 it was reported that at least ten trade unionists were murdered in the Philippines (Lamubol 2019). From the APWLD's perspective, this is reflective of a violent economic system defined by male dominance and the exploitation of the oppressed. Social and gender justice for the syndicate consequently means dismantling an oppressive system of heteropatriarchy that is being reinforced by "globalization, fundamentalism and militarism" (APWLD 2019a). The APWLD also argues that justice will only be achieved when discriminatory laws are revoked and statutes that safeguard women's rights, voices, agency, autonomy, and bodily integrity are meaningfully mainstreamed and legislated. Accordingly, the APWLD launched the Breaking Out of Marginalization program to build capacity and social movements that will assist marginalized women across rural and urban contexts (Chakma 2016). In addition, the APWLD created a Feminist Participatory Action Research (FPAR) program, which was set up to advocate for migrant, Indigenous, and peasant women, among others; document violations of human rights; collaboratively find viable solutions to pressing challenges and threats; and develop mobilization tactics and strategies to push for transformation across local, domestic, regional, and global scales (APWLD 2020a). The FPAR program analyzes labor rights and documents evidence of how current labor laws and policies impact women's rights. In detailing the impact of the FPAR program, Lamubol (2019) writes, "Through their initiatives, women workers have found that regardless of whether they belong in the formal or informal sector, manufacturing or agriculture, public or private sphere, they all share the realities of receiving poverty wages, being subject to sexual harassment, precarious employment, lack of social protection, as well as facing barriers to rights to organize." One of APWLD's main goals with FPAR is to support Indigenous and migrant women on their terms so they become effective advocates capable of influencing policy and development practices related to their rights over land, resources, decent work, democratic participation, and inclusion.

After broad-based surveys, APWLD organizers in the program realized that workers across the Asia-Pacific were unaware of, or actively being prevented from knowing, their rights (Sheill et al. 2019). Consequently, exploitative employers took advantage of power imbalances and instead of enlightening workers and sharing information, they persisted to sabotage and weaken worker initiatives to unionize and campaign for workplace improvements. As a response, the All Adivasi Women's Association of Assam (AAWAA), via FPAR, investigated the working conditions of tea plantations located in Assam, northern India from 2017 to 2019 (Lamubol 2019). Evidence of underpayment and a lack of health care provision were found. Union activists were then threatened by company management when they attempted to intervene. A similar occurrence took place in one of the biggest areas for palm oil production in Kalimantan, Indonesia. Research organized by the Palangkaraya Ecological and Human Rights Studies (PROGRESS) group found that 405 workers, including 14 union leaders, were terminated from their jobs without cause and without severance (which is a breach of national labor law) for mobilizing for decent work and living wages (Lamubol 2019). Neither of these cases is fully resolved, but women are now at least better protected and making some headway. While engaging with hostile threats and placing themselves in danger, these accounts demonstrate the awareness that can be raised and advancements that can be made when women "from below" mobilize.

Precarious employment in the Asia-Pacific region remains a major concern. This work involves short-term contracted positions, seasonal/temporary employment, and on-call/home-based labor that is poorly paid, insecure, unprotected, and generally insufficient for supporting a household (Pederson 2019). For example, the Nurse Union of Thailand discovered that one-fifth of nurses are hired on a temporary basis (Lamubol 2019). These nurses, the majority of whom were women on the frontlines of the COVID-19 pandemic, remain paid below minimum wage and have been laboring for years on end without social protection or employment benefits. The APWLD also found that textile and garment industries across the region were hiring nearly one-third of their workers, 75–90 percent of whom are women, on a contractual basis. Though their workload is the same as permanent employees, contract workers do not benefit from health care, paid leave, childcare, or the like. Neoliberal employment schemes of this nature are exploiting workers—Majority World women in particular—which hinders them from being able to financially support and socially reproduce their households, not to mention pursue creative and leisure activities they would otherwise like to spend time doing.

Environmental and Climate Justice
Environmental justice casts necessary light on the historical culpability of nations (e.g., in the Global North, the West) and members of the ruling class for their practices and patterns of industrial pollution, contamination, and extractive accumulation that have resulted in violations of human rights, shifting climate regimes, rising sea levels, and escalating disasters (Shiva 2016). It calls for wealthy countries and elites to face the music, repair the damage, and redress those groups (e.g., negatively racialized, cash-poor) who are the least culpable for climate change but typically are suffering the most from it, for example, subsistence farmers, fisherfolk, Indigenous communities, informally employed women. According to the APWLD, environmental justice also "would require immediate elimination of fossil fuel use, and resources directed toward building a renewable energy industry based on the principles of decent work and gender

equality. The just and equitable transition to renewable energy and to conserve natural resources cannot be hijacked by profit-driven interests, drawing back on the issue of corporate capture" (APWLD 2020c). In addition, environmental justice seeks to hold power brokers and decision-makers accountable, from local to global levels, to develop more ecologically just laws and policies. Here, the APWLD has submitted multiple reports on different incidences in which governments have violated international accords involving the nonconsensual removal of natural resources located on protected lands (Gahman and Thongs 2020). The Indigenous groups who reside in and depend on these lands are protesting extractivist development, which is generating irreversible environmental and climate consequences (Sharavdorj and Hakena 2018).

The APWLD aims to demonstrate that sustainable alternatives that respect local cultures are a feasible option. One of their driving motivations and ultimate goals is to transform the capitalist economy and shift away from extractivist fossil fuel burning/pollution, which contaminates ecosystems and places workers and communities at risk, and move toward low-impact renewable energy-source initiatives that are more frequently led by women. They are also aiming to eradicate the exploitation of women and negatively racialized groups in the Majority World and elsewhere through the promotion of gender-just governance systems and solidarity economies. The APWLD views the political economy as inextricably linked to the climate crisis and intensifications of what are often mistakenly referred to as "natural" disasters. On this front, they are targeting extractivist corporations that are damaging ecosystems and grabbing land. According the APWLD (2019a), one constituent aspect of environmental justice includes eliminating the "tax havens, tax holidays, trade mispricing, and profit shifting or other tax avoidance" that private capital and multinational corporations are guilty of by creating a global tax floor. Here, they (APWLD 2019a) go on to explain that the implementation of additional levies on injurious practices including "finance speculation, arms trade, shipping, and extractive industries" is a necessary step toward mitigating exploitation, war, and the continued dispossessions of land.

Related to environmental justice, the APWLD's climate justice program was created to build capacity and collect evidence on the impacts of climate change. In particular, the APWLD's climate justice initiative is aimed to serve those who hold little responsibility for the degradation of the

environment due to fossil fuel consumption and dependency yet are dispa-
rately experiencing the negative consequences of climate change (e.g.,
peasant communities, the rural cash-poor, Indigenous groups, women).
The APWLD are advocating for the involvement of all governments to
ensure that policies and laws are being implemented on a global level to
develop more sustainable low-impact economies and breathe life into what
they have termed a "Feminist Fossil Fuel Free Future" (APWLD 2019b).
Their demand for this gender-just and fossil-fuel-free future is more urgent
than ever due to worsening climate change, which continues to result in
increasingly severe and intensifying detrimental environmental impacts.
While state officials in male-dominated institutions draft policies and
slash regulations to further damage the world via industrial production
and agri-imperialism for financial gain, women are disproportionately on
the front lines of resisting these forces while simultaneously being made
more vulnerable to the harmful upshots of climate change (Acha 2017).
Drought, floods, crop loss, inaccessible potable water, and famine are
some of the outcomes marginalized women are contending with, often
alone and with little to no institutional power.

The APWLD's stance is that governments must invest in sustainable
agroecological projects to alleviate the climate crisis and refrain from
signing neoliberal agreements with wealthy corporations that are heavily
invested in profiting off resources ripped from the land, the process of
which simultaneously contaminates it. According to the APWLD (Lutvey
et al. 2015), given that women must deal with the myriad emerging challenges being generated by the climate crisis, it then follows that women
should also be placed at the fore regarding decision-making, devising, and
developing just and sustainable solutions to said climate challenges. In
turn, women farmers across the Asia-Pacific region have begun multiple
smallholder projects that implement regenerative agricultural practices
and techniques that promote food sovereignty and are aimed at balancing
the social, economic, and ecological needs of people based on their differing respective vulnerabilities and resilience differentials (APWLD 2018).
Efforts and decisions here are prioritizing and being made in relation to the
unique and situated cultural and ecological contexts in which varying
communities are living and laboring.

In sum, through APWLD climate justice initiatives, both rural peasants
and urban working people are attempting to advance low-impact eco-
friendly alternatives to conventional nonrenewable energy sources. Despite

this transformative praxis and forward-looking approach, rural peasants and the urban poor, especially women, continue to be excluded and ignored from formal decision-making processes, which is at once reducing their respective resilience and suppressing sustainable alternatives (Ramli 2016). Nevertheless, in the face of increasing climate injustice and persistent environmental racism, activists from the APWLD continue to argue that it is immoral and unjust for transnational corporations, international bodies, and state administrations to remain silent and perpetuate the liberal-capitalist status quo while expecting the marginalized, impoverished, and oppressed either to grin and bear it or correct the problems they did not create. The contention remains that states, instead of attacking and assassinating land and human rights defenders, should commit to addressing environmental injustices, violations, and crimes. The APWLD is arguing the time has come to end systems of governance that are beholden to the principles of capitalism, rooted in Western thought, driven by neoliberal logics, and that continue to exploit and oppress women and negatively racialized communities.

Accountability to Peoples
The APWLD's final transformative shift, Accountability to Peoples, involves structural change at the core of governance, which enables people to define their own realities and make decisions on their terms and preferences that will be put in the service of community well-being and livable futures (Shejni 2019). This shift necessitates empowering all people, and in particular Indigenous communities, migrant workers, disabled people, and working women across the Majority World, to be part of transparent and informed decision-making in all stages of development processes at local, national, regional, and international levels (Pederson 2019). This type of shift in governance will foster an equitable framework that promotes solidarity-driven economies that (re)value social reproduction, focus on the vitality of communities and ecosystems, and equitably distribute the means of production/distribution among the people. Transforming systems of governance so that decision-making processes are democratic and foreground accountability to the people requires a shift in priorities away from the uneven accumulation and overconsumption of resources and toward ensuring human rights and respect for the environment vis-à-vis development. That is, this final transformative shift of being accountable to people, which centers on justice, democracy, and freedom, holistically

incorporates the implementation of the four previously mentioned pillars of development justice into governance.

For the APWLD, a development justice approach places the well-being and resilience of people above notions of economic "growth" and "development" indicators that are tethered to neoliberal metrics, state GDPs, and the purported strengths of differing stock markets. That is, accountability to people under a development justice framework aspires to chart a course toward eliminating absolute poverty and the patterns of domination and overconsumption that prevail in wealthy, self-ascribed "developed" nations, which perpetuate colonial worldviews, logics, and geopolitical power relations. Land, in particular, is a key component in bringing development justice to fruition. On this point, the APWLD FPAR program has stressed a recognition of—and amplified calls for—Indigenous land rights, which is evidenced in their most recent annual report (APWLD 2020a), which asserts, "Indigenous women's land rights clearly illustrate how Indigenous women in many Asian countries are experiencing subjugation and discrimination both by external actors (both state and nonstate actors) as well as within their own community. Indigenous women's rights to access to and control over their lands, territories and resources must be recognized and protected." The APWLD goes on to mention, alongside critical Indigenous scholarship (Anaya and Puig 2017), that the establishment of new, democratic, global, and national accountability mechanisms for states will mitigate treaties and trade deals that are enabling transnational extractivist corporations to grab land, violate Free, Prior, and Informed Consent, and damage communities and ecosystems. Here the APWLD stresses that the use and management of natural resources should include and be guided by the participation of local people, in particular because they live in the contexts where extraction and its corollary damage are occurring.

States, from the APWLD's standpoint, should also provide universal public services to ensure their overall well-being, such as education, health care, water and sanitation, sustainable energy, and sexual and reproductive health care (Napier-Moore et al. 2017; Woo et al. 2010). Another factor proposed is the provision of a universal social wage and social protection. This would provide all with a dignified standard of living regardless of their employment, citizenship, and/or class status. The investment in decent work and inauguration of a universal living wage, including for laborers in the informal sector, would reduce global gender pay gaps.

The APWLD is not waiting for transparent, democratic, and corruption-free governments to miraculously appear to start their battle against neoliberal logics and capitalist states. Instead, activists from the syndicate have already embarked on a journey to fight for the excluded and oppressed by raising awareness and amplifying the voices of those who have been deliberately silenced. Concretely, the APWLD have initiated multiple campaigns to help assess and treat various concerns of systemically marginalized groups, in particular women, across a range of Asia-Pacific geographies. Such campaigns include Feminist Law and Practice (FLP), which "focuses on building capacity of women's rights advocates and organizations to transform discriminatory laws, policies and practices and increase women's access to justice" (APWLD 2019). Activists who contribute to the FLP campaign believe that law and judicial systems often institutionalize the oppression of women and the working poor, and environmental defenders yet remain crucial instruments that can be used to effect justice, promote equality, and defend human rights. This program gives rise to a consortium of activists, lawyers, policymakers, and implementers who leverage law and legal statutes to advance women's rights and justice for oppressed peoples. Knowledge of the law and of human rights will inform women with the necessary skills that are required to challenge discriminatory statutes and confront systemic injustices that are embedded within conventional jurisprudence.

Women in Power (WiP) is another program aimed at strengthening "women's political leadership and democratic participation of women in decision-making process" (APWLD 2018). Through the provision of political training to parliamentary members from a feminist perspective and via delivering resources to frontline activists in women's rights movements, the WiP aspires to transform women into leaders at every level of society so they will be capable of realizing socially just change in both administrative systems and everyday life while increasing the democratic participation of women across the board. Relatedly, Women Organizing Workers (WOW) is a labor organizing program aimed at advancing women's rights to decent work and a living wage. The majority of the women connected to this program are employed either precariously or informally, meaning the jobs they have are typically nonunionized, lower paid, higher risk, devalued, and rife with weak labor protection (Sheill et al. 2019). Moreover, due to the lack of legal security, women are susceptible to hyperexploitation that takes the form of overwork, sub-poverty-level wages, dangerous working conditions, and increased exposure to sexual harassment and assault (Ramli 2016). Despite these challenges, women in the program are determined to fight for their rights by organizing workers and collectively pushing for better and safer job conditions. In short, the WOW program is equipping women with the necessary skills and knowledge to organize labor and lead unions via the provision of feminist consciousness related to struggling against neoliberal policy, developing tactics for workplace organizing, and increasing legal literacy. Activists in the program are also building capacity and developing a network of organizers who are committed to fostering collective action for labor rights across national, regional, and global levels.

Conclusion

For the APWLD, humanity's sense of shared dignity is slowly being eroded away as states, corporations, and world "leaders" continue to remain increasingly fixated on the acquisition of power and accumulation of wealth. Many activists in the syndicate contend that if development agendas continue to undermine the rights of people and neglect the preservation of natural environments, in a few decades, we will no longer have a planet to call home. In short, global capitalism—which cannot be cleaved from the historical trajectories of colonialism, the persistent racial contempt that drove it, and the continued heteropatriarchal norms that characterize it—gives way to a profit-driven economy that privileges and rewards self-centrism, overconsumption, and the devaluation and privatization of social reproduction. Institutions, relationships, and sociospatial divides defined by repression, exploitation, and alienation are the consequence.

As noted at the outset of this article, development as we know it is not immune to injustice and arguably maintains the asymmetrical relations of domination that were forged through empire. Neoliberal foreign trade agendas, international "aid" schemes, and economic development programs continue to sanction and perpetuate extractive destruction, the unequitable distribution of wealth, and ongoing exercises of colonial power—all of which are disproportionately affecting communities of color and women (Desai 2015). Globally, women are being overworked and undervalued while being excluded from leadership roles and decision-making processes, whether they be political, social, or economic. Violence and abuse against women and girls, too, remains a pervasive and pressing issue in need of urgent and deliberate intervention. With respect to animating pathways out of realities marked by structural violence and cocreating sustainable and just futures that are imbued with emancipatory politics, compassion, and dignity for all, we end this article with an appeal to development justice by citing a social movement "from below"—the APWLD (2019c)—and a call to collective action from the feminist organizer Misun Woo, who asserts, "We are living in a dangerous world where feminism and women's human rights are being depoliticized and pink-washed by promoting terms such as 'women's economic empowerment,' or even 'feminist foreign policy.' This is the state of political manipulation. Our collective power and feminist solidarity are our hope and answer to fight back patriarchy, fundamentalism, capitalism, and militarism."

Nasha Mohamed is a University of the West Indies (St. Augustine Campus) graduate and Spanish and French teacher from Trinidad and Tobago. In addition to focusing on Arabic- and English-language studies and postcolonial literature, she has a commitment to taking the lasting legacies of empire to task across the Caribbean and beyond.

Sutapa Chattopadhyay is an associate professor in women's and gender studies and development studies at St. Francis Xavier University. Her areas of interest are migration, social movements, and political ecology, and her books include *Migration, Squatting, and Radical Autonomy* (2017) and *Politics of Development and Forced Mobility* (2022).

Levi Gahman is an affiliate with University of the West Indies and professor of emancipatory politics and environmental conflict at the University of Liverpool. His books include *Land, God, and Guns: Settler Colonialism and Masculinity* (2020) and *Building Better Worlds: Ideas and Inspiration from the Zapatistas* (2022).

Works Cited

Acha, Maria Alejandra Rodriguez. 2017. "We Have to Wake Up Humankind! Women's Struggles for Survival and Climate and Environmental Justice." *Development* 60, nos. 1–2: 32–39.

Anaya, James, and Sergio Puig. 2017. "Mitigating State Sovereignty: The Duty to Consult Indigenous People." *University of Toronto Law Journal* 67, no. 4: 435–64.

APWLD (Asia Pacific Forum on Women, Law and Development). 2013. "Women Resist the WTO, Call for Economic Justice." December 9. https://apwld.org/women-say-no-to-wto/.

APWLD (Asia Pacific Forum on Women, Law and Development). 2014. *Growing the Power of Movements Annual Report*. Chiang Mai, Thailand: APWLD.

APWLD (Asia Pacific Forum on Women, Law and Development). 2017. *ReSisters, Per-Sisters, Sisters Annual Report.* Chiang Mai, Thailand: APWLD.

APWLD (Asia Pacific Forum on Women, Law and Development). 2018. *We Learn and We Rise Annual Report.* Chiang Mai and Penang, Thailand: APWLD.

APWLD (Asia Pacific Forum on Women, Law and Development). 2019a. *Development Justice 2.0.* December 10. https://apwld.org/launch-development-justice-2-0-climate-gender-development-justice/.

APWLD (Asia Pacific Forum on Women, Law and Development). 2019b. *Feminist Fossil Fuel Free Future.* November 12. http://apwld.org/wp-content/uploads/2016/12/5Fs_briefer_v2.pdf.

APWLD (Asia Pacific Forum on Women, Law and Development). 2019c. "If Women Stop, the World Stops." May 1. https://apwld.org/press-release-labour-day-feminist-groups-call-for-a-womens-strike/.

APWLD (Asia Pacific Forum on Women, Law and Development). 2020a. "Expert Mechanism on the Rights of Indigenous Peoples." January 15. https://apwld.org/wp-content/uploads/2020/01/APWLD_submission_EMRIP-study_land_2020_15Jan_FINALLL.pdf.

APWLD (Asia Pacific Forum on Women, Law and Development). 2020b. Feminist Law and Practice (FLP). November 19. https://apwld.org/our-programmes/feminist-law-and-practice/.

APWLD (Asia Pacific Forum on Women, Law and Development). 2020c. *Twenty-Five-Year Review of the Beijing Declaration and Platform for Action.* Chiang Mai, Thailand: APWLD.

Ashiagbor, Diamond. 2021. "Race and Colonialism in the Construction of Labour Markets and Precarity." *Industrial Law Journal* 50, no. 4: 506–31.

Barry, Tessa. and Levi Gahman. 2020. "Agrarian Struggle and Food System Injustice in the Anglo-Caribbean: Centering Social Reproduction by (Re)turning to Creft and Fanon." *Human Geography* 13, no. 2. https://doi.org/10.1177/194277862092 5824.

Bhattacharya, Tithi. 2017. *Social Reproduction Theory: Remapping Class, Recentering Oppression.* London: Pluto Press.

Biccum, April. 2005. "Development and the 'New' Imperialism: A Reinvention of Colonial Discourse in DFID Promotional Literature." *Third World Quarterly* 26, no. 6: 1005–20.

Chakma, Trimita. 2016. "Feminist Participatory Action Research (FPAR): An Effective Framework for Empowering Grassroots Women and Strengthening Feminist Movements in Asia Pacific." *Asian Journal of Women's Studies* 22, no. 2: 165–73.

Chattopadhyay, Sutapa. 2012. "Adivasi Insurgencies and Power in Colonial India." *ACME: An International Journal for Critical Geographies* 11, no. 1: 55–80.

De Jong, Sara, Rosalba Icaza, and Olivia Rutazibwa, eds. 2019. *Decolonization and Feminisms in Global Teaching and Learning.* London: Routledge.

Desai, Manisha. 2015. *Subaltern Movements in India: Gendered Geographies of Struggle against Neoliberal Development.* New York: Routledge.

Douglass, Michael. 2010. "Globalization, Mega-projects and the Environment: Urban Form and Water in Jakarta." *Environment and Urbanization ASIA* 1, no. 1: 45–65.

Dutta, Madhumita. 2021. "Becoming 'Active Labor Protestors': Women Workers Organizing in India's Garment Export Factories." *Globalizations* 18, no. 8: 1420–35.

Fadaee, Simin. 2017. "Bringing in the South: Towards a Global Paradigm for Social Movement Studies." *Interface: A Journal for and about Social Movements* 9, no. 2: 45–60.

Familara, Aileen. 2014. "Organisation Profile: Asia Pacific Forum on Women, Law and Development (APWLD)." *Gender and Development* 22, no. 2: 378–82.

Fanon, Frantz. 1963. *The Wretched of the Earth*. New York: Grove Press.

Front Line Defenders. 2020. *Global Analysis 2019*. Blackrock, Ireland: Front Line, the International Foundation for the Protection of Human Rights Defenders.

Gahman, Levi, and Gabrielle Thongs. 2020. "Development Justice, A Proposal: Reckoning with Disaster, Catastrophe, and Climate Change in the Caribbean." *Transactions of the Institute of British Geographers*. https://doi.org/10.1111/tran.12369.

Godden, Naomi Joy, Pam Macnish, Trimita Chakma, and Kavita Naidu. 2020. "Feminist Participatory Action Research as a Tool for Climate Justice." *Gender and Development* 28, no. 3: 593–615.

Griffin, Paul. 2017. *The Carbon Majors Database: CDP Carbon Majors Report 2017*. London: CDP Worldwide.

Gurumurthy, Anita, and Nandini Chami. 2019. "Development Justice in the Digital Paradigm: Agenda 2030 and Beyond." *Development* 62, no. 1: 19–28.

Kujur, Joseph Marianus. 2008. "Development-Induced Displacement in Chhattisgarh: A Case Study from a Tribal Perspective." *Social Action* 58: 31–39.

Lamubol, Suluck Fai. 2019. "Decent Work Left Behind: Reality of Women Workers in Asia." *APWLD Blog*, October 7. https://apwld.org/blog-post-decent-work-left-behind-reality-of-women-workers-in-asia/.

LeBaron, Genevieve, and Ellie Gore. 2020. "Gender and Forced Labour: Understanding the Links in Global Cocoa Supply Chains." *Journal of Development Studies* 56, no. 6: 1095–1117.

Le Tran, Dalena, Joan Martinez-Alier, Grettel Navas, and Sara Mingorría. 2020. "Gendered Geographies of Violence: A Multiple Case Study Analysis of Murdered Women Environmental Defenders." *Journal of Political Ecology* 27, no. 1: 1189–1212.

Lutvey, Tanya, Kate Lappin, Camille Risler, and Aileen Familara, eds. 2015. *Women Warming Up! Building Resilient, Grassroots Feminist Movements for Climate Justice in Asia-Pacific*. Chiang Mai, Thailand: Asia Pacific Forum on Women, Law and Development (APWLD).

Mohanty, Chandra Talpade. 2003. *Feminism without Borders: Decolonizing Theory, Practicing Solidarity*. Durham, NC: Duke University Press.

Motta, Sara, and Alf Gunvald Nilsen. 2011. *Social Movements in the Global South: Dispossession, Development, and Resistance*. London: Palgrave.

Muñoz, Enara Echart, and María del Carmen Villarreal. 2019. "Women's Struggles against Extractivism in Latin America and the Caribbean." *Contexto Internacional* 41: 303–25.

Napier-Moore, Rebecca, Wardarina, Trimita Chakma, and Haley Pedersen, eds., and FPAR partner authors. 2017. *Changing Development from the Inside-Out: Feminist Participatory Action Research (FPAR) for Development Justice in Asia and the Pacific.* Chiang Mai, Thailand: APWLD.

Nilsen, Alf, Geoffrey Pleyers, and Laurence Cox. 2017. "Social Movement Thinking beyond the Core: Theories and Research in Post-colonial and Postsocialist Societies." *Interface: A Journal for and about Social Movements* 9, no. 2: 1–36.

Ossome, Lyn. 2021. "Pedagogies of Feminist Resistance: Agrarian Movements in Africa." *Agrarian South: Journal of Political Economy* 10, no. 1: 41–58.

Patel, Kamna . 2020. "Race and a Decolonial Turn in Development Studies." *Third World Quarterly* 41, no. 9. https://doi.org/10.1080/01436597.2020.1784001.

Pederson, Haley. 2019. *Promoting and Fulfilling the Right to Development.* Chiang Mai, Thailand: Asia Pacific Forum on Women, Law and Development (APWLD).

Ramli, Rashila. 2016. "Transnational Advocacy Networks: The Examples of the APWLD and NCWO. Comment on the Indian Case Study from a Malayan Perspective." In *Transnational Advocacy Networks. Transnational Social Work and Social Welfare: Challenges for the Social Work Profession,* edited by Beatrix Schwarzer, Ursula Kämmerer-Rütten, Alexandra Schleyer-Lindenmann, and Yafang Wang, 199–206. Abingdon, UK: Routledge.

Ruspini, Elisabetta. 2020. "From the Effects of Globalization on Women, to Women's Agency in Globalization." *Glocalism: Journal of Culture, Politics, and Innovation.* https://doi.org/10.12893/gjcpi.2019.3.8.

Rutazibwa, Olivia Umurerwa. 2019. "What's There to Mourn? Decolonial Reflections on (the End of) Liberal Humanitarianism." *Journal of Humanitarian Affairs* 1, no. 1: 65–67.

Seppälä, Tiina . 2016. "Feminizing Resistance, Decolonizing Solidarity: Contesting Neoliberal Development in the Global South." *Journal of Resistance Studies* 2, no. 1: 12–47.

Sharavdorj, Sarankhukhuu, and Helen Hakena. 2018. "Asia Pacific Forum on Sustainable Development: CSO Intervention." March 29. https://apwld.org/apwld-members-sarankhukhuu-sharavdorj-and-helen-hakena-speak-at-apfsd/.

Sheill, Kate. 2019. *A Dangerous Unselfishness: Learning from Strike Actions,* edited by Suluck Fai Lamubol, Trimita Chakma, and Zar Zar Tun. Penang, Thailand: Asia Pacific Forum on Women, Law and Development (APWLD).

Shejni, Lamìs. 2019. "Technology Is Not the Great Equalizer: A Feminist Perspective on the Digital Economy." *Development* 62, no. 1: 128–35.

Shiva, Vandana. 2016. *Staying Alive: Women, Ecology, and Development.* Berkeley, CA: North Atlantic.

Spivak, Gayatri. 1988. "Can the Subaltern Speak?" In *Marxism and the Interpretation of Culture,* edited by L. Grossberg and C. Nelson, 271–316. Basingstoke, UK: Macmillan.

Sulistyaningsih, Erwiana. 2019. "APWLD Member Erwiana Sulistyaningsih Speaks." February 13. https://apwld.org/apwld-member-erwiana-sulistyaningsih-speaks-at-the-preparatory-meeting-for-csw63/.

Taguiwalo, Judy, and Trimita Chakma. 2019. APWLD: *Herstory 1986–2017*. Chiang Mai, Thailand: Asia Pacific Forum on Women, Law and Development (APWLD).

Wattimena, Patricia. 2018. "Redefining Development: A Perspective from Indigenous Peoples in Asia." *Indigenous Policy Journal* 29, no. 3: 338–40.

Wilson, Kalpana. 2012. *Race, Racism, and Development*. London: Zed.

Woo, Jong Min, Jeong Ho Chae, and Soo Chan Choi. 2010. "Crisis Intervention for Workers in Severely Stressful Situations After Massive Layoffs and Labor Disputes." *Journal of Preventive Medicine and Public Health* 43, no. 3: 265–73.

Yazzie, M. K. 2018. "Decolonizing Development in Diné Bikeyah: Resource Extraction, Anti-capitalism, and Relational Futures." *Environment and Society* 9, no. 1: 25–39.

Debjani Chakravarty and Christine Standish

Consumption as Changemaking and Producers as Artists
Theorizing Alt-Profit Corporations from a Transnational Feminist Perspective

Abstract: In this article the authors perform a transnational feminist analysis of marketing strategies deployed in compassionate consumption. This strategy communicates to the consumer that consuming equals doing good. Using public-facing website data, the authors conduct a discourse analysis of *alt-profit* corporations, a term they coined to demonstrate yet another widespread strategy of late capitalism. Applying a transnational feminist perspective, they postulate that these alt-profits (meant to invoke "alternative" and "altruistic" actions by corporations) *McDonaldize* their marketing strategies to capitalize on consumer interests for sustainability, fair trade, "women's empowerment," and a desire to consume artisanal goods. They further argue that artisans from the Global South serving consumers in the Global North are framed as gendered and globalized in a way that helps sales. This is done purposefully using text and graphics, including digital storytelling, buzzwords, and vibrant photography. Contrary to the Marxist framework of alienation, artisans are presented as workers who find joy in their work. Alt-profits invite consumers to buy products and appreciate the unique experience of "meeting the artists." The authors conclude that the formulaic pattern of communication used by alt-profits is both distinct to them yet also common in publicizing any compassionate consumption and ultimately negates the reality of current global markets necessitating exploitative capitalist structures such as opaque and unsustainable supply chains.

MERIDIANS · feminism, race, transnationalism   23:2 October 2024
DOI: 10.1215/15366936-11266412 © 2024 Smith College

Introduction

In this article we explore the notion of compassionate consumption that positions consumption as "doing good" and fulfilling a socio-spiritual purpose beyond personal gratification and economic participation. This aspect of consumption can be understood as contributing to the greater common good. Through critical discourse analysis of public-facing information available on the websites of twelve corporations, we are investigating how their rhetoric of conscious and conscientious consumption uses the same set of keywords to do a kind of public relations damage control for global capitalism. We narrowed these twelve corporations based on their presence and publicity on social media, their large US consumer base, and their separation of sales and production operations between the US and elsewhere—in places loosely termed as belonging in the "Third World." We name these corporations that claim to be using a business model of people over profits and relationships over revenue as *alt-profits*. The *alt-* in *alt-profit* stands for *alternative* as well as *altruistic*. The mission of these corporations involves profit making through alternative and altruistic means. If the notion of altruism does not seem compatible with profit making, the business model as communicated to consumers persuasively argues for using fair trade practices, creating relationships with producer-artisans that are not exploitative but "mutually beneficial," "respectful," "trusting," and "transparent." This lexicon of altruism and alternative practices—alternatives presumably to commonly used ones in global capitalism—sets the alt-profits apart for consumers who are able to pay a premium on globally sourced goods that also represent goodness and humanity, products that appeal to not just necessity but nicety, not to a need for consumption as much as to the value of compassion. We theorize alt-profits as corporations with the following characteristic features:

1. They seem to present an alternative to the complex, anonymous, and exploitative supply chains of large global corporations by being global corporations with a strong local base featuring trust and transparency of local relationships.
2. They emphasize the human element of production and consumption by centering producers and their craft. In addition, this human element is reinforced with human-interest stories from the lives of founders and artisans along with other relatable elements for consumers/audience in the Global North.

3. They create conditions for compassionate consumption where the
    customer is given an ideal of humanitarianism and sustainability
    that they can live up to. Thus, consumption becomes an act that is
    broader than the mere act of consuming; it becomes an act of altru-
    ism, transformation, and intervention. Consumption becomes less
    about the product and more about the production processes that
    apparently create dignified livelihoods and decent incomes for
    producers.

The above characteristics are deeply embedded in alt-profit corporations' customer-facing communiqué, for example, "Creating go-to ward-
robe pieces that empower both women who wear them and make them,"
deploying the terms "women" and "empower[ment]." Alt-profits make
optimal use of new media to advertise, publicize, trade, and communicate.
They do this through dedicated company websites, social media, and
hyperlinks (e.g., to websites of partner organizations and informational
websites such as UNwomen.org). What we find on the dedicated websites
is repetitive, predictable, uniform rhetoric that we term *McDonaldized rhetoric*, given its similarity to George Ritzer's (2019) notion of efficient and predictable institutions and processes. McDonaldization is very much implicated in economic and cultural globalization, so it is an important
framework for our purposes. Our overall critique of these strategies
deployed to promote charitable and exotic consumption draws from both
sociological and transnational feminist frameworks. The former often
misses the gendered aspect of consumption and global capitalism; and,
while the latter framework considers these issues, it is more
focused on gendered production than the meanings and processes of
consumption.

Consumption: A Review of Literature

Within sociological studies of consumption, Sharon Zukin and Jennifer
Smith Maguire (2004) argue that consumption is a social, collective process
that should be seen as an institutional field. They also allude to a global
consumer culture and society facilitated by pervasive media. Mette H.
Jacobsen and Anders R. Hansen (2021) explain, using Pierre Bourdieu's
(1977) notion of *habitus*, that the collective, internalized histories that
social actors embody, connected to their status, form their habitus and this
is what ultimately drives consumption patterns. Consumption patterns

create "cultural classes" that distinguish consumption of the exotic vis-à-vis the regular, and as progressive versus regressive (May 1996).

Nina Bandelj and Christopher W. Gibson (2019: 163) explain that "in a broad stroke, studies of consumption vary by their starting point, either taking the consumer, or the process of consumption, as a point of departure. If the starting point is the process of consumption, this is a less circumscribed target of study. It includes consumer behavior, a bread-and-butter of consumption studies, but also the intriguing worlds in which commodities are experienced." They further argue that consumption should be understood as relational, emotional, and experiential. A relational turn in consumption studies can bridge the gap between understanding cultural identities and a social context—both necessitating the study of power. Consumption is expanded and patterns of consumption are modified with the expansion of new media and online marketplaces (McQuarrie 2015; Ritzer 2019).

Delving into literature about compassionate consumption reveals commentary on the kind of cultures global capitalism generates. Compassionate consumption driven by compassionate consumerism is a project of unequal global economies. Japhy Wilson (2015) critiques cause-related marketing (CRM), which is the practice of attaching social cause(s) to the commodity being sold and consumed so that the consumer experiences compassionate consumption—consuming toward contributing to a cause—which in turn demonstrates compassion and conscience. Kathleen M. Kuehn (2009: 28) explains that "CRM campaigns are effective not because they offer new or better products but because they infuse the brand with new qualities and experiences that consumers appropriate into the assemblage of their own identities." Conscientious consumers are motivated by values such as sustainability to shape their consumption choices, and this is becoming a critical field of study (Hume 2010; Evans 2011; Watkins, Aitken, and Mather 2016). These varied forms of ethical consumer practices are influenced by people's personal moral compass as well as prevalent social, political, and economic discourses and activism.

The notion of morality is complicated, and when there is a connection between individual morality and consumption we do wonder about the performance and manifestation of morality in and through consuming. There also seems to be a connection between a consumer's quest for truth, uniqueness, meaning, identity, and consumption—so much so that consumption and consumerism become akin to religiosity and/or spirituality in some cases (Jhally 1989; Bruce 2002; Choudhury 2019). This also manifests itself in a marketplace for "healing," "recharging," and "spiritual" products, mainly for white consumers, that simultaneously represents a space for cultural appropriation and a form of consumerist "new age" spiritual secularism (Bruce 2002). In our research we noticed that there is a convergence of such marketplaces for "mindfulness" and compassionate consumption. Certain manifestations of neoliberal feminisms also center notions of spiritual well-being and self-care that apparently require use of what are loosely termed *artisanal products* and *traditional practices* (Fisher 2017). Of course, whose tradition and what counts as artisanal can be complicated.

The literature on compassionate consumption is scarce, and our research tries to address gaps in theoretical and substantive approaches in understanding how new media promotes a certain form of compassionate consumption that requires repetitive, McDonaldized rhetoric. We also argue that strategies deployed to make products and producers valuable to the end consumer include exoticizing the unfamiliar, and utilizing gendered tropes of aid, empathy, and empowerment.

Theoretical Framework: Globalization as Theorized in Transnational Feminist and Sociological Thought

Globalization is understood as social, economic, political, and cultural processes on a planetary scale. By no means are these processes mutually exclusive, and they are indeed co-constitutive. Globalization creates a global marketplace of/for goods and services, and a global supply chain driven by oligopolistic business practices. A global culture is seen as composite and heterogeneous, yet is increasingly homogeneous and predictable because of cultural imperialism and structural adjustments. Globalization is also an unequal process that reinvigorates colonial binaries of us and them, self and other, civilized and uncivilized, developed and underdeveloped. Inequalities of globalization are results of deepening neocolonial and neoliberal policies—economic drain and exploitative and extractive markets masquerading as "free" markets. For the purposes of our research, we are utilizing two frameworks of globalization: (1) transnational feminist critique drawn from the works of Chandra Mohanty, Inderpal Grewal, and others, and (2) sociology of globalization, drawn from George Ritzer, Leslie Sklair, and others. We also discuss scholarship where the two converge.

Transnational feminism is a result of the Western academy evolving as a site of feminist struggle responding to globalization, re-creating the everyday material/ideological conditions of intellectual and activist work (Mohanty 2003; Desai 2007). This discourse critiques the inevitable forces of corporate capitalism and neocolonial globalization that are oblivious of—or purposely devaluing and exploiting—the natural environment, women's and minorities' labor, knowledge, and images. It draws from postcolonial theories that argue, among other things, that the idea of the "West" becomes more composite yet pervasive through various processes of globalization and transnational neoliberalism creating dependencies between colonizing nations and nations colonized by them after formal declarations of independence. Mohanty's (2003: 43) appeal for an oppositional feminist movement consisting of "imagined communities of women with divergent histories and social locations, woven together by the threads of opposition to forms of domination that are not only pervasive but also systemic" forms a basis for transnational feminist movements as well as theorizing. Grewal and Caren Kaplan (1994), who used the terms *transnational* and *feminism* together for the first time, state that *postcolonial* "can serve as a term that positions cultural production in the fields of transnational economic relations and diasporic identity constructions. It is particularly useful in projects that delineate fields of reception in the west (United States, Europe, and Australia). Critiques of Western reception can deconstruct the aesthetic and political mystiques that govern the marketing and distribution of cultural artifacts from the 'Third World'" (1994: 15). Mohanty's (1988) early transnational feminist theorizing aligns with Gayatri Spivak's (1988) postcolonial critique of the monolithic, perpetually oppressed "Third World women." Both Mohanty and Spivak critique Western feminist notions of scapegoating subaltern, Third World women and men as homogeneous and powerless without discussing the colonialist and capitalist origins (largely) of such powerlessness. Western (or "global") feminists are often moved by Third World women's poverty and oppression through what Uma Narayan (1997) terms *death by culture*, women becoming victims of their own regressive "uncivilized" culture. Thus, one of the crucial transnational feminist perspectives, closely connected to critique of colonialism, global capitalism, and global/Western feminisms, is a critique of actively othering the imagined spaces of the Third World and Third World women. Yet, such representation is also inextricably connected to ideas of deep concern for the Other and for "doing good," as summed up by a statement in one of the websites we studied, discussing the life-changing travel of the founder to Uganda as a teenager.

> It was there that I met a Ugandan woman named Sarah. Sarah lived her life with great meaning and purpose. She sacrificed everything she had to care for 24 children who slept on her floor. There I was, a girl who had been given so much, standing before a woman who had so little but gave what she had away so that others could live. I only spent ten minutes with Sarah, but I was forever changed. I knew that there were poor children in the world. But for the first time, I SAW them. I saw their mats, distended stomachs, and their sores. I wanted to help.[1]

These forms of centering one's *self* also create displacement of the *Other* whereby the distant non-Western *they* as opposed to the familiar, Western *we* are reduced to uncomplicated objects of charity. In addition, transnational feminist critique of consumer citizenship explains how blurring the meaning and nature of identities and citizenship replaces political thinking and action with discourses of neoliberal choice and consumption. For instance, Grewal (2005: 81) argues that

> consumer citizenship, simultaneously transnational and national, enabled increased levels of connectivity with transnational consumer culture. This version of citizenship, in which liberal democracy could only be imagined or made possible through consumer culture and its focus on choices between alternative goods or through the work of the market, produced liberal subjects in various parts of the world.

When these liberal subjects are gendered, there is a possibility of analyzing the nature of gender, globalization, liberalism, and neoliberal capitalism simultaneously. Websites that sell artisanal products deploy varied ideologies of "feminism" and "liberalism," and use gender as a crucial identity to mobilize support for their causes and consumers for their products, globally.

   With that, we segue into issues of globalization as a backdrop and necessary condition for "compassionate consumption" and a type of "compassionate capitalism" that implies capitalist practices as a pathway toward global and environmental justice. The processes of globalization, analyzed sociologically, are seen here as international and transnational— both prefixes to *national* implying among or within sovereign territorial nations, but also nations without states. Globalization is conceptualized in terms of transnational practices, practices that cross state borders but do not necessarily originate with state agencies, actors, or institutions. These practices are analytically distinguished by Sklair (2002) as three levels: economic, political, and culture-ideology—constituting the sociological totality. The culture-ideology of consumption and consumerism is carefully crafted and disseminated by a transnational capitalist class, which is a ruling class focused on profit and political domination (Sklair 2010). Information communication technologies (ICTs) play a major role in this culture-ideology by creating connectivity and decentralized information between local and global actors and building a network society and/or a postindustrial information society (Bell 1980; Castells 2000; Sassen 2007).

Ritzer's sociological perspectives on globalization as McDonaldization, and globalization as *grobalization* featuring something/nothing are important to consider. Ritzer (2003) complements the notion of *glocalization*, a term used by theorists of globalization to signify interplay of heterogeneous global and local processes, with *grobalization*, which "focuses on the imperialistic ambitions of nations, corporations, organizations, and other entities and their desire—indeed their need—to impose themselves on various geographic areas. Their main interest is in seeing their power, influence, and (in some cases) profits grow" (2003: 194). This is connected to previous sociological analyses of consumer capitalism and late capitalism whereby consumption as well as exploitation become embedded capitalist ideologies (Horkheimer and Adorno 2002; Mandel 1999). "Nothing" is a conceptual formation that is empty of meanings and devoid of distinctive cultural content that can be easily globalized. "Something," on the other hand, contains substance, meaning, and context—examples being specific places, things, people, and services that are grounded and cannot be easily globalized. Nothing, meanwhile, would be "non-thing," "non-people," and so on, demonstrating automation and homogenization aimed at economic growth more specifically (Ritzer 2003). Global capitalist processes also display what Ritzer (2019: 2) terms *McDonaldization*, which "is the process by which the principles of the fast-food restaurant are coming to dominate more and more sectors of American society as well as the rest of the world." The five principles of McDonaldization are efficiency, calculability, predictability, control, and irrationality of rationality. While McDonaldization creates some economic and social advantages, it also suppresses creativity and humanity, and increases cultural gatekeeping. In recent discussions of this phenomenon, Ritzer (2019) discusses how digital McDonaldization, in the form of ecommerce corporations such as Amazon, creates "platform capitalism" which allows control of not just transactions but also social participation, interaction, and other material realities of social life.

We will apply Ritzer's frameworks to understand the proliferation of digital compassionate consumption, but we must also subject the very notion of McDonaldization to feminist critique and revision. Transnational feminists go deeper into how globalization (and McDonaldization) pries open localities and regions, spreading the new hegemony of neoliberalism that pushes freedom, choice, and ability (often to consume and design the "self"). The cost of such production and consumption enabling "free markets" is something rarely discussed or discussed nebulously as "human costs," which can obscure realities of gender—whether it be women in maquiladoras in Mexico or women in Bangladesh's garment factories exploited by mostly male supervisors trying to meet global demand for cheap fashion. No discussion of globalization can be complete without a discussion of gender as well as feminist praxis in a global context (Grewal and Kaplan 1994; Nagar and Swarr 2010). Transnational feminist theory can be considered a robust critique of globalization utilizing marginalized standpoints of actors marked by gender, sexuality, socioeconomic class, and occupation, as well as geopolitical and global supply chain location. Manisha Desai (2007) contends that there is an uneasy, messy relationship between feminisms and globalization, marked by complicity of feminism with global capital as well as the possibility for feminist critique of agency building in global capital, commerce, and consumption. Nira Yuval-Davis (2009) also discusses similar paradoxical effects of "globalization" and "social change" vis-à-vis gender rights and feminist activism.

Transnational feminist praxis often exists both in close ties and in tension with global civil-society organizations such as the World Social Forum (Conway 2013). In pursuit of global justice, such civil society organizations sometimes follow Western feminist ideas and capitalist market logic, losing sight of local contexts. Vrushali Patil (2011) contends that there are three overlapping transnational feminist sociological positions. The first focuses on the notion of nation and on the histories of colonialism, neocolonialist global capitalism, and neoliberalism, critiquing militarism and war as well the neocolonial positions of transnational governance, for example, the United Nations. This approach brings together textual and empirical sociological methodology of inquiry. The second position focuses on women's transnational organizing and transnational feminist praxis as well as successes, complexities, and limits of such organizing. The third approach brings together, overlaps, and sometimes synonymizes transnational, global, and international feminisms and their prospects for gender justice. Our analysis draws from this complexity of sociological and transnational feminist congruences and departures and argues that in a perverse way, McDonaldized consumerist rhetoric draws from the language of global feminism—global women's rights and justice—while placing the idea of the struggling Third World woman (Mohanty 1988) at the center of their appeal to consume without referencing "the myriad ways women are organizing against the gendered, racialized, and regionalized processes of global capital expansion" (Naples 2002: 12). In other words, alt-profit corporations are often framing the issue of women's rights and justice as limited to the right of women in the "Third World" to produce items for (mostly) women in the "First World" who have the right to consume such products in the name of justice and altruism.

Compassionate Capitalism and Passionate Consumption: A Critical Discourse Analysis

As argued above, globalization is a necessary condition for the kind of compassionate capitalism we are analyzing in this article, peddling artisanal handmade goods locally produced and globally dispersed. The "globality" of the products—imported from faraway "exotic" places—adds a special value to this kind of consumption, as does the idea of "doing good." We analyzed claims and terminology found in twelve popular websites that advertise and sell products that have value beyond their materiality and usability. This value is positioned as making positive social change, whether through providing income for women in poverty or using sustainable production practices that takes the environment into account.

Our criteria for finding businesses were that (a) they claimed that their products were value-added, the value being a greater social good and a better society; (b) their inventory was handmade products created by artisans in the Global South; and (c) they had detailed websites that did not serve only as e-commerce sites but also as informational sites providing details about their business ethics, business practices, and business models—all oriented toward a specific cause or multiple causes. Most of these businesses have been operational for a decade or more, some are certified B Corps (e.g., https://shopsoko.com/), and some are connected to cause-based foundations and nonprofits that intervene in specific Global South locales—working with other organizations such as the Mines Advisory Group, which clears unexploded mines and cleans post-conflict lands.

In our critical discourse analysis, we analyze the informational politics of these cause-based businesses in the context of capitalist globalization and compassionate consumption, attempting to understand how/whether these processes are co-constitutive. What discourses are emerging through the companies' communiqués as they exhort consumers in the Global North to buy products as a way of producing positive social change? How do these discourses on compassionate consumption fold into existing discourses about globalization and capitalism—phenomena that make such consumption possible?

We focused on (a) the company's mission statements—also presented in the format of "our story," "about us," and "founder's message/letter"; (b) further information provided about the causes being espoused and the company's impact, often in the format of attractive and accessible representation of numerical data; and (c) descriptions of products, which most often included narrative about the producer. We noticed that the textual content of (a) and (b) are often buzzword ridden, and similar words, phrases, and expressions repeat themselves across all twelve websites. Descriptions under (c) are steeped in assumptions about producers and potential consumers.

Next, we proceeded to analyze the commonly occurring buzzwords using a transnational feminist approach that pays attention to inequities of representation and rights. Overall, the websites focus on consumption as an activity that is not merely personal or individual but that fulfills a greater common good. They also focus on a narrative of production as a process of joy, fulfillment, and creativity—quite distant from a Marxian notion of grim alienation generated by the capitalist production process. In this narrative, producers (artisans, craftspeople, makers) are whole human beings who are in control of their own work and destiny in a holistic and purpose-driven production process that is ethical and empowering. To complete the narrative loop, the products are ethically distributed in the form of sales by the companies through their own and other e-commerce websites. The fond hope is that there are compassionate consumers who can be persuaded, tempted, and challenged to buy these high-impact products that are apparently life-changing for producer, distributor, and customer alike. In this narrative the capitalist system of production needs some ethical fine tuning to be able to bring opportunities and prosperity (and in a couple of instances, "happiness" and "fulfillment") for all. This win-win narrative blends business and charity as well as consumption and conscience to frame global capitalism as a purveyor of humanistic values and social good. The globality of capitalism allows consumers to connect with distant makers and producers of exotic goods, and it allows consumers to provide life-changing benefits to these producers through the very act of consuming.

Table 1 shows the most commonly occurring words and expressions on these websites, occurring in more than five instances per website.

Other commonly occurring expressions on these websites that occur in three instances or fewer per website are: *accountability, authenticity, children, connection, courage, craftsmanship, developing/underdeveloped, dream, employment, fair trade, gender, happiness, income, inequality, making a difference, poverty,* and *upliftment.* The patterns that emerge from critical discourse analysis can be discussed under three phenomena: 1) consumption as life-changing, digitized, and compassionate; 2) producers as gendered and globalized; and 3) justice and equity as a matter of technological innovation and goodwill. We discuss them as follows.

Consumption as Life-Changing, Digitized, and Compassionate

Consumption as a crucial economic activity under capitalism can be studied sociologically by relating it to socioeconomic class—especially when we are discussing consumption of necessities. This theme of alt-profit communication aligns with several sociological frameworks of globalization including McDonaldization and culture-ideology of consumerism. Consumption of comfort and luxury goods can be associated with social status and cultural capital, impression management and self-consciousness. It is usually connected to the self through notions of fulfillment as well as participation in a material culture. Compassionate consumption creates another layer of significance, loosely understood as consumption as life-changing and consumption as a greater common good. This life-changing aspect is twofold: changing the lives of makers and producers as well as changing the lives of consumers themselves. The former is achieved, expressly, through creating fair and ethical conditions of production and distribution, the

Table 1. Repetitive Website Rhetoric Encouraging Compassionate Consumption

Expressions/Buzzwords	On How Many Websites (n = 12)	Related Expressions/Example of Use
Artisan	8	Artist Traditional art E.g., "Artisans are agents of change, healing their land, making it safe to play and grow rice."
Community	6	Community-focused Community building E.g., "That means you can trust that every hand-made purchase and donation you make directly impact the life and community of its maker in a developing country."
Empowerment	6	Empowering E.g., "We're a way for you to shop with intention for ethically-sourced wares—and to share in the joy of empowering makers."
Ethical	7	Ethics E.g., "We are committed to these ethical practices—and hope you are, too."
Global	11	Globally (inspired/driven) E.g., "Impact the world by purchasing handmade products directly from global artisans!"
Handmade	7	Handcrafted E.g., "Handcrafted with love by young women escaping human trafficking."
Opportunity	6	Employment opportunity E.g., "As a social entrepreneur she has helped hundreds of women and girls to use their talents to find opportunities for success."
Sustainable	7	Sustainability E.g., "We travel to Nepal every year to maintain relationships and make sure our sourcing is ethical and sustainable."
Women	10	Woman Women in poverty E.g., "By supporting jobs that guarantee fair wages by fair trade, women are able to proudly contribute to their families, encouraging their communities to flourish."

latter through creating an ideology of self-care and spirituality that needs consumption of faraway, exotic, intriguing products connected to unfamiliar cultures.

Consumption as having a greater social good is emphasized in neoclassical economics as an activity that keeps national economies healthy and productive. What we are seeing under the compassionate consumption trend is a greater social good that has cross-border significance, as an activity that allows economically and socially oppressed people such as people in poverty to turn their lives around—lives that are existing at the periphery of society and in a brutal, competitive capitalist economy. The brutality of capitalism is emphasized in how artisans are generally not compensated fairly for their work and how the local/national economy is exploitative and/or unable to provide enough opportunities for all. Therefore, to address issues of exploitative policies and intermediaries, entrepreneurs from the Global North are creating businesses where they themselves become the ethical intermediaries, paying the artisans a fair price and providing opportunities for growth and realization of human potential. One website explains a founder's work in the following manner: "Prior, she worked with an Italian non-profit, focusing on maternal health: the Women's Maternity Waiting Home Center and Weaving Group. Her role also included organizing skills training for women around weaving and other crafts."[2] There is a certain not-for-profit positioning of the products being sold, so much so that initially we had mistaken the majority of the companies we looked at as nonprofits with "gain divisions," or operations that generate a revenue stream. We realized as we got into details that these are corporations that brand themselves as doing community work, as being more ethical than regular corporations, and in some cases doing charity work through associated trusts and foundations. Some businesses are *certified* B *Corps*, which according to the certification body, "are a new kind of business that balances purpose and profit. They are legally required to consider the impact of their decisions on their workers, customers, suppliers, community, and the environment. This is a community of leaders, driving a global movement of people using business as a force for good."[3] Thus, businesses that have a compassionate consumption model are based on ideals of social good and justice. Some businesses have emphasized this by going beyond their commitment to makers and producers by pledging their commitment to the environment and issues of sustainability. Most state that they are doing this through the ethical sourcing of raw materials and the reducing of carbon footprints. One corporation avers that "the Earth sustains us, and we believe it's courteous to return the favor. We focus on the use of locally sourced, recycled and renewable materials in our products. We promote creative re-use and energy efficiency in artisan workshops and our supply chain to minimize our environmental footprint."[4] Another approach to emphasize blending of social and environmental good is to distance one's operations from China, a country with a checkered environmental and human rights record. However, there is no mention at all of countries in the Global North that overconsume, create excessive waste at individual and industrial levels, and create disproportionately high carbon footprints. It is easy to see why. Sharing responsibility or claiming complicity in capitalist processes that exploit human beings and the environment while encouraging customers to consume more as a way of doing more social good is ironic, ridden with obvious contradictions. A simplistic rhetoric of compassion and care can contain neither irony nor contradictions.

One company states that their business is "different because our main priority is to support artisans directly, and we travel to Nepal every year to maintain relationships and make sure our sourcing is ethical and sustainable. We never buy from Chinese factories or street vendors. We go directly to the artists themselves."[5] This sort of rhetoric has the dual purpose of demonstrating care and accountability while setting a business apart from capitalism as usual. Thus, the altruistic motive takes precedence over a profit motive.

We understand that the purpose of these corporations is to brand and sell products, and their websites are set up to do just that. What sets their publicity rhetoric apart is disproportionate emphasis on how consumption as an activity is akin to changing the world and changing lives, a form of value-added consumption where the value does not reside in the product alone. Thus, this branding rhetoric does not merely create brand loyalty and visibility for a specific corporation or their products, it also brands and publicizes the very process of consumption as compassionate and transformative. It goes beyond traditional economics of consumption out of necessity, for comfort, or as luxury and conspicuous consumption to consumption as a compassionate life-changing intervention (Hudson and Hudson 2021). This can alleviate guilt or doubts associated with overconsumption, commercialization of most human activity, and normalized consumerism to position consumption as a noble pursuit.

The digitized nature of consumption and communication accelerates the pace and scale of distribution not just of the products but also of the ideology of compassionate consumption. The consumers and producers, separated by oceans, can connect through the websites, although this connection is manifested through buying from an intermediary. However, to discount this commercial connection and underscore a human and humane one, the websites deploy a rhetoric of connection and compassion by creating narratives of the makers' lives—lives as struggling yet fulfilled, hardworking yet joyful, precarious yet comfortable. Excessive discussion of struggles, precarity, and poverty might turn off consumers looking for jewelry with meaning and art with spiritual significance to be purchased sight unseen and to be paid a premium for; therefore, these narratives are tempered by heavy emphasis on the company's mission, ethics, and business practices that apparently transform communities. Another way of doing this is emphasizing the gender of producers, a point we take up in the next section.

Producers as Gendered and Globalized

Putting the producer and their work (often qualified as artistic and creative—and hence joyful and fulfilling) at the center of a business model, the life-changing aspect of consumption is emphasized heavily by alt-profit companies. This particular practice, analyzed through the lens of transnational feminisms, reveals several repetitive manipulative features. Most alt-profits work with female producers who are more likely to be impoverished and exploited in all societies, and the Global South is no exception. Helping impoverished women is a worthy mission, and the websites ensure that the gender of the producers is repetitively emphasized. This is done through vibrant photography, evocative personal stories, and discussions about how the corporation is intervening in gender equity. The following are examples of how the corporations are apparently not just enhancing ethical production and distribution practices but also providing something that goes beyond mere buying and reselling of products: "When a woman is employed by Akola, she is more likely to keep her kids in school, gain the skills to generate additional income, and operate as a leader in her community. Akola creates jobs that help women rebuild inner confidence, strength, and the determination to realize their full potential."[6]

Thus, concrete claims about additional income are blended with unverifiable claims about inner confidence and strength. More often than not, the poverty of the female producers is emphasized more than their artistry and creativity. Some websites emphasize how women are empowered through their association with the corporation. One corporation claims that women, "largely from rural communities, are given dignified employment and living wages. Akola's vision is to create a female empowered workforce that will be a strong contributor to Africa's economic development." Yet another describes the work of a partner organization, "which is to create an all-natural product and empower women in the process. Their workflow is beautiful. Working from an open and airy home outside of Kathmandu, a team of women create each batch of soap by hand using traditional Tibetan and Nepalese ingredients."[7]

Another interesting aspect we noticed about the representation of gender on these websites was the marked difference in how producers and consumers are depicted. While most producers of items are women because many alt-profits champion a "women's cause," so are the target customers—positioned as women consuming wisely and prolifically. One website sums this up in three words, that their fashion products are "Functional. Feminine. Forward."[8] However, there seem to be two varieties of femininity on display. One is upper-class or middle-class femininity of customers, represented by mostly white female models who are shown in serene, luxurious surroundings—looking content as they use the products on sale (e.g., wearing jewelry, carrying handbags, drinking out of hand-crafted wine glasses or mugs). They are usually pictured alone in well-crafted glamour shots, enjoying leisure. The female artisans, who are often shown hard at work, are visibly nonwhite women in over 89 percent of the images (of producers), dressed in local or "traditional" attire, often shown in a group of other women. One commonality among the subjects of the photograph would be their radiant smiles, which is more common in images of consumers than producers. This contrast between white and Other femininity, work and leisure, individuality and community, is immediately noticeable.

Processes of unequal globalization have thrown societies in the Global South in disarray, creating relationships of exploitative dependency and deepening existing social inequities. Poor women's lives are often the most upended (Mohanty 2003). The alt-profit corporations whose websites we studied depend on these very processes of globalization to produce and distribute products. The operation of the alt-profits usually entails a relationship between the Global South and the Global North. This interaction portrays a fundamental aspect of globalization, which is globalization in service of the Global North. All the website content is written in English, containing specific cultural references and explanations to be palatable and accessible to Western audiences. The gender of the consumers of the products made by women in underdeveloped, impoverished, or disadvantaged countries is often presumed to be feminine because of the preponderance of products often marketed toward women (e.g., feminine jewelry, dresses, scarves, bags, and artistic knickknacks).

However, globalization for the gendered producers is presented as a narrative of opportunity and opulence where processes of globalization allow women from the Global South to create intricate and expensive extravagant products for women in the Global North. This is presented as a win-win situation for all involved. There is no reference to colonial occupation and colonization, relationships of dependence and exploitation that create barriers for women in the Global South. When these barriers are discussed on the websites, it is as if they are failures of innovation in the local society and products of regressive local cultures that do not value women's rights. For instance, a website claims this about the artisans' lives before their company stepped in: "They worked hard, digging in a field for almost nothing, and it was never enough. I realized that meaningful job creation is critical. Women in poverty need living wage employment, training and support to meet the needs of their children and transform their lives."[9] This seems to imply that there were no local jobs or job trainings for women, a claim that is dubious and condescending.

We use the adjective *globalized* for producers in the sense of global characteristics ascribed to people just as *racialized* is used in the sense of imposing assumed racial characteristics on people. *Global* or *international* are often used colloquially in the United States to signify people, places, products, and processes outside the United States, where "global" women's narratives of struggle can become products too. As one website recounts about an orphaned artist who has children of her own,

> If Zandra still has questions about what happened to her mother and father, she bears no bitterness over her circumstances. Her dreams are not those of luxury. She treats herself to small rewards in life: a delicious cake after an especially busy season. But she does hold onto one important dream, as much for her children as for the child that still lives within her: a trip to Disney World.[10]

The stories of artisans are vibrant and touching, and they capture universal experiences with some amount of unfamiliarity and intrigue. These stories are curated with a purpose, and we speculate that stories which are relatable to consumers who too perhaps enjoy Disney World trips would be beneficial for sales. Some of the stories are in first person, capturing the sheer joy of creativity despite adversity:

> I married into a farmer's family and we had to struggle to make ends meet. I helped by working from home as well as in farming. At night, we would paint. As they say, life is a struggle and there is nothing like the joy and satisfaction of overcoming your difficulties . . . [I] am now able to sell my creations in my own name and get a better price as well. The best thing about my work is seeing people who admire and display them in their homes—what a joy![11]

This joy and pleasure of creativity, on the one hand, represent the wholeness and aspirations of artists, not merely as suffering human beings in need of aid, but artistic human beings who are resourceful and resilient. This presents a contrast to production processes of global corporate capitalism that—whether in a large factory farm, a windowless factory, or a gigantic warehouse—reduce people to expendable nameless machinal resources for hard labor. Instead, the people featured in the online narratives are often women who are fulfilling their potential, in charge of their own destiny with a little help from alt-profits.

Justice and Equity as a Matter of Technological Innovation and Goodwill

Alt-profits often present issues of economic and social justice as problems that can be solved by technological and corporatist innovation, goodwill, and altruism. Sociologically, we can analyze this as a form of technological determinism that also displays the "irrationality of rationality" aspect of McDonaldization. This dimension of McDonaldization demonstrates how the rightly controlled, rational, calculable, predictable systems of capitalism are often inefficient, dehumanizing, and resistant to changes (Ritzer 2019). Discussion of justice and equity in alt-profit websites is similarly predictable and controlled—quickly and efficiently signaling the corporations' commitment to corporate social responsibility. Justice is positioned as fairness embodied in fair trade practices, represented by statements suggesting that people "working together" can solve economic injustices. Of course, practices of transparent price agreement, interest-free microfinance investment, payment in full before export are indeed helpful to address exploitation, as embraced by one of the older and well-established alt-profits that we studied. However, pervasive as economic injustice is, not every issue of equity is strictly connected to economic issues. This repetitive communication sounds inexorably like lip service.

The impact that the alt-profits claim in providing livelihoods and dignity obscures how their reach is statistically/geographically limited. Under the circumstances, making tall claims about changing countries and societies seems disingenuous. Ideals such as "the things we love should be made with love, in environments free of harassment, discrimination, and forced labor, regardless of gender, location, or economic status"[12] minimize multiple issues of local social stratification as well as existence of producers at the intersection of oppressive global systems of capitalism, colonialism, racism, and so on. Presenting globalization as unfettered opportunity and a solution to problems created by globalization including unfair "free" trade practices and structural adjustments misrepresents the inequitable nature of globalization. Of course, to critique the very process that makes the alt-profit business model profitable would require acknowledging the complicity of consumers and traders in unequal globalization. It is easier to critique "local culture" and "gender inequality" that need intervention than acknowledging the limitations of interventional and informational politics embedded in alt-profit communiqué and logic.

The goodwill aspect of the business model is directly associated with customers whereby they are expected to pay a premium while enjoying fruits of "good" globalization that involves opportunity, equity, justice, and empowerment. This empowerment, as discussed before, is something that producers experience through working in an equitable environment created by the alt-profit(s). It also is something consumers experience, signified in the following rhetoric:

> The ethical consumer ideal implies that individual customers can have a significant role, through their daily purchasing decisions, in promoting ethical corporate practices. Products that make sure that all the stakeholders in the value chain are treated fairly constitute whether a product is considered ethical . . . and when our members choose to use their purchasing power for good it encourages innovative companies like ours, while discouraging others that ignore the social and environmental consequences of their business model.[13]

This presents a dynamic interaction and partnership among customers, producers, and intermediaries, as well as between the Global South and Global North—the former as a space of consumption and ethical consciousness while the latter is a space for production and painstaking progress. The e-commerce company is a conduit for consciousness raising as well as "combatting" poverty and other injustices that afflict the lives of producers.

Consciousness raising of customers happens through attractively presented data on global poverty rate, women's poverty, and women's education, often drawn from UN Women, UN Development Programme, and other transnational organizations. There is also an abundance of descriptive quantitative data on the company's impact presented in numerical or narrative format. Sometimes the impact is measured vis-à-vis national numbers, for example, "93% of artisans are able to send their children to school (national average is 50%)" or "Starting artisan wages are 3x above the national minimum wage."[14] Article 22, a company that sells jewelry created from unexploded ordnance in Vietnam and Laos, states under "Our Story": "250 million bombs dropped. 80 million failed to detonate. Each Peacebomb helps clear UXO from land in Laos. Peacebomb is the name of a necklace; UXO stands for unexploded ordnance." Some corporations such as Article 22 feature the UN Universal Declaration of Human Rights on their website. Issues of equity and social justice are seamlessly woven into digital narratives, and the customer is invited to join in through consumption. Narratives and storytelling about justice display characteristics of McDonaldization—especially efficiency and predictability. These qualities are achieved through technological innovation in the realm of digitization, big-data-driven social justice, and other formats of mediatization.

In Conclusion: Critiquing the Gendered Discourse of Global Compassionate Consumption

A transnational feminist critique of globalization includes discussions about the economic, environmental, and political effects of globalization that are also often gendered. Processes of injustice and exploitation are often obscured by the hegemony of pervasive good-for-everyone grobalization. Transnational feminists also critique cosmopolitan feminism, notions of global "sisterhood," and neoliberalism. The products and related discourses created by alt-profits that focus on gender rights and equality seem to embody some of these problematic ideologies that position globalization as development and empowerment, inequities as temporary—waiting for innovative solutions.

The alt-profit companies who trade in these goods are often established and/or run by women from the Global North who claim partnership with women in the Global South. This is reminiscent of global sisterhood and indeed strategic sisterhood that encourages liberation through economic and political partnerships when the conditions of such partnerships are laid out by those with more power and privilege (Ong 2006; Mohanty 2003). This privilege is very apparent in the alt-profit founders' stories that repeat a tale, with minor variations, of the desire to do good, the desire to bring equity and equality, the desire to intervene in an unfamiliar and "unfortunate" society, the desire to count one's "blessings" and give back. Of course, meaningful acknowledgment and utilization of privilege is useful to build communities and social justice movements, but performative humility is not. The desire to obscure profit motives, economic stakes, and structural issues while speaking about justice work is suspect.

For alt-profits, "local traditions" become commoditized as simultaneously aesthetic and oppressive, with rich potential for consumption and profit making. The rhetoric presented on the websites—the chief conduit of trading and publicity for most alt-profits that do not have physical stores—creates imagined transnational communities of struggling, resilient, creative women waiting for liberation. This is a branding strategy, and as with any consumer/household goods business, branding is usually associated with product visibility, maintaining or increasing sales, and sometimes charging a premium for a product over its generic counterparts. Our analysis of alt-profit rhetoric also reveals branding of ideologies (such as globalization as good, cultures in Global South as exotic, nations and women in the Global South as perpetually "developing" with help from developed nations and women from the Global North). In some cases, people or target constituencies are branded as "29% of Akola women hold leadership position in their community" or "79% of Akola children are in school." Therefore, associated women and children are represented online as faceless, nameless employees and beneficiaries of transnational trading corporations. Even when women are named, they are represented, as we mentioned before, as the Other.

Simplistic connections, such as when a woman is employed by an alt-profit she is more likely to educate herself and her children, are reminiscent of claims made by larger transnational companies trying to establish goodwill and/or trying to steer clear of controversies related to the use of sweatshop labor or flouting of environmental norms. Nike Foundation's

"Girl Effect" comes to mind where a snappily produced video in 2008 created a clear cause-and-effect relationship between young girls in Third World countries getting educated, achieving social and economic stratus, and therefore escaping societal ills such as early marriage and AIDS. The use of stereotypes and faulty neoliberal logic abounds in development and women's empowerment discourses emerging from the Global North where exploited and oppressed parties are shown as carriers of potential, provided they receive just a little charitable help. In addition, Michelle Murphy (2017) has argued that the vision of a girl who is able to exercise the liberal feminist promise of individual agency represents not just individual welfare but also human capital, which "designates the embodied capacities of a person that can produce future economic benefits for that person, her employer, and even her national economy" (115). Such discourses make the heterosexualized "girl" an undervalued stock for the future of economic recovery and national wealth. Such discourses launch foundations and projects and rarely, if ever, look at global and local structural issues. Heather Switzer (2013) states that the "Girl Effect narrative reaffirms the agency of the postfeminist viewing subject in the global north by encouraging her to invest in the recuperation of the authentic victim" (347).

The producers who create items for alt-profits also are positioned as succeeding in neoliberal-capitalist-approved ways, by selling their creativity and "culture," working hard, and enjoying the fruits of their labor. These producers are gendered, heterosexualized, and localized. Their customers are a world away enjoying the fruits of such "personal agency," in the form of leather goods, pottery, and metalwork. Products are "something," as Ritzer (2003) theorizes, imbued with meaning, as opposed to meaningless "nothings" created by ruthless supply chains of exploitation in a "grobalized" environment. Products that are positioned as spiritual, cultural, impactful, beautiful, and even, in some cases, feminist, can take away the guilt of consumerism or unfettered consumption that greater purchasing power and privileged lifestyles can afford. The privileged "feminist" consumers can also signal their worth in the realm of spirituality and empathy, social justice and equity. If one consumes toward spiritual and altruistic ends, is that really consumption? If one is mindful of products that are also coincidentally used to increase mindfulness and well-being, is that really consumption? If consumption is equated with social activism and altruism, then surely consumption is compassionate, meaningful, and necessary? Subscription services that ask potential customers to "join the movement" and to subscribe to "a box with a heart" make compassionate consumption an urgent call to action as well as a gentle reminder, asking consumers to grapple with the questions above.

Our purpose with this article is not merely to critique consumption or alt-profit business models. Reading impact reports from some alt-profits leads us to conclude that they have partially followed up on their claims of providing income and livelihoods, that they engage in fair trade practices and pay verified fair trade wages, that they are mindful of gender and disability rights. Companies like Article 22 work with local organizations and transnational foundations to clear up land in "the most heavily bombed country in history per capita."[15] Some alt-profits (e.g., Able) publish their living wage calculation model as well as actual wages. Companies such as Same Sky and Purpose Jewelry are connected to foundations and nonprofits that do targeted work such as assisting survivors of human trafficking.[16] Most of these alt-profits operate as social enterprises that have a justice mission that complements their profit motive. What we are questioning are the flawed discursive formations of globalization, accountability, authenticity, community, and empowerment that these companies utilize to sell products. Indeed, we argue that they create and contribute to neoliberal ideologies of individual responsibility and economic efficiency of free trade without holding social structures (governmental, economic, epistemological, and technological, to name a few) accountable. In fact, their ideal of individual responsibility is masked in the language of "a proactive corporate social responsibility" (Murphy 2017: 126). Corporate social responsibility is an effective strategy used by corporations including alt-profits to engage with consumer activism/political consumerism such as boycotting of exploitative brands—a way of signaling ethical operations (Hudson and Hudson 2021).

We also question compassionate consumption as a trend that blurs the boundaries between global and local, individual and community, citizenship and clientship, as well as the Global South and the Global North in a sea of feel-good buzzwords that foreground altruism and alternativeness of alt-profit companies. These buzzwords equate consumption with compassion, activism, spirituality, well-being, and global intervention. They deepen the north-south divide conceptually and operationally while rationalizing the need for connection and commonality. We worry that the implications of such flawed discourse and representation can end up adding to the harms of globalization, can expand complicity of target audience and consumers as they fancy themselves as positive changemakers.

Our transnational feminist critique connects the operation and rhetoric of alt-profits to processes of extractive neocolonialist globalization and cosmopolitan Western feminist discourses of global sisterhood. Analyzing persuasive and spectacular text and images utilized by alt-profit websites also demonstrates that ideologies of racism, colorism, classism, and nationalism can subtly intersect within narratives of women's empowerment, now more pervasive and accessible through new media. Statements we analyzed such as "conscientious purchases are part of the solution to global economic injustice" are illogical and incorrect, demonstrating irrationality of rationality, given the current pace and scale of economic globalization and extractive oligopolies. It is this kind of misinformation and tall claims in the service of unequal globalization and the transnational capitalist class that we critique. We also anticipate future research directions that trace connections among corporate social responsibility, corporate legitimacy, neocoloniality, and gender justice. Converging sociological and transnational feminist perspectives can offer rich analysis of globalization, gendered production, and consumption, as well as neoliberal performances and co-optation of social justice, as so richly demonstrated by alt-profits.

....

Debjani Chakravarty is an associate professor of gender studies at the University of Utah. Her academic and activist interests span gendered and racialized globalization, feminist pedagogy and epistemology, and new media, citizenship, and belonging. Chakravarty has published academic and artistic works exploring the topic of transnational feminisms, collaborative research ethics, and epistemic justice. Her current research focuses on invisible labor and trauma-informed pedagogies. She is a coeditor for Frontiers, A Journal of Women Studies.

Christine Standish is an independent scholar working at UC San Diego as a program evaluation specialist. She graduated from Utah Valley University with her undergraduate degree in behavioral science with a concentration in anthropology, and a minor in gender studies. Her research interests and experience include gender representation, nongovernmental/nonprofit organization development and sustainability, religion, identity, phenomenology, and fear-based decisions.

Notes

Both authors contributed equally to this work. Chakravarty described the specific type of businesses studied as "alt-profits" while Standish created the notion of "gain divisions" for nonprofits. The authors express deep gratitude to the anonymous reviewers for their helpful comments and suggestions for revision, which made this a stronger, better article. We would also like to thank the journal's editors and editorial assistants for their time and care.

1   Brittany Underwood, "Founder's Letter," https://akola.co/pages/founders-letter (accessed July 15, 2020).
2   Article 22, "Story" and "About," https://article22.com/ (accessed July 21, 2020).
3   Certified B Corporation, https://bcorporation.net/ (accessed August 1, 2020).
4   Ten Thousand Villages, "Homepage" and "Maker to Market Stories," https://www.tenthousandvillages.com/ (accessed July 20, 2020).
5   Dharma Shop, "About Us," https://www.dharmashop.com/ (accessed July 21, 2020).
6   Akola, "Homepage," "Shop," and "Our Mission," https://akola.co/ (accessed July 20, 2020).
7   Dharma Shop, "About Us," https://www.dharmashop.com/ (accessed July 21, 2020).
8   Able, "Shop" and "About," https://www.livefashionable.com/ (accessed June 30, 2020).
9   Akola, "Homepage," "Shop," and "Our Mission," https://akola.co/ (accessed July 20, 2020).
10 Novica, "Our Mission" and "Catalog," https://www.novica.com/ (accessed June 30, 2020).
11 Novica, "Our Mission" and "Catalog," https://www.novica.com/ (accessed June 30, 2020).
12 Causebox, "Impact," https://causebox.com/ (accessed December 1, 2020).
13 Causebox, "Impact."
14 Causebox, "Impact."
15 Article 22, "Story" and "About," https://article22.com/ (accessed July 21, 2020).
16 Same Sky, "Our Story," https://www.samesky.com/ (accessed on July 12, 2020); Purpose Jewelry, "Behind the Brand," https://www.purposejewelry.org/pages/who-we-are (accessed on July 12, 2020).

Works Cited

Bandelj, Nina, and Christopher W. Gibson. 2019. "Relational Work and Consumption." In *The Oxford Handbook of Consumption*, edited by Frederick F. Wherry and Ian Woodward, 151–66. New York: Oxford University Press.

Bell, Daniel. 1980. *The Winding Passage: Essays and Sociological Journeys, 1960–1980.* Cambridge, MA: Abt.

Bourdieu, Pierre. 1977. *Outline of a Theory of Practice.* Cambridge: Cambridge University Press.

Bruce, Steve. 2002. *God Is Dead.* Oxford, UK: Blackwell.

Castells, Manuel. 2000. *The Rise of the Network Society: The Information Age Economy, Society, and Culture.* West Sussex, UK: Blackwell.

Choudhury, Koushiki. 2019. "Materialism, Consumerism, and Religion: A Buddhist Vision for Nonprofit Marketing." *International Journal of Nonprofit and Voluntary Sector Marketing* 24, no. 3. https://doi.org/10.1002/nvsm.1634.

Conway, Janet. 2013. *Edges of Global Justice: The World Social Forum and Its Others.* New York: Routledge.

Desai, Manisha. 2007. "The Messy Relationship Between Feminisms and Globalizations." *Gender and Society* 21, no. 6: 797–803.

Evans, David. 2011. "Thrifty, Green, or Frugal: Reflections on Sustainable Consumption in a Changing Economic Climate." *Geoforum* 42, no. 5: 550–57.

Fisher, Melissa. 2017. "White Corporate Feminine Spirituality: The Rise of Global Professional Women's Conferences in the New Millennium." In *Ethnographies of Conferences and Trade Fairs,* edited by Høyer Leivestad and Anette Nyqvist, 43–63. London: Palgrave Macmillan.

Horkheimer, Max, and Theodore Adorno. 2002. *Dialectic of Enlightenment.* Stanford, CA: Stanford University Press.

Hudson, Ian, and Mark Hudon. 2021. *Consumption.* Cambridge, UK: Polity Press.

Hume, Margee. 2010. "Compassion without Action: Examining the Young Consumers Consumption and Attitude to Sustainable Consumption." *Journal of World Business* 45, no. 4: 385–94. https://doi.org/10.1016/j.jwb.2009.08.007.

Grewal, Inderpal. 2005. *Transnational America: Feminisms, Diasporas, Neoliberalisms.* Durham, NC: Duke University Press.

Grewal, Inderpal, and Caren Kaplan. 1994. *Scattered Hegemonies: Postmodernity and Transnational Feminist Practices.* Minneapolis: University of Minnesota Press.

Jacobsen, Mette H., and Anders R. Hansen. 2021. "(Re)introducing Embodied Practical Understanding to the Sociology of Sustainable Consumption." *Journal of Consumer Culture* 21, no. 4: 747–63.

Jhally, Sut. 1989. "Advertising as Religion: The Dialectic of Technology and Magic." In *Cultural Politics in Contemporary America,* edited by Ian Angus and Sut Jhally, 217–29. New York: Routledge.

Kuehn, Kathleen M. 2009. "Compassionate Consumption: Branding Africa through Product RED." *Democratic Communiqué* 23, no. 2: 23–40.

Mandel, Ernest. 1999. *Late Capitalism.* London: Verso.

May, Jon. 1996. "'A Little Taste of Something More Exotic': The Imaginative Geographies of Everyday Life." *Geography* 81, no. 1: 57–64.

Mohanty, Chandra Talpade. 1988. "Under Western Eyes: Feminist Scholarship and Colonial Discourses." *Feminist Review* 30, no. 1. https://doi.org/10.1057/fr.1988.42.

Mohanty, Chandra Talpade. 2003. *Feminism without Borders: Decolonizing Theory Practicing Solidarity.* Durham, NC: Duke University Press.

Murphy, Michelle. 2017. *The Economization of Life.* Durham, NC: Duke University Press.

Nagar, Richa, and Amanda Swarr. 2010. Introduction to *Critical Transnational Feminist Praxis,* edited by Amanda and Richa Nagar, 1–18. Albany: SUNY Press.

Naples, Nancy A. 2002. "Changing the Terms: Community Activism, Globalization, and the Dilemmas of Transnational Feminist Praxis." In *Women's Activism and Globalization: Linking Local Struggles and Transnational Politics,* edited by Nancy A. Naples and Manisha Desai, 3–14. New York: Routledge.

Narayan, Uma. 1997. *Dislocating Cultures.* London: Routledge.

Ong, Aihwa. 2006. *Neoliberalism as Exception: Mutations in Citizenship and Sovereignty.* Durham, NC: Duke University Press.

Patil, Vrushali. 2011. "Transnational Feminism in Sociology: Articulations, Agendas, Debates." *Sociology Compass* 5, no. 7: 540–50.

McQuarrie, Edward F. 2015. *The New Consumer Online: A Sociology of Taste, Audience, and Publics.* Northampton, MA: Edward Elgar.

Ritzer, George. 2003. "Rethinking Globalization: Glocalization/Grobalization and Something/Nothing." *Sociological Theory* 21, no. 3, 193–209.

Ritzer, George. 2019. *The McDonaldization of Society: Into the Digital Age.* Thousand Oaks, CA: Sage.

Sassen, Saskia. 2007. *A Sociology of Globalization.* New York: W. W. Norton.

Sklair, Leslie. 2002. *Globalization: Capitalism and Its Alternatives.* Oxford: Oxford University Press.

Sklair, Leslie. 2010. "Iconic Architecture and the Culture-Ideology of Consumerism." *Theory, Culture and Society* 27, no. 5: 135–59. https://doi.org/10.1177/0263276410374634.

Spivak, Gayatri. 1988. "Can the Subaltern Speak?" In *Marxism and the Interpretation of Culture*, edited by Cary Nelson and Lawrence Grossberg. Urbana: University of Illinois Press.

Switzer, Heather. 2013. "(Post)Feminist Development Fables: The Girl Effect and the Production of Sexual Subjects." *Feminist Theory* 14, no. 3: 345–60. https://doi.org/10.1177/1464700113499855.

Watkins, Leah, Robert Aitken, and Damien Mather. 2016. "Conscientious Consumers: A Relationship between Moral Foundations, Political Orientation, and Sustainable Consumption." *Journal of Cleaner Production* 134, part A: 137–46. https://doi.org/10.1016/j.jclepro.2015.06.009.

Wilson, Japhy. 2015. "The Joy of Inequality: The Libidinal Economy on Compassionate Consumption." *International Journal of Žižek Studies* 9, no. 2: 1–26.

Yuval-Davis, Nira. 2009. "Women, Globalization, and Contemporary Politics of Belonging." *Gender, Technology and Development* 13, no. 1: 1–19. https://doi.org/10.1177/097185240901300101.

Zukin, Sharon, and Jennifer Smith Maguire. 2004. "Consumers and Consumption." *Annual Review of Sociology* 30: 173–97. http://www.jstor.org/stable/29737690.

Guadalupe Escobar

....

The Unforgetting of Claribel Alegría
Reckoning with Capitalist Catastrophe in El Salvador

Abstract: This essay examines women's perspectives on Salvadoran memory struggles that reckon with enmeshed military repression and US colonial capitalism. The two texts by Central American writer Claribel Alegría investigated here, the novel *Ashes of Izalco* (1966; trans. 1989) and the *testimonio* *They Won't Take Me Alive* (1983; trans. 1987), expose the entanglements of state terror and foreign interests, providing an opportunity to critique the coffee regimes in the 1930s and the intimate apparel industry in the 1960s and 1970s, respectively. The author claims that both of Alegría's texts can be understood as narrative acts of "unforgetting" that not only recuperate neglected labor histories often overshadowed by militarized spectacles but also break seeming silences. Consolidating critical interventions in memory studies and Marxist feminisms, the author argues that Alegría's narratives invite an undoing of the memory paradigm premised on transnational oblivion.

The work of Central American writer Claribel Alegría has often been associated with constructions of Salvadoran female subjectivity, including portrayals of women as armed militants. Yet her writing also depicts women's perspectives on *capitalist catastrophe*, by which I define transnational economic enterprises that undergird world-shattering military violence, if not imperialist war. This article focuses on two primary events in El Salvador: *La Matanza* (The 1932 Massacre), retold in the novel *Ashes of Izalco* (1966; trans. 1989), and the US-backed civil war (1980–92), recounted in the testimonio *They Won't Take Me Alive* (1983; trans. 1987; hereafter *Alive*). These are both events of memory trouble, difficult recall accompanying not

MERIDIANS · feminism, race, transnationalism   23:2 October 2024
DOI: 10.1215/15366936-11266404 © 2024 Smith College

simply militarized spectacle overshadowing colonial capitalism but also enforced and voluntary silences.

I demonstrate how both of Alegría's texts can best be understood as narrative acts of "unforgetting," which the Salvadoran journalist and memoirist Roberto Lovato (2020: 289) has likened to forensic recovery, a kind of suturing of the dismembered. Such active remembering not only requires reattaching disjointed state-constructed histories and personal memories but also piecing together (often painful) transnational remembrances of Salvadoran Americans. Although El Salvador has never been a formal colony of the United States, its national development, as elsewhere in Central America, has been "historically disrupted and interrupted to promote U.S. economic interests" since the nineteenth century (Alvarado, Estrada, and Hernández 2017: 6). Consequently, erasure of empire and evasive accountability have been all too common. Lovato (2020: 299) adds, "Salvadoran violence is, in no small part, an expression of forgotten American violence." For its part, the Salvadoran government has enacted obliteration of its own by passing a postwar amnesty law to bury evidence of state crimes and "forget the totality of the past" (Huezo 2021: 64). I argue that unforgetting in Alegría's work enables confronting traumatic histories, uncovering international economic conditions, and rethinking memory practices.

The late Claribel Alegría was best known as a poet—given the success of *Sobrevivo* (*I Survive*, 1978), *Woman of the River* (1989), and *Sorrow* (1999)—but her commitment to the urgent and the concrete also encompassed her fiction and nonfiction. During a lifetime of publishing over forty works, she received the prestigious Casa de las Américas Award for Poetry in 1978 and the Neustadt International Prize for Literature in 2006. Alegría was born in Estelí, Nicaragua, in 1924, but was mostly raised in Santa Ana, El Salvador; her father, Daniel Alegría, was a Nicaraguan medical doctor, and her mother, Ana María Vides, was a Salvadoran member of the coffee-growing elite. Since her father opposed US occupation in Nicaragua in 1924 and supported the anti-imperialist national leader Augusto Sandino, the family was forced to relocate to El Salvador when Claribel Alegría was just nine months old. This mixed Nicaraguan-Salvadoran lineage made her well-positioned to reflect critically on US interventionist histories beyond the nation-state. Following a self-imposed exile, Alegría attended George Washington University in Washington, DC, where she earned a BA in philosophy and letters and met her partner (and later frequent translator and coauthor) Darwin J. Flakoll.

The present article expands critical conversations about the violent intersections between military rule and foreign capital as well as the conjunction of memory and gender. To establish deeper lines between memory and materialism, I first provide a brief contextualization of the two texts analyzed to understand how transnational memory has been influenced by historical and economic processes. I then turn to *Ashes of Izalco* to examine how Alegría's version of unforgetting works in line with what Michael Rothberg (2009) calls "multidirectional memory," drawing attention to both the malleability of discursive space and the continual remaking of collective memory in a transnational sense. For Rothberg, collective memory is "subject to ongoing negotiation, cross-referencing, and borrowing" (3). I argue that the novel calls attention to the limits of the narratable and of one-sided memory construction; by reimagining female narrative voices and multidirectional memory instead, the novel allegorizes US-Salvadoran relations. Alegría's experimentation with collective memory gives rise to what I call *polywitnessing*, wherein a critical reader beholds a character bearing witness, opening up speculation about the subtleties of implication.

In the remainder of the article, I consider how *Alive* reflects anticapitalist critique revolving around the economic exploitation of women garment workers. By depicting how US companies like the brassiere manufacturer Maidenform established export processing industries in El Salvador in the 1960s and 1970s, the literary narrative sheds light on the precarity of invisible international labor not as separate from but as coconstitutive of revolutionary movements, driving many women to join the national liberation movement. Read together, Alegría's texts rewrite women into the transamerican imaginary, disrupting geopolitical hierarchies, and invite an undoing of the memory paradigm premised on transnational oblivion.

Troubling Memory

In January 1932, *campesinos* in western El Salvador, most of whom were Indigenous (Nahuat) and male, challenged the coffee plantation regime—its wage cuts, food shortages, and evictions from communal lands. In response, military dictator Maximiliano Hernández Martínez ordered state forces to murder an estimated forty thousand people in the Nahuat-Pipil coffee highlands. The threat of US intervention drove the Martínez government and armed vigilante bands to extreme measures in order to maintain some semblance of control (Chomsky 2021: 29).[1] What came to be known as La Matanza, amid the global economic depression, marked one of the darkest episodes of genocidal dictatorship in modern hemispheric history, the reverberations of which would haunt future generations.[2] La Matanza established the dialectics of insurgency and counterinsurgency, the cultural logic of communist containment, and the idea of Indigeneity as "subversive" (Grandin 2010). Moreover, this key event set the infrastructure that ushered in unceasing military tyranny in the ensuing decades that would culminate in the civil war, when the state killed nearly 75,000 people and disappeared another 10,000.

As patron of military training and economic aid, the United States orchestrated systematic terror in El Salvador, especially under the Reagan administration. Colluding with the Salvadoran state and landed elites, death squads radically transformed the national landscape into deathworlds. Throughout the 1980s and 1990s, the Salvadoran civil war escalated political disorder, combatting "communism" while at the same time enabling yet erasing US military and economic interventions. With the advent of war, social roles changed considerably: unprecedented numbers of women participated in the armed revolution and the transnational labor force. The revolutionary era in El Salvador and in its neighbors Nicaragua and Guatemala resulted in more than one million people internally displaced and more than two million resettled in the United States, Canada, and Mexico (García 2006: 1). The growing presence of US Central American constituencies in the wake of these civil wars has in turn shaped Latinx diasporic imaginaries deeply rooted in cultural memory.

Extreme violence in El Salvador has left a disquieting legacy marked by fragmentation and ineffability, but also endurance. Literary scholars Arturo Arias, Claudia Milian, Maritza Cárdenas, Yajaira Padilla, and Ana Patricia Rodríguez have highlighted textualities of resistance—other historiographies, diasporic reimaginings, and feminist genealogies—that intersect with the intricacies of nation-states, race, class, language, gender, and sexuality in the disruption of silencing. Building on this foundational scholarship in general, and on previous criticism on Claribel Alegría's oeuvre in particular, I add to this body of knowledge by highlighting insights into the interlinked issues of the international division of labor and gendered insurgencies. Inasmuch as *Ashes of Izalco* and *Alive* rely on the nuanced subject positions springing from Salvadoran women's standpoint to further historical explorations of economic, military, and linguistic control, in all their variegated power inequities, I view both texts as examples of a transamerican imaginary, anticipating future stakes of forced displacement. A rereading of Alegría's work reckons with the social aphasia in El Salvador that prevails from social suffering rooted in capitalist global relations that are too easily subsumed by the surplus violence of militarism complexly enmeshed with US colonialism.

More broadly, the interplay between state repression and silenced memory in the twentieth century is not restricted to El Salvador: it extends across the Central American isthmus (Nicaragua, Guatemala) and other political geographies of Latin America (Chile, Peru). Jean Franco (2013: 11) reminds us that capitalist modernity saw state-sponsored killing sprees that eliminated labor movements in Latin America, from the Argentine petroleum workers in 1932 to Bolivian miners in 1942, while Cold War Latin America witnessed mass atrocity, most centrally targeting "communists" and their alleged support networks, in the second half of the twentieth century. As Franco (2013: 7) clarifies, "even though acts of cruelty have changed little, their justification has." Not least, reckoning with such mass cruelty largely depends on memory struggles. Giving voice to muted memories is a powerful form of resistance.

Ashes of Izalco: Coffee Barons and Colonels

Alegría has explained in interviews that the aim of *Ashes of Izalco* has been to "fill a gap in historical memory," to restore a "cultural lobotomy" (McGowan 1994; Flores y Ascencio 2000). In an exchange with fellow poet Carolyn Forché (1984: 12), Alegría not only recalled the indelible impression of witnessing the 1932 massacre as a seven-year-old girl but also addressed a longer genealogy of US-Latin American relations: "Latin Americans are forced to live in the shadow of an enormously rich, imperial power that has continuously intervened in the internal political affairs of each Latin American nation over the past 150 years, and has been intervening more crudely during the last 25 years to install in power and support oligarchic parties and military dictatorships that will maintain the status quo." What is notable here is Alegría's prescient grasp of two distinct patterns of US imperialism in Latin America: its hidden "soft power" (e.g., sponsorship) and hypervisible "hard power" (e.g., military might) (Grandin [2006] 2021). Though she clearly incorporates personal memory, inviting and refusing autobiographical readings of *Ashes of Izalco*, I would suggest, her reimagining of the 1932 insurrection investigates how US subjects and the Salvadoran agro-financial elite are differentially implicated. Rothberg (2019: 1) formulates the concept of the "implicated subject" to describe the ambiguous situatedness beyond the facile victim/perpetrator binary. Implicated subjects, for Rothberg, "occupy positions aligned with power and privilege without being themselves direct agents of harm; they contribute to, inhabit, inherit, or benefit from regimes of domination but do not originate or control such regimes." Indeed, Arias (1994: 36) has asserted that Alegría is an implicated subject herself, though not in those very terms, in stating that her "social origins were closer to those of the exploiters than the exploited." Nevertheless, Alegría often used her privileged position to highlight class oppression and working-class experiences in her writing. Her complex positionality, including her marriage to a US leftist, did not foreclose an alignment with incipient Central American revolutionary movements. Given this intersectional inheritance of Central American identity and class origins, Alegría's narrative practices of unforgetting occupy a unique position at the crossroads of histories of victimization and histories of perpetration.

Ashes of Izalco has been regarded as ahead of its time even as it has been frequently characterized as a lyrical historical novel. It was published a year before Gabriel García Márquez's *Cien años de soledad* (*One Hundred Years of Solitude*, 1967), a landmark novel set in a small hamlet in Colombia, the memorable "Macondo," about a banana massacre that alludes to the 1928 strike of the United Fruit Company. Both novels offer valuable representations of parallel moments dealing with the brutality of commodity production for the global market. *Ashes of Izalco* reimagines the coffee empire in Santa Ana, El Salvador: a sleepy, stagnant town ten kilometers from the volcano Izalco and where La Matanza will unfold. Patricia Varas (2013: 50) notes that "it precedes by a few years the revolutionary movements in which the Central American nations would be involved." Alegría's novel tells the story of Carmen Rojas, a diasporic subject who travels from Washington, DC, to her childhood home in Central America to bury her mother, Isabel. While there, she inherits a secret diary, which becomes a site of intergenerational transmission as it details the romantic interlude between Carmen's mother and an alcoholic Oregon-based writer, Frank Wolff. The novel invites readers to approach transnational memory construction anew by bifurcating Carmen's and Frank's visions, proceeding backward in order to redress histories of injustice.

The protagonist in the narrative present (the early 1960s), Carmen, is an upper-middle-class Salvadoran American married to Paul, a North American "good provider" yet uncritical supporter of US foreign policy in Latin

America (Alegría 1989: 59). Importantly, Carmen's voluntary migration to Washington, DC, marks her as a precursor of the *pioneras*, pioneering migrants from Central America who arrived in the United States after the 1965 Immigration and Nationality Act. Carmen's early migration experience indexes the "history of the isthmus in relationship to the United States," originating in the late nineteenth century with the construction of the Panama Canal Zone and the commodification of bananas, coffee, and the like (Alvarado, Estrada, and Hernández 2017: 5).

The novel's other protagonist, Frank, is a blue-eyed struggling writer, who travels to Central America on a whim to see his distant friend Virgil, a US missionary, and to also "tour the Mayan ruins" (Alegría 1989: 55). Nancy Saporta Sternbach (1994: 68) has compellingly argued that "Frank can be read as a representative of the political, cultural, and religious presence that the United States has exercised in the region." As readers, we first learn of the novel's nonteleological storyline midway through the opening chapter, when Carmen interrupts the narrative flow to express her disorientation wrought by reading Frank's diary, containing surprising revelations of her mother, and remarks, "I need to order my memories, trace each feature and characteristic, rescue [mother] from chaos and oblivion" (Alegría 1989: 7). Such temporal dissonance creates a textual gap even as it merges the two narrative lines. The alternating chapters that follow scuttle between Frank's diary, recorded in 1931 and 1932, and Carmen's simulated reading of it in 1962.

What, then, is the purpose of unforgetting through the intertwining of US-based narrators? Attuned to transnational gender dynamics from the 1980s on, Yajaira Padilla (2012: 5–6) has argued that Salvadoran women often "function as national allegories—whether they represent a Salvadoran nation in conflict and in need of liberation or a postwar nation in transition and decline." In my view, the prewar novel *Ashes of Izalco* follows this trend of allegorizing US-Salvadoran relations, too, but does so by calling attention to the limits of the narratable and one-sided memory construction, allowing for a reimagining of female narrative voices taking part in multidirectional memory. Unpacking US representational regimes of Central America matters because, as Padilla has recently argued, such perceptions influence systemic and symbolic exclusions of US Central Americans. According to Padilla (2022: 8), US Central Americans were largely illegible in popular discourse before the refugee crisis of the 1980s; since then, they have frequently been cast as "threatening and undesirable citizen-subjects of the nation"—in a word, Other. Whereas Frank's gaze in *Ashes of Izalco* gives us a glimpse of the undermining, enduring image of the isthmus as "backward," Carmen counters an impending "cultural politics of unbelonging" (4) for US Central Americans by learning to belong to herself through recovering personal memories.

Frank's diary serves as a cornerstone for conveying multidirectional memory. What begins as travel writing, with much navel gazing, transforms into love letters addressed to Isabel, which then inadvertently changes into a family heirloom for her daughter. Finally, Frank's diary produces cultural memory for us as readers. It is no wonder that Roy Boland Osegueda (2005: 172) regards *Ashes of Izalco* as "the first major testimonial novel," fusing "interior monologues, diary entries, folktales, Amerindian myths, and a rich network of Western literature and art to 'bear witness' to 'La Matanza' of 1932." The fictionalization of Frank's testimony anticipates the archetypal woman as witness that would become a defining feature of late twentieth-century Latin American testimonios like those of Rigoberta Menchú, María Teresa Tula, and Domitila Barrios de Chungara. Rather than centering the voices of "the oppressed," who have witnessed state terror galvanizing social action, however, Frank's diary sets in motion a chain of polywitnessing: we, as readers, see Carmen carefully scrutinizing Frank's witnessing of La Matanza. If the novel positions Carmen as a secondhand witness, we as the audience are thirdhand observers. Mieke Bal (1999: x) insists that "witnessing can become a model for critical reading." That Frank rearticulates the Salvadoran history of the 1932 massacre of the Indigenous and political dissidents, of course, risks appropriating cultural memory and indirectly enhances US domination. Yet, Frank's growing attachment to Isabel seems solidaristic, even if tropicalizing the topography and romanticizing her rescue. Frank's private repository of the past gives way to the construction of collective memory.

Interlocking systems of oppression—the militarized government, local elites, and US influence—are nowhere better illustrated than in Frank's first diary entry. Overhearing a politically heated conversation at a dinner party hosted by Dr. Rojas (Carmen's father and Isabel's husband), Frank notes,

> Dr. Rojas' brother-in-law, Eduardo Valdés, is assistant manager of the Santa Ana newspaper, and he was citing the comings and goings of certain "barons" and military officials to sustain his thesis that a political crisis was brewing in the country. It gradually became clear that his "barons" were the small clique of immensely rich coffee planters who seem to

control Salvadoran politics from behind the scenes. . . . I was amused.
The vision of generals, colonels, and "barons" skulking about at night,
laying plans to overthrow the government of this absurd little country,
while the entire population followed and commented on their every
move, seemed a delightful, comic opera touch. (Alegría 1989: 31–32)

Frank's phrase "absurd little country" expresses a certain condescension
toward El Salvador and trivializes the coming coup d'état that would overthrow President Araujo and install General Martínez. His very presence at
the dinner party recenters white supremacy and patriarchal narrative
authority. Additionally, Frank's ambivalence corresponds with the hesi-
tancy of US military interference in 1932 due to heavy criticism around its
involvement with the neighboring country, Nicaragua. Ericka Beckman
(2012: 30), in another context, posits that "from the mid-nineteenth-
century onward, coffee was not grown for consumption in the country, but
for export to Europe and the United States." Thus, commoditized coffee
would come to signify the status of El Salvador in the world market and,
more specifically, El Salvador's dependency on US markets. As Salvadoran
poet-rebel Roque Dalton (2007: 267) remarks, "Little by little, North American imperialism displaced the other powers in the Central American
area until it alone remained as the exclusive and dominant foreign factor."
Here, Dalton's words resonate with Alegría's earlier observation about the
soft shocks of US economic control in El Salvador long before military
intervention.

The allusion to the anti-imperialist icon Farabundo Martí, deeply
ingrained in Salvadoran insurgent imaginaries, reinforces the novel's
alignment with the revolutionary left. Before a firing squad executed him in
the aftermath of La Matanza, Martí fought alongside General Sandino
against the US Marines in Nicaragua and later became one of the founders
of the Salvadoran Communist Party in 1930 and leaders of the 1932 uprising. His legacy of resistance would continually be invoked with the Farabundo Martí National Liberation Front (FMLN), a wartime guerrilla group
that transformed into a prominent postwar political party. It is through
Frank's conversations with Farabundo that the novel exposes readers to the
poverty and mistreatment of the countryside peasants by the oligarchy.

Multidirectional memory is most explicitly apparent in chapters 16
and 17, comprising four epistles in which Frank rearticulates his traumatic recall of La Matanza. Rothberg's (2009: 11) concept—"the dynamic
transfers that take place between places and times during the act of

remembrance"—provides a useful framework for understanding the afterlives of apocalyptic violence in El Salvador entwined with the prevailing problem of corporate extraction from the economic base. In these two chapters, Frank not only directly conveys his narrative memory to Isabel but also indirectly transmits it to Carmen. In a letter addressed to Isabel, dated January 27, 1932, Frank relates how on a bus ride between San Salvador and Santa Ana, several men armed with machetes terrorize the passengers. He attempts to make sense of this traumatic experience: "I remembered the arc of the machete swinging down on the bus driver's head, the screams of the girl who was dragged away into the darkness" (Alegría 1989: 154). This image of dismemberment and disappearance foreshadows the grisly practices of state terror that would become all too familiar during the civil war. It also brings to mind Joan Didion's *Salvador* (1983), locating El Salvador as a site of dark tourism, not only serving as an influential point of reference, but also revealing how US subjects, like Alegría's character Frank, tend to be regarded as legitimate recordkeepers of the isthmus for posterity's sake. In this segment of Frank's diary—the key site of cultural memory in the novel—broken bodies reflect mutilated memory, or "the machete of memory," as Roberto Lovato (2020: xvii) evocatively puts it. Just as the aforementioned girl's body is snatched away into the shadows, so, too, does the novel invite readers to search for voices that have disappeared from Salvadoran storytelling.

Thus, Frank's diary lays bare discrepancies of memory modification and grapples with the limits of representing collective horror. In *Tangled Memories*, Marita Sturken (1997: 7) argues that difficult memorialization cannot be reduced to a "replica of an experience that can be retrieved and relived." Instead, memory making is by and large a narrative act. In Frank's case, intoxication interferes considerably with the witnessing of La Matanza. He confesses, "I had spent the two days of the brief, bloody civil war sleeping in ravines and on hillsides, limping through the sulphurous wilderness, unaware of it all" (Alegría 1989:152). Consequently, the two-day blackout renders Frank's eyewitness account partly incomplete and inaccessible. When he fully awakens, he enters Izalco only to find it a ghost town and fails to comprehend the magnitude of the moment. In her review of the novel, Barbara Harlow (1990: 91) suggests that "in the end the socially confined Isabel is no more able to change her domestic situation than Frank is able to grasp for himself the political consequences of the brutal history into which he has unwittingly intruded and with which he is now complicit."

Centering Frank's one-dimensional construction of memory, obscuring Isabel's record, reveals a tacit hierarchy within a gendered dialectic of narration and silence. It bears mentioning, however, that Frank vividly recalls Isabel commenting on women's lack of voting power in the 1930s, suggesting a widespread political silencing of women in El Salvador. Despite Isabel's apparent aporia, her daughter searches for signs of her subjectivity. Upon closely examining Frank's diary, she discovers that the "pages [had been] dog-eared, worn with much handling and rereading," implying that her mother responded not with indifference but private passion (Alegría 1989: 115). While the past cannot change, its interpretation can. In *The Struggle for the Past*, Elizabeth Jelin (2021: 1) contends that multiple memories often "appear as recollection, silences and words unspoken, or traces, shaped by the scenarios and the social struggles that are going on at each historical moment." Only by reading between the lines of silences can we see how interpretations of events are not fixed but fluid.

Retracing matrilineal memory through intergenerational reading practices triggers Carmen to investigate women's narrative agency. For instance, in a pivotal scene, Carmen wonders whether her mother recorded her selfhood on her own terms:

> "Did she ever leave any of her diaries, Eugenia? She always kept a diary, but I've looked everywhere."
> "She must have burned them."
> "Didn't she even leave me a letter?"
> "Nothing." (Alegría 1989: 132)

Here, Carmen calls out the uneven power relations embedded in Frank's diary. She consults with another character who was her mother's confidante, Eugenia, to corroborate Frank's narrative memory, cocreating communal responsibility over unforgetting. It becomes increasingly clear that the limited access to her mother's viewpoint stages "the confrontation of the lack of women's history" (Barbas-Rhoden 2003: 26). In this sense, Alegría's treatment of multidirectional memory creates an alternative way of reclaiming women's suppressed perspectives in traditional historiography. Arias (2007: 9) has pointed out that "the novel displaced the centrality of a masculine gaze in favor of a feminine one, which was unheard of in Central American fiction, particularly in narratives with a political focus." Considered this way, Carmen is a rather bold narrator: she breaks seeming silences of double negation for US Central American women.

Multidirectional memory again becomes evident when Carmen identifies with her mother's marital entrapment and reaches an epiphany about her own self-disavowal. Given that she is a genealogically implicated subject, Carmen belatedly benefits financially from El Salvador's structural inequality. And yet, this structural implication coexists with the dynamism of US colonialism as a Salvadoran American diasporic subject. Even so, Carmen's relative privilege, even her US residency, cannot fully shield her from the social abjection of womanhood. Marxist feminist Silvia Federici (2020: xv) reminds us that after World War II it became "a widespread phenomenon" for women to challenge "housework as women's natural destiny." As Carmen begins tracing the parameters of domestic life as a bourgeois housewife, she contemplates how she might have lost her self-identity to marital dependency, capitalist consumption, unrealized potential, and perhaps even *proto-pionera* anxiety and fraught inheritance. In her reading of Alegría's women-centered fiction, including *Ashes of Izalco*, Ana Patricia Rodríguez (2020) observes that the female protagonists "learn about their own complicity in the exploitative socioeconomic system and are forced to break free from the constraints placed on them from family, husband, home, tradition, and nation." It is the introspective mode of diary writing that opens a site for Carmen to remember and reimagine her gendered subjectivity and positionality in the social order.

Alegría's literature of memory, foregrounding women as *rememberers*, has resonated far beyond the borders of Central America, especially within the United States. For example, Sandra Benítez's novel *Bitter Grounds* (1997) compresses the residual effects of 1932 with the emergent civil war into a single literary text from a postwar perspective. Through three generations of women that the novel chronicles, readers come to recognize a continuity of racialized class conflicts. Benítez's novel not only dramatizes the familial restructuring from patriarchy to matriarchy in the wake of capitalist catastrophe, but also suggests that sheer survival positions women as political agents of collective memory. According to Lyon-Johnson (2005: 207), writers like Sandra Benítez, Graciela Limón, and Demetria Martínez engage in transnational practices of cultural commemoration in which they "transform the disappeared and the tortured Salvadoran body into a representation of the disfigured and disappeared Salvadoran collective memory." In so doing, women's practices of unforgetting enliven what should be dead and bring new subjects into life.

Returning to *Ashes of Izalco*, Alegría discursively disrupts the routine exclusion of women and Global South subjects in official historical discourse. The novel demonstrates not only how the construction of memory is a gendered struggle, but also that language itself is contested terrain. If Rothberg is concerned with how we remember and rearticulate historical injustice, Alegría is preoccupied with *who we remember* and *who are the rememberers*. It is tempting to read two US-based narrators as instantiating hegemonic forms of disremembering, but the novel ultimately conveys subversive memory practices in reconfiguring the monologic into the dialogic. Whereas this text offers a portrait of bourgeois feminisms, partly tethered to imperial intimacies, *Alive* asserts the value of proletarian women's voices beyond the realm of domesticity.

They Won't Take Me Alive: Maidenform Made in El Salvador

Alegría reworks the form of the historical novel in *Ashes of Izalco* to represent the coffee massacre of the early twentieth century, while using a peculiar narrative structure of polywitnessing to convey a relational comparison of the Global North looking south, attuned to profound complexities of privilege. Employing the diary form within the novel disrupts "feminine" associations of the genre, unsettles the totalizing view of history, and facilitates privacy to unflinchingly reflect on elite Salvadoran Americans as implicated subjects. *They Won't Take Me Alive*, on the other hand, portrays the capitalist exploitation of urban poor women in the late twentieth century. The testimonio draws attention to storytelling from the bottom of global hierarchies without the implicated weight for US Salvadoran subjects, registering the dramatic shift of Salvadoran transnational mobility from voluntary migration to mass war displacement. The aesthetic forms of this pairing express distinct relationships to the proximity of catastrophic histories under capitalism. In contrast to viewing the distant suffering of coffee workers through Frank's fictionalized testimony, readers of *Alive* access a firsthand account of Marina, a woman worker in foreign-owned factories, however mediated that may be. In this instance, Alegría offers a more intimate perspective to the economically marginalized themselves and gestures toward restoring the voice of those silenced. This vantage point of Global South women looking north widens our understanding of the relationship between the peripheralization of global economic systems and gendered marginalizations.

In the "Historical Introduction," the British translator and editor Amanda Hopkinson situates the military repression of the 1930s and the 1980s, suggesting that *Alive* works as a sequel to *Ashes of Izalco*. "The real horror," Hopkinson asserts, "is that the army still continues to behave much as it did in 1932, only equipped with all the sophisticated weaponry another half-century of United States' technology (and money) can buy" (Alegría 1987: 15). As with *Ashes of Izalco*, the latter text sets out to excavate the economic restructuring beneath the surface of catastrophic conflict.

Alive is a heteroglossic *testimonio* that mainly chronicles the process of becoming a *guerrillera* (woman combatant) for "Eugenia" (nom de guerre of Ana María Castillo Rivas). In this regard, Alegría "challenged the andro-centric revolutionary narrative and sought gender equality, sexual libera-tion, and equitable division of labor, while also highlighting the contra-dictions and tensions embedded in conventional revolutionary and patriarchal narratives" (Rodríguez 2020). Alegría's testimonio largely commemorates the primary protagonist Eugenia yet, as the subtitle "Sal-vadoran Women in Struggle for National Liberation" indicates, it also contains secondary testimonies of other female comrades. For instance, Alegría (1987: 117) dryly extrapolates, "If President Reagan and his advisors really want to know why the Salvadoran people are up in arms, they'd understand a lot more from Marina González's biography than from searching for proof of hypothetical conspiracies of Cuban and Russian origin." Alegría gives us a biography of Marina that is as much about join-ing the armed struggle as it is about working in the global system of labor, even as her authorial control, alternating between omniscient third-person to first-person interlocutor, filters all the perspectives presented in the text.[3] That said, however, the bulk of Marina's unforgetting consists not of armed resistance but of voicing the unspoken, attritional destruction of capitalist exploitation.

The critical treatment of *Alive* has usually focused on addressing gender-based oppression through the main character Eugenia—attending to the image of the *guerrillera*, militant motherhood, and bourgeois women-centered protagonism—yet the minor character Marina González has been underexamined. This oversight may stem partly from the narrative struc-ture: most of the book chapters orbit around remembering Eugenia, reserving the penultimate chapter to spotlighting Marina. Even so, relating the ravages of the Salvadoran export system that allow a critique of histor-ically invisibilized women's work is central to Alegría's memory project. While the text indicates that Marina knew *of* but did not personally know

Eugenia, they likely crossed paths in "the mass demonstrations of 1976" (Alegría 1987: 117). This likelihood is significant because it implies an interconnected mass mobilization in which women evolved into key players in radical movements. This shared public space provides an occasion for shared feminist knowing and the formation of what Verónica Gago (2020: 164) describes as "collective intelligence": "what is experienced in an assembly, in a march, or in a strike, when we feel that we are part of a movement of thinking."

Marina's entrance into the testimonio presents a different case of unforgetting from that of Carmen in *Ashes of Izalco*. In contrast to Carmen's (and the central character Eugenia's) bourgeois upbringing, Marina is "a typical Salvadoran proletarian woman" who starts life with fewer resources and faces the burden of overwork from an early age (Alegría 1987: 117). Such differences and fluidity of class identities reinforce Chandra Talpade Mohanty's (2003: 31) point that the category "women" is rather unstable and "assumes an ahistorical, universal unity between women based on a generalized notion of their subordination." Marina's narrative arc begins with working at a candy factory at age thirteen and ends with forcibly fleeing the country as a mother of four in 1980. Throughout her job history, from candy packager to cleaner to seamstress to toy vendor to food vendor, the testimonial narrative uncovers patterns of malnourishment and mistreatment, as well as underpaid and unpaid work. Her employment episodes reveal intricate racialized and gendered dimensions of global capitalism. This emphasis on the bodily dimensions of ordinary women in the global economy reflects the sociologist Barbara Sutton's (2010: 195) observation that the female flesh is both "a site of oppression and a vehicle for social change."

Female undergarments have long been loaded symbols evoking women's roles, whether closely associated with oppression or liberation. When Maidenform began popularizing brassieres through mass production in the early twentieth century, the bra replaced the nineteenth-century Victorian corset, shapewear simultaneously condemned as a painful constrictive device and recently celebrated as a reclaimed erotic object. In *An Intimate Affair: Women, Lingerie, Sexuality*, Jill Fields (2007: 272) argues that "intimate apparel shapes and sexualizes female bodies and figures centrally in women's conformity to particular historic notions of embodied femininity." In 1968, the bra wielded symbolic power when women dramatically discarded such "feminine" accoutrements in the "Freedom Trash

Can" in protest of the Miss America Pageant. Following the 1965 Hart-Celler Act, capitalist exploitation progressively intensified for largely working-class immigrant women from Asia and Latin America in the US garment industry.

Meanwhile, sweatshop labor, with the neoliberal turn of the 1970s, increasingly went global, while remaining a feminized workforce. Marxist geographer David Harvey (2005: 169) explains that "under neoliberalism, the figure of the disposable worker emerges as prototypical upon the world stage." The hyperexploitation in sweatshops, particularly offshore apparel production, hinges on low wages and degrading work environments for women workers, most of whom are brown, young, impoverished, uneducated, isolated, and living in the Global South. Typical working conditions at a *maquiladora* (foreign-owned assembly factory) entail long hours, unpaid overtime, termination of employment without payment, inadequate housing, food insecurity, lack of healthcare, and nonexistent safeguards against sexual harassment.[4] Political economist Stephanie Barrientos (2019: 95) argues that the "societal undervaluation" of such "feminization of labour," correlating with patriarchal perceptions of women's cheapness and compliance, increases value extraction while deepening subordination. Given its proximity and high unemployment driving down wages, Central America has been an attractive region for US corporate interest (Mendez 2005: viii). Prefiguring the contemporary anti-sweatshop activism of the 1990s, *Alive* uses the bra to unravel lesser-known knowledges of Salvadoran women as international intimate apparel workers.[5]

Founded in 1922 by Russian immigrants, the bra brand Maidenform had had an unconventional business history tangled with gender and militarism. What is peculiar about Maidenform is that during World War II it also manufactured artifacts of militarism: silk parachutes and pigeon vests (O'Connor 2013). In *Alive*, the bra appears as a politicized material object inseparable from the rise of the globalized apparel industry. Alegría captures the convergence of Cold War endeavors and intimate apparel production when Marina observes,

> They were even making soldiers' kits to be sent out to Vietnam. These were large, olive-green knapsacks. They sent some special machines over for this and needed to take on extra staff. Those who'd learned most about making bras were transferred to the soldiers' kits. I was assigned to putting the clips on to the elastic. They sent over everything we needed.

At first they paid me two and a half *pesos* a day, and later on three *pesos* and 20 cents. This was the highest rate I received. Once the war in Vietnam was over, no more knapsacks were produced (Alegría 1987: 119).

The text asserts connections between seemingly disparate instances of the US military industrial complex, "chillingly point[ing] at," as Amanda Hopkinson explains, "the overlap between U.S. investment and military policies throughout the world" (25). At the same time, this scene suggests that Marina's employment in El Salvador, itself a product of US-led capitalist globalization, indirectly impacts the US imperialist war machine in Vietnam. Alegría's engagement with the intersection of the Vietnam War and the Salvadoran armed conflict further illustrates Long Thanh Bui's (2015: 144) claim that the labor power of maquila workers in the Global South (Mexico, Malaysia) is often appropriated as "interchangeable labor pools to be used and abused by capitalism at will." Inasmuch as global capitalism is *racial*, it is also distinctly *gendered*. Rather than urging competition, however, *Alive* reveals colonial affinities and cross-cultural resonance among offshore producers when we again see the overlap of East Asian and Latin American regions as Marina later sells "a load of little toys from Hong Kong" (Alegría 1987: 125).

Through the voice of Marina, the text mounts a materialist critique of economic globalization, recording the historical transition of US corporations gradually moving to production overseas. As historian Aviva Chomsky (2021: 125–26) has recently shown, the emergence of the Central American Common Market in 1960 kicked off free-trade zones without taxes or unions; consequently, "U.S. companies like Maidenform and Texas Instruments established the first export processing industries in El Salvador, taking advantage of the low cost of labor and other incentives." Since then, El Salvador has manufactured many popular labels, including The Gap, Fruit of the Loom, Liz Claiborne, and Macy's, just to name a few (Armbruster-Sandoval 2005: 70). In *Alive*, Marina explains that whereas a US Maidenform employee would have earned $35 per day, she and her other coworkers make $1 per day. Her testimonio also intimates that the factory's expansion and relocation to a concentrated industrial zone increases the risk of exposure to concentrated toxic chemicals. In making visible economic inequalities and gradual adverse health effects of "out of sight, out of mind" free-trade zones, Marina dwells on the slow wearing away of the female body under US financial expansionism.

In presenting an image of Marina's deplorable living conditions, Alegría registers the human cost of free trade in the Americas. Even with a dual income, Marina and her husband can only afford a small hovel without electricity or running water in the outskirts of Soyapango. The location of these slums, Plan del Pino, requires a two-hour bus ride to Marina's *maquila* worksite. Her makeshift dwellings illustrate the dire poverty underlying the accumulated wealth of foreign investors, but also urge the reader to consider their own implicated position as a consumer. As Ileana Rodríguez (2009: 167) asserts, the *maquila* factory system generates "migrations, demographic saturation, urban restructuring, reordering of gender relations, sociocultural segregations, and overall disorder." If survival is a daily crisis under the *maquila* labor structure, war compounds the social disorder.

As Marina challenges the dehumanization of the global assembly line, she finds new ways to assert her dignity. After working at a Maidenform factory for five years, Marina asks for a raise, but management only doles out higher quota standards per day. This cheapening of women's labor mirrors neoliberalism gaining ground in the other Americas, which "in many cases reinstated an extractive export-driven model of growth" (Beckman 2012: xi). Without the option of joining the International Ladies' Garment Workers' Union, a privilege exclusively available to US Maidenform employees, Marina tries to organize others to demand better pay and working conditions, but from that moment on, "the management viewed [her] as a 'subversive' for not being satisfied" (Alegría 1987: 119). In retaliation, the management suppresses Marina by isolating her and withholds a raise for another two years. Eventually, she quits and, under such dire financial straits, joins the guerrilla movement. "I'm in the struggle," Marina states, "so that my children won't have to be" (127). After joining the armed resistance out of economic necessity, however, death squads threaten to murder her, forcing her to flee to Nicaragua, where she reinvents herself as a cook and street vendor of *pupusas*. Mobilizing such memories of labor under world capitalism signals an insurgent imaginary arising from Global South women.

Marina's memory practices reveal how globalized labor and armed resistance at times assume a female face. She practices a range of dissidence, from demanding better wages to denouncing military rule, from migrating to Nicaragua and expressing solidarity with their revolution to storytelling. Marina's narrative powerfully reframes economic hardship as a mixed blessing, discovering "in crisis opportunities for personal and social change" (Sutton 2010: 63). If imperial capitalism often disregards the voices of the dispossessed, Alegría's narrative makes a compelling case for a broader acknowledgment of the material consequences of free trade in transamerican historic patterns between the US and El Salvador leading up to the civil war. As in *Ashes of Izalco*, unforgetting in *Alive* counteracts the denial of dignity of laborers in a global capitalist system. In this case, women are more prominently positioned on the frontlines of memory culture. Just as both texts trace the underbellies of US economic control, so too do they illuminate rationales for radicalism.

Against Forgetting

In June 2021, Vice President Kamala Harris visited Guatemala seeking to better understand the root causes of Central American migration to the United States. At a press conference with the Guatemalan president Alejandro Giammattei, she stated, "I want to be clear to folks in this region who are thinking about making that dangerous trek to the United States-Mexico border: Do not come. Do not come" (Taylor and Keith 2021). Harris's statement reveals how the policing of memory services US immigration policies, even under less austere administrations. The Biden administration's deliberate disregard of the long history of US colonial presence in Central America distills how transnational oblivion works now: a persistent kind of colonial gaslighting, a systematic concealment of US interventions in the geopolitical region that blurs accountability and clouds how predatory transnational relations often spur coerced migrations.

Dissatisfied with the strategic omission of US interventionist histories, Representative Alexandria Ocasio-Cortez (2021) tweeted, "The U.S. spent decades contributing to regime change and destabilization in Latin America. We can't help set someone's house on fire and then blame them for fleeing." Here, AOC's words convey an unforgetting that presses for an acknowledgment of how the US has been implicated with the history and destiny of Central America. Focusing on how Harris's visit lays bare lasting neocolonial interests from the Global North, Suyapa Portillo Villeda and Miguel Tinker Salas (2021) insist that, "rather than grappling with root causes, the U.S. government continues to view Central America as a source of cheap labor, an exporter of raw commodities, and an investment opportunity for companies like Nestlé." In this respect, Harris's visit upholds uncurbed foreign investment in the region, neoliberal practices that may well merely redistribute wealth with devastating effects—deepening income inequality and exacerbating environmental degradation—rather than alleviate poverty and stop migration. While dominant discourse might present the Biden administration as benevolently offering employment opportunities for poor people in the Global South, turning to Alegría's *Alive* reminds us of occluded histories of US colonial capitalism, most notably portrayed in Marina's export-driven experience culminating not in upward mobility but in profound precarity.

Alegría's literature of memory remains necessary in the present to help us dig more deeply into the tension between state memory and unforgetting that is still happening. To think about Central American studies at this time is to confront its association with stigmatized migrants, such as unaccompanied children and transnational gangs. Rather than view Central Americans as merely recent arrivals, decontextualized economic migrants denied refugee status, it is instead crucial to comprehend the historical dimension of US empire that has contributed to contemporary inequality. Alegría's oeuvre provides valuable anti-capitalist and anti-colonial awareness for the present era that urges us to reconsider the United States' longstanding relationship with El Salvador, and more broadly with postconflict societies in Latin America. The agricultural product of coffee and the industrial product of shapewear in El Salvador register genealogies of Latin American export commodities—sugar, silver, cattle, cacao, rubber, and so on—linked to legacies of US capitalist imperialism.

Ashes of Izalco and *They Won't Take Me Alive* establish a new reorientation of the twentieth century, pointing to a much larger context of unbroken military rule and continuous US corporate capitalism that more fully accounts for racialized, gendered, and classed imbrications. These texts are set roughly fifty years apart but share an obsession with troubling memory around distinct moments of capitalist transition intervolved with societal collapse. They each interact with events of catastrophic conflict, transmuting harrowing experiences of peripheral labor, addressing concealed colonial-patriarchal power relations, and challenging differential marginalization: the targeting of Indigenous peoples, the subordination of women, and the subjugation of the poor. Heeding Ann Laura Stoler's (2006: 16–17) reminder that "empire is a gendered history of power," my analysis, stressing portrayals of women's memory practices, shows that Alegría's work illuminates a much-needed anti-colonial perspective for discussions about the nexus between economic globalization and political violence. Ongoing asymmetrical accumulation and rising extracted labor (increasingly of women) still impinge strongly in the neoliberal capitalist present. Ultimately, unforgetting counters unethical historical amnesia, bringing forth possible futures beyond enduring legacies of economic exploitation, political terror, and imposed silence.

....

Guadalupe Escobar is assistant professor in the English Department and the Gender, Race, and Identity Department at the University of Nevada, Reno. She specializes in contemporary Latin American and Latinx cultural expression. Her current research project is on *testimonio* as a human rights genre.

Notes

1   It should be noted that in the prologue to Roque Dalton's Miguel Mármol, Salvadoran writer Manlio Argueta (1987: xvii) similarly describes the menace of US intervention in 1932 as "North American warships arrived off the Salvadoran coast, prepared to disembark troops if the military government failed to put down the rebellion."
2   For an insightful historical analysis that situates Salvadoran authoritarianism before the civil war, see Chávez 2017.
3   For further discussion of testimonio, see Escobar 2021.
4   I use the term maquiladora (or, maquila for short) interchangeably with fábrica. Maquila is often associated with the Mexican side of the borderlands, but it is not restricted to this geopolitical location.
5   According to Ralph Armbruster-Sandoval (2005: 3), US anti-sweatshop activism can be traced back to the aftermath of the 1911 Triangle Shirtwaist Factory fire resulting in the deaths of 146 immigrant women in New York City, effectively banishing poor work practices at the domestic level until the 1970s. After the global shift of the garment industry, this labor movement took on transnational dimensions.

Works Cited

Alegría, Claribel, and Darwin J. Flakoll. (1966) 1989. *Ashes of Izalco*. Translated by Darwin J. Flakoll. Willimantic, CT: Curbstone Press.
Alegría, Claribel, and Darwin J. Flakoll. (1983) 1987. *They Won't Take Me Alive: Salvadoran Women in Struggle for National Liberation*. Translated by Amanda Hopkinson. London: Women's Press.
Alvarado, Karina, Alicia Ivonne Estrada, and Ester Hernández, eds. 2017. *US Central Americans: Reconstructing Memories, Struggles, and Communities of Resistance*. Tucson: University of Arizona Press.
Argueta, Manlio. 1987. "Prologue." In *Miguel Marmol* by Roque Dalton, translated by Kathleen Ross and Richard Schaaf, xiii–xviii. Willimantic, CT: Curbstone Press.

Arias, Arturo. 1994. "Claribel Alegría's Recollection of Things to Come." In *Claribel Alegría and Central American Literature: Critical Essays*, edited by Sandra M. Boschetto-Sandoval and Marcia Phillips McGowan, 22–44. Athens: Ohio University Center for International Studies.

Arias, Arturo. 2007. *Taking Their Word: Literature and the Signs of Central America*. Minneapolis: University of Minnesota Press.

Armbruster-Sandoval, Ralph. 2005. *Globalization and Cross-Border Labor Solidarity in the Americas: The Anti-Sweatshop Movement and the Struggle for Social Justice*. New York: Routledge.

Bal, Mieke. 1999. Introduction to *Acts of Memory: Cultural Recall in the Present*, edited by Mieke Bal, Jonathan Crewe, and Leo Spitzer, vii–xvii. Hanover, NH: University Press of New England.

Barbas-Rhoden, Laura. 2003. *Writing Women in Central America: Gender and the Fictionalization of History*. Athens: Ohio University Press.

Barrientos, Stephanie. 2019. *Gender and Work in Global Value Chains: Capturing the Gains?* Cambridge: Cambridge University Press.

Beckman, Ericka. 2012. *Capital Fictions: The Literature of Latin America's Export Age*. Minneapolis: University of Minnesota Press.

Boland Osegueda, Roy. 2005. "The Central American Novel." In *The Cambridge Companion to the Latin American Novel*, edited by Efrain Kristal, 162–80. Cambridge: Cambridge University Press.

Bui, Long Thanh. 2015. "Glorientalization: Specters of Asia and Feminized Cyborg Workers in the U.S.–Mexico Borderlands." *Meridians: Feminism, Race, Transnationalism* 13, no. 1: 129–56.

Chávez, Joaquín. 2017. *Poets and Prophets of the Resistance: Intellectuals and the Origins of El Salvador's Civil War*. New York: Oxford University Press.

Chomsky, Aviva. 2021. *Central America's Forgotten History: Revolution, Violence, and the Roots of Migration*. Boston: Beacon Press.

Dalton, Roque. 2007. "Document 3-3: Roque Dalton, El Salvador, 1963. Excerpt." In *Remembering a Massacre in El Salvador: The Insurrection of 1932, Roque Dalton, and the Politics of Historical Memory*, edited by Hector Lindo-Fuentes, Erik Ching, and Rafael Lara-Martínez, 266–68. Albuquerque: University of New Mexico Press.

Escobar, Guadalupe. 2021. "Testimonio at Fifty." *Latin American Perspectives* 48, no. 2: 17–32.

Federici, Silvia. 2020. *Revolution at Point Zero: Housework, Reproduction, and Feminist Struggle*. Oakland, CA: PM Press.

Fields, Jill. 2007. *An Intimate Affair: Women, Lingerie, and Sexuality*. Berkeley: University of California Press.

Flores y Ascencio, Daniel. 2000. "Claribel Alegría." *Bomb Magazine*, January 1. https://bombmagazine.org/articles/claribel-alegr%C3%ADa/.

Forché, Carolyn. 1984. "Interview with Claribel Alegría." *Index on Censorship* 13, no. 2: 11–13.

Franco, Jean. 2013. *Cruel Modernity*. Durham, NC: Duke University Press.

Gago, Verónica. 2020. *Feminist International: How to Change Everything*. New York: Verso.

García, María Cristina. 2006. *Seeking Refuge: Central American Migration to Mexico, the United States, and Canada.* Berkeley: University of California Press.

Grandin, Greg. (2006) 2021. *Empire's Workshop: Latin America, the United States, and the Making of an Imperial Republic.* New York: Picador.

Grandin, Greg. 2010. "Living in Revolutionary Time: Coming to Terms with the Violence of Latin America's Long Cold War." In *A Century of Revolution: Insurgent and Counterinsurgent Violence during Latin America's Long Cold War,* edited Greg Grandin and Gilbert Joseph, 1–44. Durham, NC: Duke University Press.

Harlow, Barbara. 1990. "Claribel Alegría's and Darwin J. Flakoll's *Ashes of Izalco:* Gioconda Belli, *La Mujer Habitada.*" *Race and Class* 32, no. 1: 91–93.

Harvey, David. 2005. *A Brief History of Neoliberalism.* New York: Oxford University Press.

Huezo, Stephanie M. 2021. "Remembering the Return from Exodus: An Analysis of a Salvadoran Community's Local History Reenactment." *Journal of Latino/Latin American Studies* 11, no. 1: 56–74.

Jelin, Elizabeth. 2021. *The Struggle for the Past: How We Construct Social Memories.* New York: Berghahn.

Lovato, Roberto. 2020. *Unforgetting: A Memoir of Family, Migration, Gangs, and Revolution in the Americas.* New York: HarperCollins.

Lyon-Johnson, Kelli. 2005. "Acts of War, Acts of Memory: 'Dead-Body Politics' in US Latina Novels of the Salvadoran Civil War." *Latino Studies* 3, no. 2: 205–25.

McGowan, Marcia Phillips. 1994. "Closing the Circle: An Interview with Claribel Alegría." In *Claribel Alegría and Central American Literature: Critical Essays,* edited by Sandra M. Boschetto-Sandoval and Marcia Phillips McGowan, 228–45. Athens: Ohio University Press.

Mendez, Jennifer Bickham. 2005. *From Revolution to the Maquiladoras: Gender, Labor, and Globalization in Nicaragua.* Durham, NC: Duke University Press.

Mohanty, Chandra Talpade. 2003. *Feminism without Borders: Decolonizing Theory, Practicing Solidarity.* Durham, NC: Duke University Press.

Ocasio-Cortez, Alexandria (@AOC). 2021. "This Is Disappointing to See." Twitter, June 7, 2021, 4:16 p.m. https://twitter.com/aoc/status/1402041820096389124 ?lang=en.

O'Connor, Maureen. 2013. "Back When Pigeons Wore Bras." *The Cut,* September 4. https://www.thecut.com/2013/09/back-when-pigeons-wore-bras.html.

Padilla, Yajaira. 2012. *Changing Women, Changing Nation: Female Agency, Nationhood, and Identity in Trans-Salvadoran Narratives.* New York: State University of New York Press.

Padilla, Yajaira. 2022. *From Threatening Guerrillas to Forever Illegals: US Central Americans and the Cultural Politics of Non-Belonging.* Austin: University of Texas Press.

Rodríguez, Ana Patricia. 2020. "Diasporic Social Imaginaries, Transisthmian Echoes, and Transfigurations of Central American Subjectivities." *Oxford Research Encyclopedia of Literature,* September 28. https://oxfordre.com/literature/display/10.1093 /acrefore/9780190201098.001.0001/acrefore-9780190201098-e-439.

Rodríguez, Ileana. 2009. *Liberalism at Its Limits: Crime and Terror in the Latin American Cultural Text.* Pittsburgh, PA: University of Pittsburgh Press.

Rothberg, Michael. 2009. *Multidirectional Memory: Remembering the Holocaust in the Age of Decolonization*. Stanford, CA: Stanford University Press.

Rothberg, Michael. 2019. *The Implicated Subject: Beyond Victims and Perpetrators*. Stanford, CA: Stanford University Press.

Sternbach, Nancy Saporta. 1994. "Engendering the Future: *Ashes of Izalco* and the Making of a Writer." In *Claribel Alegría and Central American Literature: Critical Essays*, edited by Sandra M. Boschetto-Sandoval and Marcia Phillips McGowan. Athens: Ohio University Press.

Stoler, Ann Laura. 2006. *Haunted by Empire: Geographies of Intimacy in North American History*. Durham, NC: Duke University Press.

Sturken, Marita. 1997. *Tangled Memories: The Vietnam War, the AIDS Epidemic, and the Politics of Remembering*. Berkeley: University of California Press.

Sutton, Barbara. 2010. *Bodies in Crisis: Culture, Violence, and Women's Resistance in Neoliberal Argentina*. New Brunswick, NJ: Rutgers University Press.

Taylor, Brian, and Tamara Keith. 2021. "Kamala Harris Tells Guatemalans Not to Migrate to the United States." NPR, June 7. https://www.npr.org/2021/06/07/1004074139/harris-tells-guatemalans-not-to-migrate-to-the-united-states.

Varas, Patricia. 2013. "*Ashes of Izalco*: Female Narrative Strategies and the History of the Nation." In *Redefining Latin American Historical Fiction: The Impact of Feminism and Postcolonialism*, edited by Helene Carol Weldt-Basson, 47–64. New York: Palgrave Macmillan.

Villeda, Suyapa Portillo, and Miguel Tinker Salas. 2021. "The Root Cause of Central American Migration is U.S. Imperialism." *Jacobin*, June 8. https://www.jacobinmag.com/2021/06/kamala-harris-central-america-guatemala-visit-us-imperialism.

Henrikke Sæthre Ellingsen

....

Response to Kuokkanen

On Structural Violence, Bad Faith, and Strategic Ignorance
in Norwegian Wind Power Development

Abstract: In this response to Rauna Kuokkanen's (2022) critical reading of Henrikke Sæthre Ellingsen's (2020) master's thesis on wind power development in Norway, Ellingsen elaborates on what theoretical terms could have been used in the thesis to better elucidate a systematic pattern in Norwegian politics for the Saami population and illuminate the Fosen case to describe how the Norwegian government handles the knowledge provided by the Indigenous South Saami reindeer herders at Fosen when developing wind power in the latter's essential winter pastures. The use of the term *lack of knowledge* helps make the Saami knowledge invisible, so instead, Ellingsen argues, several other theoretical perspectives can highlight the power asymmetry between the Saami community and the Norwegian government.

I thank Rauna Kuokkanen (2022) for her critical reading of my master's thesis on wind power development in Norway. My thesis (Ellingsen 2020) explored the uneven power dynamics between the Norwegian government and South Saami reindeer herders at Fovsen/Fosen in Trööndelage/Trøndelag County during the establishment of Europe's largest onshore wind power facility.[1] I argued that throughout the process of developing onshore wind power in Norway, the government has deliberately disregarded the knowledge held by the South Saami reindeer herders. This deliberate action resulted in a Supreme Court verdict in 2021 that declared the development at Fosen violated the South Saami reindeer herders' right to practice their culture, as outlined in Article 27 of the United Nations

MERIDIANS · feminism, race, transnationalism   23:2 October 2024
DOI: 10.1215/15366936-11266420 © 2024 Smith College

International Convention on Civil and Political Rights (HR-2021-1975-S). However, in my master's thesis, I used the term *lack of knowledge* to describe the disparity between the South Saami reindeer herding knowledge and the knowledge the administration uses to justify wind power development in Saami Indigenous areas.

Kuokkanen (2022) critiques my use of this term, suggesting that it obscures the agency of the Norwegian state and its deliberate disregard for and marginalization of Saami knowledge regarding these areas and herding practices. She also points out that this term may inadvertently imply that there is no knowledge about Saami reindeer herding practices within the Norwegian government body, which was never my intention. I concur with Kuokkanen's perspective that the term *willful disinterest* more accurately characterizes the ongoing production of power imbalances between the Norwegian government and the South Saami reindeer herders. Furthermore, I believe that concepts like Lewis Gordon's bad faith, the sociological notion of strategic ignorance, and Johan Galtung's (1969, 1990) concept of structural and cultural violence can help elucidate a systematic pattern in Norwegian politics for the Saami population. This short response will illustrate how these concepts can illuminate the Fosen case.

The Drawbacks Associated with Employing
Lack of Knowledge as a Term

Writing this response allows me to critically examine the narrative I have contributed by employing the term *lack of knowledge*. First, the term can be seen as positivist, implying that more knowledge in the departments and administration would solve the problem. However, conversations with the Saami herders at Fosen reveal that they have been sharing their knowledge about the reindeer movement and life with various bureaucrats over the past thirteen years. This suggests that there is no desire or willingness on the part of the Petroleum and Energy Department and the Norwegian Water Resources and Energy Directorate (NVE) to listen and act on the knowledge provided by the Saami community on the effects of wind energy development in reindeer herding areas. Second, when terms like *lack of knowledge* or *knowledge gap* are used when the relevant information is already supplied, it implicitly places an expectation and burden of evidence on the Saami reindeer herders to provide even more knowledge. Frantz Fanon (2004) noted that the colonial system often requires the colonized to prove their innocence. In this context, the South Saami herders at Fosen need to justify their right to exist by continually providing more knowledge to a system that marginalizes their community. This implication contradicts my original intention behind my master's thesis and exposes the colonial narrative the term represents.

The Dynamics of Colonial Relations in Norwegian Wind Energy Development

To better elucidate the current colonial relations between the state and the South Saami reindeer herders in Norway, I would like to build on Kuokkanen's concept of epistemological ignorance. The concepts of structural violence and cultural violence are valuable for describing the current situation at Fosen, as they encompass structural abuse into institutional structures, which manifests as unequal power dynamics and relationships. These forms of violence are categorized as either *direct violence*, which includes physical or psychological harm; *structural violence*, which pertains to discriminatory societal systems; or *cultural violence*, which justifies both direct and structural violence (Galtung and Fischer 2013; Sehlin MacNeil 2017). Structural and cultural violence can be understood as perpetuating unjust societal structures and fostering racist and discriminating attitudes. Cultural violence often diminishes and discriminates against Indigenous cultures and worldviews, often by imposing expectations connected to notions of "primitiveness" (Sehlin MacNeil 2017). For Fanon (cited in Mbembe 2001: 174–75), colonial violence is inherent in structures and institutions, producing a culture and becoming a cultural praxis. In essence, colonialism operates as a complete system of violence (Fanon 2004). By highlighting forms of violence that may go unnoticed and unrecognized, we expand the field of visibility and reveal the forms of invisible violence, making structural violence visible and demonstrating its intergenerational impact (Winter 2012: 198).

Additionally, the concept of bad faith can illuminate the violence in the state-Saami relationship. Bad faith captures the inherent logic of the Norwegian government's structure, wherein actions are taken independently of the individual's intentions. While individual bureaucrats may or may not act in good faith, there is always an individual responsibility to recognize how power and colonialism influence their work. However, emphasizing individual agency and legal responsibility in a positivist manner is an unsatisfactory criterion for determining agentive intentionality and fails to adequately address the invisible instances of violence. Susanne Normann's (2021) research illustrates how the institutional dimension of bad faith in the state-Saami relationship is rooted in collective attitudes stemming from the colonial legacy and the history of the Norwegian government. Thus, the persistence of bad faith in the consultations between the Saami reindeer herders at Fosen and the Norwegian government leads to dehumanizing the Saami herders (Gordon 1995: 8; Normann 2021).

As Fanon (2004) noted, the dehumanization of the colonized served as the colonial system's rationale for seizing land and subjugating its people. The ongoing suppression of the South Saami culture and the presence of institutional and structural violence are imbued with elements of racism and alienation, repressing agency (Gordon 2010: 184). Racism, as Fanon (2004) demonstrated, often involves denying even the humanity of certain groups of other people. Moreover, as Elsa Reimerson (2015: 1) argued, portraying Indigenous peoples as inferior has historically positioned them in ways that made it difficult "or even impossible to be recognized as knowledgeable, authoritative, or politically relevant actors."

In my thesis, I interviewed one of the South Saami reindeer herders at Fosen who had participated in consultations on a joint venture between a private development company, Fosen Vind DA, and a state-owned one, Statkraft. The "dialogue meetings" are required by Norwegian consultation law and are intended to function as a forum where the Saami community can meet and discuss development plans in their respective areas. During the meeting, the South Saami reindeer herder had the opportunity to indicate on a map which areas were crucial for the Northern part of the development plans. He left the meeting believing that he had achieved a shared understanding and an agreement on which grazing areas should remain undisturbed by wind turbines because of the critical value of the areas during the winter. However, later, the very same areas were included in the development with the full knowledge that the areas were essential winter pastures. This example underscores how bad faith may prevail in the establishment of wind power parks in Indigenous areas. Forms of bad faith that emerge under structural and institutionalized racism in Norwegian wind power development involve making promises with no intention of fulfilling them, systematically and strategically ignoring the input of the South Saami reindeer herders.

The Production of Strategic Ignorance and Epistemic Violence

I concur with Kuokkanen that her concept of *willful disinterest* aptly describes the lack of political consequences of the Fosen verdict. As Kuokkanen (2008: 64) rightly puts it, the lack of inclusion and respect for Indigenous knowledges constitutes epistemic ignorance at both the institutional and individual levels. Ignorance is not merely a passive lack of understanding; it often involves actively avoiding other knowledges and worldviews, a pattern known as strategic ignorance. The positivist solution to ignorance typically suggests that inclusion and respect will follow once more knowledge is obtained. Kuokkanen criticizes my master's thesis for adhering to the positivist tradition, implying that uneven power relations can be rectified with more knowledge. Nevertheless, despite the Supreme Court ruling in 2021 and research highlighting the disparities the Saami reindeer herders face in the Norwegian energy transformation, Saami knowledge remains marginalized. This underscores the importance of making the violence visible (Fjellheim et al. 2020; Fjellheim 2023). I agree with Kuokkanen (2008) that these uneven power relations, rooted in epistemic ignorance, are a colonial legacy that frequently manifests as strategic ignorance in the Norwegian energy transformation, which I aimed to demonstrate through my thesis.

According to Perl, Howlett, and Ramesh (2018: 585), the significance of willful ignorance, where facts and evidence that contradict or undermine firmly held opinions and beliefs are denied, obstinately contested, or simply ignored, has been largely overlooked by policy scientists and analysts. Upholding the epistemology of ignorance prolongs the mystification of Saami cultures and knowledges and indicates a problem of denial by the Norwegian government (Fjellheim 2020; Perl, Howlett, and Ramesh 2018). Consequently, a culture of domination persists, undermining the Saami's rights. For Indigenous communities, dehumanization through denial of their meaning systems and self-determination materializes in epistemological and ontological violence, which can lead to epistemicides and the destruction of existing knowledge (Normann 2021). What results is the knowledge systems of dehumanized groups hold little to no value for most of society. Gaining more knowledge of the effects of large-scale industrial development on the Saami reindeer herding communities is not the problem. The issue at hand revolves around the importance of acknowledging and creating a place for diverse knowledge systems and worldviews to be valued in the transition away from fossil fuels.

The Continuation of Colonial Patterns in Norway

The ongoing human rights violation at Fosen underscores the predominance of Western knowledge hegemony. Therefore, situating bad faith, strategic ignorance, and structural violence within a broader framework of green colonial rationalization enables an exploration of the social and historical conditions underlying contemporary forms of violence. This approach helps bring to the forefront and analyze epistemic and ontological violence experienced by the Saami reindeer herding community at Fosen. The Norwegian state actively ignores both the Saami knowledges and the Fosen verdict. Consequently, parts of Norway's onshore wind power development remain embedded in colonial relations of injustices under the name of "green" development and industrialization (Zografos 2022).

As I write this response, over two years have passed since the Fosen verdict was handed down, and the lack of political response from the Norwegian government makes it evident that the recurring neo-colonial patterns are hard to ignore in Norway. The process of institutional violence and structural ignorance of the Saami community are still present. The most troubling outcome arising from the strategic ignoring of the Fosen verdict is the absence of safeguards against the abuse of power and the oppression experienced by the Saami in Norway.

Decolonization requires acknowledging that we live in a colonizing state and that oppression occurs in a colonial system. As I have emphasized throughout my response, decolonization entails listening to the affected communities at the frontline (Zografos 2022: 47), a commitment I will continue to uphold in the future. As Linda Tuhiwai Smith (2012) has already established, researchers working within Indigenous methodologies and communities must be attentive to their role as researcher, which necessitates an ongoing exploration of ethics and community sensibilities, which I apply while critically examining my research practices, including the selection and application of theories and terms.

. . . .

Henrikke Sæthre Ellingsen is a PhD candidate at the Norwegian University of Technology and Science in the Department of Political Science. Her work focuses on how green colonialism operates in Norway today and how this affects the South Saami reindeer herders at Fosen.

Notes

1   Saepmie, the Saami people's ancestral land, spans Norway, Sweden, Finland, and Russia. The Saami are Indigenous and constitute an ethnic minority in these nations (Hansen and Olsen 2022). For the purpose of this response, when

I use *Saepmie* I am referring explicitly to the portion of Saepmie located within the borders of the Norwegian nation-state.

Also, I give both the South Saami and Norwegian spelling of these names here to underscore the presence of the South Saami community in Trøndelag County.

Works Cited

Ellingsen, Henrikke Sæthre. 2020. "Resistance to Wind Power Development in Norway: Exploring Power, Knowledge Production, and Injustice at Fosen and Frøya." MSc thesis, Institute of Sociology and Human Geography, University of Oslo.

Fanon, Frantz. 2004. *The Wretched of the Earth*. New York: Grove Press.

Fjellheim, Eva Maria. 2020. "Through Our Stories, We Resist: Decolonial Perspectives on South Saami History, Indigeneity, and Rights." In *Indigenous Knowledges and the Sustainable Development Agenda*, edited by Anders Breidlid and Roy Krøvel, 207–26. London: Routledge.

Fjellheim, Eva Maria. 2023. "Wind Energy on Trial in Saepmie: Epistemic Controversies and Strategic Ignorance in Norway's Green Energy Transition." *Arctic Review on Law and Politics* 14: 140–68.

Fjellheim, Eva Maria, Florian Carl, and Susanne Normann. 2020. "'Green' Colonialism Is Ruining Indigenous Lives in Norway." Al Jazeera, August 1. https://www.aljazeera.com/opinions/2020/8/1/green-colonialism-is-ruining-indigenous-lives-in-norway/.

Galtung, Johan. 1969. "Violence, Peace, and Peace Research." *Journal of Peace Research* 6, no. 3: 167–91.

Galtung, Johan. 1990. "Cultural Violence." *Journal of Peace Research* 27, no. 3: 291–305.

Galtung, Johan, and Dietrich Fischer. 2013. *Johan Galtung, Pioneer of Peace Research*. London: Springer.

Gordon, Lewis Ricardo. 1995. *Bad Faith and Anti-black Racism*. Amherst, NY: Humanity Books.

Gordon, Lewis Ricardo. 2010. "Sartre and Fanon on Embodied Bad Faith." In *Sartre on the Body*, edited by K. J. Morris, 183–200. London: Palgrave Macmillan.

Hansen, Lars Ivar, and Bjørnar Olsen. 2022. *Samenes historie: Fram til 1750*. 2. Oslo: Cappelen Damm Akademisk. HR-2021–1975-S (Fosen).

Kuokkanen, Rauna. 2008. "What Is Hospitality in the Academy? Epistemic Ignorance and the (Im)possible Gift." *Review of Education, Pedagogy, and Cultural Studies* 30, no. 1: 60–82.

Kuokkanen, Rauna. 2022. "Is the Reindeer the New Buffalo? Climate Change, the Green Shift, and Manifest Destiny in Sápmi." *Meridians* 22, no. 1: 11–33.

Mbembe, Achille. 2001. *On the Postcolony*. Berkeley: University of California Press.

Normann, Susanne. 2021. "'Time Is Our Worst Enemy': Lived Experiences and Intercultural Relations in the Making of Green Aluminum." *Journal of Social Issues* 78, no. 1: 163–82.

Perl, Anthony, Michael Howlett, and M. Ramesh. 2018. "Policy-Making and Truthiness: Can Existing Policy Models Cope with Politicized Evidence and Willful Ignorance in a 'Post-fact' World?" *Policy Sciences* 51, no. 4: 581–600.

Reimerson, Elsa. 2015. "Nature, Culture, Rights: Exploring Space for Indigenous Agency in Protected Area Discourses." PhD diss., Umeå University.

Sehlin MacNeil, Kristina. 2017. "Extractive Violence on Indigenous Country Sami and Aboriginal Views on Conflicts and Power Relations with Extractive Industries." PhD diss., Umeå University.

Tuhiwai Smith, Linda. 2012. *Decolonizing Methodologies: Research and Indigenous Peoples.* Dunedin, New Zealand: Zed.

Winter, Yves. 2012. "Violence and Visibility." *New Political Science* 34, no. 2: 195–202.

Zografos, Christos. 2022. "The Contradictions of Green New Deals: Green Sacrifice and Colonialism." *Soundings: A Journal of Politics and Culture,* no. 80: 37–50.

Aisha A. Upton Azzam

"Enhancing Human Dignity Here and Around the World"

The Black Sorority as International Uplift Movement

Abstract: In the second half of the twentieth century, Black sororities began establishing chapters and social programs across the globe, an intentional social action that Aisha A. Upton Azzam conceptualizes as the Black sorority movement (BSM). In this piece, Upton Azzam explores the style and extent of such international engagement. She illuminates the marginalized aspect of the movement's international activism while clarifying how such activism may have also employed the very neoliberal, neocolonial, and patriarchal ideas and practices that the movement explicitly stated that they wished to resist and overturn.

Introduction

Recognizing that national borders did not limit the struggles for Black female dignity and human rights, in 1948 Zeta Phi Beta sorority became the first Greek-letter sorority to charter a chapter in Africa (Monrovia, Liberia). Two years later, in 1950, Delta Sigma Theta sorority established a chapter in the capital of the first free Black republic in the Western Hemisphere— Port-au-Prince, Haiti. In the second half of the twentieth century, Black sororities continued to establish chapters and social programs across the globe, an intentional social action that I conceptualize as the Black sorority movement (hereafter BSM).[1] The BSM had grown its influence beyond US borders to promote basic literacy, reproductive rights, and political agency, alongside many other civil and human rights programs for Black communities in general and often for Black women specifically.

MERIDIANS · feminism, race, transnationalism   23:2 October 2024
DOI: 10.1215/15366936-11266452 © 2024 Smith College

The extant literature on Black international human and civil rights movements has largely ignored female actors and organizations. An examination of the global activities of the varied organizations that constitute the BSM promises to reconceptualize Black internationalism beyond the current registers of masculine and patriarchal agency and activism. Through a content analysis of Alpha Kappa Alpha's national organ, the *Ivy Leaf*, Delta Sigma Theta's national organ the *Delta*, Zeta Phi Beta's national organ the *Archon*, and Sigma Gamma Rho's national organ the *Aurora*, the BSM reveals a Black feminist-led shift from the conventional discussion of US civil rights within the sphere of legal protections, to a narrative about existentially deserved human rights on an international scale.

With varied technique, the four sororities altered their focus from legal and domestic concerns to concentrate on collaborations with the Non-Partisan Council and the American Human Rights Council of the United Nations and other international agencies, and they labored to establish their international chapters to expand their activism. For example, Marjorie Parker (1990: 166), author of *Alpha Kappa Alpha through the Years 1908–1988*, contends,

> The Boule adopted a series of resolutions which reflected the Sorority's concept of an ever-widening community of service. Alpha Kappa Alpha went on record in support of the "democratic way of life" and efforts to "enhance human dignity here and around the world." Other resolutions urged members to "make every effort to enhance human dignity" and to support aid to education in developing nations.

I explore the style and extent of such international engagement. Moreover, while I attempt to illuminate the marginalized aspect of the BSM's international activism, I do not engage in that analysis uncritically. I judiciously outline the modes of BSM engagement, clarifying how such activism may have also implicitly employed the very neoliberal, neocolonial, and patriarchal ideals and practices the BSM explicitly stated they wished to resist and overturn.

An Overview of the Black Sorority Movement

The early twentieth century bore witness to the genesis of Black sororities. Like members of the Black women's clubs that preceded them, the women who began these sororal organizations faced myriad obstacles due to their unique social location as Black women. That is, the intersection of both de jure and de facto white supremacy and patriarchy limited the economic, political, and social upward mobility, if not the basic human rights, of Black women (White 1999). Most Black women who sought employment worked privately as domestic workers or sharecropping farm laborers (Hine 1994). Moreover, by 1900, only 5.9 percent of Black women (aged 18–21) were enrolled in higher education (compared to 10.4 percent of white men and 8.6% of white women) (Integrated Public Use Microdata Series Census samples for 1900). Of that small percent that went to college, a reduced portion organized to overcome these obstacles, meet their culturally specific needs, and intentionally create an organization based on fictive kinship ties of sisterhood and the advancement of Black womanhood (Neumann 2008).

Alpha Kappa Alpha (AKA) sorority, the first of four still extant Black sororities, was founded in 1908 on the campus of Howard University in Washington, DC. Nine women, led by Ethel Hedgeman, formed an organization dedicated to forging a community of sisterhood and serving humanity through their motto *Askosis Kai Axiosis*, which translated from Greek means "by culture and by merit" (Parker 1990). In 1913, the members of AKA banded together to incorporate the sorority—the first to be nationally incorporated.

At its inception, the organization was only known for participating in other organizations' service projects, including the Young Women's Christian Association and the National Association for the Advancement of Colored People (Evans 2008; Parker 1990). Parker (1990: 163) explains that although "the earliest AKA programs were cultural in nature, . . . soon after the organization was formed . . . [the members] marched for women's rights in the suffragette parades." During the 1930s, AKA turned much of its attention toward taking on the racially based human rights work already organized under the aegis of the Black women's club movement, such as the self-help-based Mississippi Health Project (Parker 1990). The sorority also founded the Non-Partisan Committee on Human Rights, which worked to protect the rights of Blacks by lobbying for US congressional legislation (Parker 1958, 1990; White 1999). AKA chapters pursued health initiatives throughout the South between 1935 and 1942—and lobbied for the Women's Reserve of the United States Navy to end its exclusionary practices that disallowed Black women in the service (Collier-Thomas 2001; White 1999). The sorority was active in both national and local projects including war efforts for World War II and the founding of the Cleveland Job Corps Center for Women in Cleveland, Ohio.

Delta Sigma Theta (DST) sorority was founded at Howard University in 1913 when twenty-two undergraduates led by Edna Brown left AKA hoping to begin their own intentional community of sisterhood (Giddings 1988). Social activism became a cornerstone of DST's involvement as they participated in the suffragette movement and worked closely with organizations like the National Association for the Advancement of Colored People and the National Urban League (Harris 2008). DST advanced their legacy of social activism through their work with the National Council of Negro Women and the Non-Partisan Committee on Human Rights (Collier-Thomas 2001; Jones 2009)

Also at Howard University, in 1920, five women led by Arizona Cleaver overcame significant strife to form Zeta Phi Beta sorority (ZPB). From their founding ZPB was invested in cultivating "finer womanhood" and working to improve Black communities through their work with organizations like the National Association for the Advancement of Colored People and the National Negro Caucus (Hughey 2008). ZPB worked closely with Phi Beta Sigma fraternity to enhance and promote fellowship, equal rights, and service to all humankind (95). Shortly following, Sigma Gamma Rho (SGRho) sorority was the first and only Black sorority to be founded at a predominately white university—the campus of Butler University in 1922. Bernadette Pruitt, Caryn E. Neumann, and Katrina Hamilton (2008: 125) tell the story of seven schoolteachers who "formed a self-help organization that sought to promote intellectual distinction among female schoolteachers and education majors."

As the four sororities grew in both membership and strength, the BSM expanded. From its roots in the early twentieth century as a cluster of organizations focused on self-help and creating intentional spaces for sisterhood, the BSM began to undertake causes specifically geared toward women and families outside of themselves. After spending the beginning of the century focused on race work such as integration and other domestic civil rights, the BSM sororities expanded physically through the creation of chapters abroad and ideologically by embracing aspects of women of color's struggles to obtain human rights in their own nations.

Scholarship on the Black Sorority Movement as International Black Feminist Organizations

Extant scholarship on Black feminist organizing tends to focus on the period of 1968 to 1980, a moment in which explicitly Black feminist organizations like the National Black Feminist Organization, the Third World

Women's Alliance, and the Combahee River Collective were active (Springer 2005). While a focus on this time period helps to delineate a space for the Black feminist movement proper, it does not fully address the presence of Black protofeminist organizing before the radical feminist movement of the 1960s and post–civil rights era. Accordingly, scholarly interpretations of pre–civil rights and first-wave feminist organizations are often stuck at the juncture of androcentric views of internationalism, first-wave views of feminism as centered primarily on the work of white women's organizations, and the short historical view of Black feminist organizing. Hence, it is important to interrogate the international work of the BSM to reveal a much more nuanced and entrenched form of racial and gender-based organizing throughout the first half of the twentieth century.

Scholarship on Black women's civic engagement reveals that Black women have a long history of working within civil society to improve the lives of other Black women and the conditions of various Black communities (Higginbotham 1993; Scott 1990; Gilkes 2001). Early Black protofeminism included creating organizations that allowed women to design and orchestrate the activism from which they were disallowed participation within male-led organizations (Collins 1998). The formation of their own organizations became paramount in order to engage in a specific Black feminist praxis—activism that addressed the intersections of both race and gender on equal terms. Patricia Hill Collins (1998) contends that this type of organizing by Black women worked to break the silence placed on them due to their subordinated position in the social order (43). The first Black women's organizations, mutual aid societies and women's club organizations, exemplified the Black feminist ideal of breaking the silences about racism and sexism. The women in these organizations engaged in activism focused on self-help and mutual aid (Higginbotham 1993; Scott 1990; White 1999).

Black sororities continued the work of early first-wave Black feminist organizations like the National Association of Colored Women. They built on the work laid by the organizations before them and expanded their focus beyond teaching domestic skills and creating settlement houses (White 1999). As they grew their organizations, the sororities formed national projects geared toward creating and enhancing education, access to health care, and civil rights law (Giddings 1988). While they took on the duty of "race work" writ large, as the waves of feminism shifted, they intentionally focused on issues that affected Black women and children specifically

(White 1999). The attention toward the experiences and issues directly pertaining to women's and children's lives was both cause and consequence of a growing internationalist focus that sought to challenge "heteronormative and masculinist articulations of nationalism while maintaining the importance, even centrality, of national liberation movements for achieving Black women's social, political, and economic rights" (Higashida 2011: 2). They expanded its boundaries—from lobbying for US civil rights to taking on the Black feminist movement's push for human rights across the globe.

Such articulations were manifest in diverse forms of activism. First, given that the movement aimed to connect local Black female struggles with the oppression of women globally (Collins 1998; Higashida 2011), the immediate task was to define the contours of those issues without being either overly abstract or too locally tailored. Collins (2000) identifies the core themes of Black feminism as revolving around the social arenas of work, family, and oppression. Interwoven with these issues is the notion of intersectional thought—the ability to see that the Black woman is "confronted by both a woman question and a race problem, and is yet an unacknowledged factor in both" (Cooper 2017: 76).

Scholarship on Black sorority activism is limited, but some research does focus on their involvement with the spheres of work, family, and human rights. Regarding work, Black fraternities and sororities sprung out of the tension of Du Boisian and Washingtonian models that promoted either intellectual or industrial labor, respectively. Michael H. Washington and Cheryl L. Nuñez (2005) contend that either way, early Black fraternal organizing emphasized a "Gospel of Work" that eventually resulted in the formation of Black-led fraternities and sororities, Black newspapers such as "the *Chicago Defender, Boston Guardian, New York Amsterdam News, St. Louis Argus,* Cincinnati's *Union,* and the NAACP's *Crisis,*" the establishment of mutual aid and insurance companies, and fifty-five Black-owned banks by the year 1914. In Black sororities, these women members led and worked at "black hospitals and preventive health programs to combat tuberculosis, venereal disease, infant mortality, and malnutrition. They established schools from kindergartens to postsecondary institutions" (163–67).

Additionally, scholarship emphasizes the sororities' interests in families. Neumann (2008) details the sororities' wide array of programs geared specifically at children. Other scholarship describes the organizations' health work, explaining that their work, especially in the rural south, was geared toward keeping Black families and communities healthy (Harris and Mitchell Jr. 2008; White 1999). Another example of their commitment to families was AKA's Project Family. This project was a collaborative effort between the sorority and social workers, where they "adopted twenty families and administered adult education, providing advice on birth control, budgeting, and career opportunities" (Whaley 2010: 46).

In regard to the theme of human rights and oppression, Deborah Elizabeth Whaley (2010) contends that AKA "took on activist work out of necessity owing to their subordinated position as sexualized, gender, ethnic, or racial minorities" (31). For Whaley, Black sororities' work against racism and sexist oppression separates them from the club women who preceded them in that sorority women's "goals went beyond nebulous ideas of sisterhood and individual achievement; these women sought to transform the society in which they lived" (38).

Marybeth Gasman (2011: 29–30) also shows that the Black sororities were at the forefront of pushing Eisenhower to sign the United Nations covenant on human rights. When Eisenhower refused, the sororities—through their involvement in the American Council on Human Rights (ACHR)—stated that "the decision not to sign the human rights covenant could be construed only as a setback for the cause of human rights in this country and throughout the world" (in Gasman 2011: 30). Interestingly enough, by 1957 all the Black fraternities left the ACHR, leaving it a mostly Black-women-led organization. Accordingly, DST sorority put more heat on the Eisenhower administration, when they unveiled a five-point plan for increasing African American job opportunities and curbing human rights abuses before Eisenhower's Committee on Government Contracts—the plan included "an educational campaign on employment, support of mental health facilities, increased community service, and an emphasis on *international aid*" (31; my emphasis).

The aforementioned literature shows an "organizational life cycle of Black Greek-Letter Organizations" (Roberts and Wooten 2008). Through a close examination of the history of Black Greek-letter organizations in select periods of time—intersected by Black sororities' focus on labor, education, family, and various other forms of racial and gender activism—Laura Morgan Roberts and Lynn Perry Wooten (2008: 280) posit that "organizational behavior in the mature years of the BGLOs focused on strengthening the community service ethos and their identity." A crucial part of the organizational life cycle was expanding these organizations' community service and domestic activism to an international scale.

Gaps, Extensions, Disputes

The aforementioned scholarship provides only a few insights on Black sororities' national and international activities, thus making for several challenges. First, this scholarship has typically followed the "good deeds" model (Tindall, Hernandez, and Hughey 2011). This scholarly approach toward Black sororities focuses on the philanthropic work of these organizations, painting "a positive picture of membership" that functions as a form of praise for these organizations but does not address possible negative repercussions of this work or how such philanthropy might serve as a glossy veneer to these organizations' more complex and paradoxical activities at best, or as a smokescreen for more insidious and counterproductive activities at worst (Tindall, Hernandez, and Hughey 2011). This good-deeds model tells an aspect of the Black sorority narrative, but it shrinks from a critical understanding of their international involvement.

Second, a focus on the philanthropy and good deeds of the organizations neglects these women's social location as middle- and upper-class Black women. Taking into account their class position necessitates a closer look at their politics and their practices. It necessitates delving deeper into their motivations and structural constraints that enabled and inhibited their work—especially if their work (intentionally or unintentionally) reified their racial, gender, or class positionality (Kendall 2002). While scholarship has outlined BSM activities as leading forces in twentieth-century women's activism, the engagement of the sororities was often limited and may have implicitly reinscribed the neoliberal, neocolonial, and patriarchal ideals these women supposedly sought to redress (Frazier 1957; Kendall 2002; White 1999). Toward that end, there is a gap in our scholarly understanding of the BSM in relation to Black internationalism. Illuminating the factors that pushed or pulled the BSM away from or toward reactionary "politics of respectability" or radical Pan-Africanist stances is a crucial next step in reclaiming the legacy of the BSM from hagiographic accounts that would either romanticize or demonize their praxis.

Third, and as a counterweight to the previous point, almost no scholarship focuses on the BSM as an international movement. While a bevy of work accounts for BSM-led activism within the confines of the American nationalist project or liberal democratic practice (Harris 2005; White 1999; Whaley 2010), few scholarly expeditions have tried to map the undulations of the BSM's increasingly global vision. The few scholarly attempts that have mentioned black sorority involvement in global affairs have concentrated on organizational mechanisms (Roberts and Wooten 2008) and recounting organizational history (Giddings 1988; Parker 1990). I alter tack to demonstrate why and how the BSM rationalized and legitimated a move from the conventional discussion of domestic civil rights to a narrative about human rights on an international scale.

I detail how the BSM moved toward internationalism in several different ways: reporting back through their organs about the international travel of other members, establishing international chapters around the world, working with the United Nations on projects like International Women's Year, and focusing their efforts on improving the lives of women in Africa. Discussing these methods of international engagement addresses gaps in the literature about Black women's internationalism more generally, and more specifically addresses the gaps in the literature regarding the BSM's international involvement.

Data and Methods

I employed a content analysis methodology to analyze AKA's national organ the *Ivy Leaf* (n = 364), DST's national organ the *Delta* (n = 124), ZPB's national organ the *Archon* (n = 20), and SGRho's national organ the *Aurora* (n = 52). The dates of the sororities' organs I analyzed ranged from 1921 (the earliest publication of the *Ivy Leaf*) over ninety years to 2011.

While the *Ivy Leaf* was available via microfilm, the organs the *Delta*, the *Archon*, and the *Aurora* were obtained via archival research. Because the collections of these organs were incomplete, they were less accessible than the *Ivy Leaf*. For this reason, the *Ivy Leaf* is overrepresented in the sample. Each of the organs was analyzed for mentions of internationalism. After recording each instance of internationalism, the instances were grouped into the larger themes of (1) reporting back, (2) establishing international chapters, (3) working with the United Nations, (4) International Women's Year, and (5) focusing on Africa. After delineating these themes, I also took a critical stance toward these forms of "internationalism" to illuminate inconsistencies and paradoxes. I find that while the BSM moved toward a critical womanist internationalism, such activism was not one-dimensional; they simultaneously engaged in (1) *a politics of respectability* (see Higginbotham 1993) and (2) *bourgeois organizing and philanthropy as window dressing* (see Frazier 1957).

Sororities' national organs are useful sources for content analysis on this topic because they operate as a form of direct contact from the organization's national level to the general membership and are published regularly (Bracey, Harley, and Meier 2000). These factors make the national organs of Black Greek-letter sororities excellent primary sources for gaining an understanding of how sorority women viewed internationalism.

The national organs of each organization are published at varying frequencies, with some of them like the *Ivy Leaf* and the *Aurora* being published quarterly, and the *Archon* and the *Delta* being published monthly. The overall frequency of these organs allows us an examination of the variance in how the organizations identified, proposed solutions, and issued calls to action toward the civil and human rights issues of an international scale.

Toward Internationalism

Black sororities urged their members to develop "world-mindedness" (Zeta Phi Beta Sorority 1957)—or to engage in the "task of building a world society" (Zeta Phi Beta Sorority 1957: 3). Developing this "world-mindedness" came to mean a wide array of different things for each sorority. Paula Giddings (1988: 218) explains sororities' international involvement, contending that, "the late forties and fifties were a time of tremendous interest in international affairs." Beginning in this time period, Black sororities moved through laboring for civil rights domestically toward working for human rights internationally. During this time period these sororities all took part in several activities that illustrated this shift including establishing international chapters, moving from working with domestic civil rights organizations to making connections with international human rights organizations and causes, and focusing explicitly on working within the African continent to improve the lives of women.

Through a content analysis of the *Ivy Leaf*, the *Delta*, the *Archon*, and the *Aurora* a shift in both ideology and practice can be seen. The sororities of the BSM moved from work on domestic civil rights through organizations like the Non-Partisan Council and the ACHR to working on projects to aid women internationally through entities like the United Nations. This shift can be seen in different ways including using the organs as a space for members to report back about their international travel. Each of the organizations created international chapters as they expanded their philanthropic interests. After these organizations began to see themselves as global citizens, the BSM worked closely with the United Nations and took part in projects like International Women's Year. In addition, the BSM often focused explicitly on projects to improve women's lives in Africa.

"Reporting Back"

One of the ways the sororities began connecting themselves internationally was through publishing stories about members who had traveled abroad, explaining the cultural and political lessons those members learned about that they thought would enhance the world knowledge of other members. Through their publication of members' experiences in destinations like Africa, Europe, Asia, and the Caribbean, the sororities aimed to develop a "world-mindedness" of their members. An April 1957 issue of ZPB's *Archon* describes this world-mindedness as how members could embrace a "one world spirit" through integrating themselves at the individual, national, and global levels (Zeta Phi Beta Sorority 1957: 3). Embracing the one world spirit meant that members would be reporting back to their sorority sisters about their travels abroad and that their experiences would inspire the organizations' international work.

In 1963, the *Delta*—in an issue focused on internationalism—reported that forty-six of its members took part in a 1962 African Study Tour showing how the forty-six members traveled to countries like Egypt and Nigeria. Members visited pyramids, met dignitaries, and rode camels in the desert (Delta Sigma Theta Sorority 1962: 45–48). The forty-six women took trees with them, called friendship trees, and brought them to the countries they visited "as a symbol of the sorority's aspirations for peace and brotherhood" (47). Similar offers of friendship were made by sorority members in the United States as they sent hospital supplies to clinics in Kenya, contributed to a school in Uganda, and helped foreign students at Tuskegee Institute adjust to local life (49).

In addition to inspiring service work of the organizations, members also reported back about their travels to share their experiences as tourists and to educate other sorority members about international travel. An early issue of the *Ivy Leaf* featured a story written by a member who received the 1928–29 foreign scholarship from the sorority. The member wrote about how she used the scholarship to go to Germany to take classes in mathematics (Alpha Kappa Alpha Sorority, Inc. 1930: 15–16). A May 1955 issue of SGRho's *Aurora* shared that a member visited seven European countries and that "the trip was educational and valuable. It gave one an altogether different aspect of the countries and their people" (Sigma Gamma Rho Sorority 1955: 6). A member who participated in ZPB's 1960 trip to the Philippines, Hong Kong, and Japan wrote that the trip enlightened her about the way that the economic, social, and political situations of the people shaped their daily lives (Zeta Phi Beta Sorority 1960: 5). Reporting back on travels abroad was important to the BSM as it helped them expand their members' knowledge about different countries and combat a sense of complacency about world affairs (Zeta Phi Beta Sorority 1960: 5). Reporting on members' travels was the earliest form of internationalism by the BSM.

Establishing International Chapters

A large part of beginning to think internationally for Black sororities meant seeing their organizations at the international level. Each of the four sororities expanded their organizations to include international chapters during the twentieth century. ZPB was the first Greek-letter organization to charter a chapter on the continent of Africa, when they established a graduate chapter in Monrovia, Liberia, in 1948. DST chartered their first graduate chapter, Delta Zeta Sigma chapter, in Port-au-Prince Haiti in 1950 (Giddings 1988). AKA established a graduate chapter, Eta Beta Omega, in Monrovia, Liberia, in 1957 (Parker 1990). SGRho also established international graduate chapters.

Chartering chapters internationally was the way that these sororities expanded their service on an international scale. For example, DST used the chapter they established in Haiti as a site for their first Haitian relief fund after Hurricane Hazel in 1954 (Giddings 1988). Since they began branching out internationally, the sororities have established chapters in Africa, Europe, Asia, and in the Caribbean (Bracey, Harley, and Meier 2000; Giddings 1988; Parker 1990). Chartering of international chapters was often done by American members who relocated to the locations. Members of international chapters were sometimes women who moved into locations because of their husbands' military service (Sigma Gamma Rho Sorority 1949: 4). Additionally, sororities recruited citizens of respective countries where the chapters were chartered for membership.

The establishment of international chapters worked toward facilitating a greater sense of world-mindedness among BSM members. It also facilitated the BSM's global feminist lens through expanding their fictive networks to women in other countries (the Alpha Kappa Alpha Sorority, Inc. 1958: 10–11). As each BSM sorority chartered new chapters abroad, their engagement with international feminism expanded.

Working with the United Nations

AKA began the National Non-Partisan Council on Public Affairs in 1938. It was formed in the hopes of getting Black people better able to participate in the democratic process (Parker 1958). The Non-Partisan Council worked with other Black organizations including the National Association for the Advancement of Colored People, the National Association of Colored Women, the Brotherhood of Sleeping Car Porters, and the Urban League (Parker 1958). Whaley (2010) summarizes the achievements of the National Non-Partisan Council between its founding and 1945:

1. Planning and sponsorship of conferences on race and gender issues;
2. dissemination of information about Black disenfranchisement, including speeches given on radio programs;
3. cooperation with other women's and civil rights organizations;
4. funding of education and encouragement of Black activity in public politics;
5. use of civic, political, economic, and educational activities on behalf of racial integration in all places of public life in the United States;
6. planning and work that helped improve life for Black men and women in the armed forces; and
7. stimulation of thought and planning for the adequate solution of problems in peace and in anticipation of the postwar era. (Whaley 2010: 48)

Following World War II the council began to move from thinking about civil rights domestically to involving itself in international affairs. Parker (1958: 57) claims that there are two reasons for this move from being concerned domestically to internationally:

> First the council realized quite clearly that America could never command the respect necessary to a position of leadership in the free world if one-tenth of her own population was cut-off from, or indifferent to, conditions of the rest of the world. In the second place, the Council firmly believed that a minority group in this country could strengthen its own position through concern for, and action in co-operation with, similar minorities in other countries.

Due to their increased interest in international affairs, the Non-Partisan Council became the first organization created by a fraternal organization to be an observer in the United Nations (UN). This status of observer in the United Nations meant that the council not only was represented at General Assembly meetings but was also able to participate in the process of drafting the Declaration of Human Rights (Parker 1958).

With the success of the National Non-Partisan Council, AKA wanted to include other organizations in their work for civil and human rights, which was growing internationally. Together with other fraternal organizations, the American Council on Human Rights (ACHR) was formed. Member organizations of this body included Alpha Phi Alpha, Sigma Gamma Rho, Delta Sigma Theta, Phi Beta Sigma, and Zeta Phi Beta (Parker 1958; Gasman 2011).

The ACHR fulfilled a similar role as the Non-Partisan Committee as it lobbied Congress to pass legislation for civil rights. The ACHR worked domestically to combat segregation through lobbying Congress and encouraging African Americans to vote (Harris 2005). Sororities, through their national organs, encouraged their members' participation in the ACHR by suggesting that local chapters advocate for integration, educational reform, and voting in their communities. The ACHR pushed for federal funds to be denied to school districts that refused to admit students to schools without regard for race (Zeta Phi Beta Sorority 1957: 7). A May 1960 issue of the *Archon* discussed how the council pushed for protest aid, saying that "the nation approaches a crossroads in the serious domestic problem of racial discrimination and injustice." It states that the action must be "decisive . . . to bring an end to lynchings, bombings, desecration of places of worship, denial of the right to vote, ghetto housing, inequalities in employment and education" (Zeta Phi Beta Sorority 1960: 33). The council made plans to support student activists who participated in sit-in protests, as well as launched a nationwide letter-writing campaign—a "write for civil rights"—to send one million letters to Congress about segregation (Delta Sigma Theta Sorority 1960: 31).

The ACHR's international involvement included the continued push for "the United States' Acceptance and implementation of the Universal Declaration of Human Rights" (Harris 2005: 225). Having also become an observer in the UN, the ACHR worked on projects including the UN Educational, Scientific, and Cultural Organization conferences, and "sought independence for colonized nations of Africa and the Caribbean and to end apartheid in South Africa" (Harris 2005: 225).

The sororities who made up the ACHR had already begun shifting their focus toward international relations by the time the ACHR disbanded in 1964. The organization's disbanding did not spell the end of the sororities' involvement with international organizations like the UN and did not stop them from moving forward with their international involvement.

Giddings (1988: 207) contends "the establishment of the United Nations, and the principles it would abide by was seen by Blacks as a new opportunity to redress racism and discrimination—this time in the international arena." She argues that Delta's new focus on internationalism impacted the sorority greatly—that Delta began incorporating ideas of human rights into their overall program structure (207–8). This same international consciousness affected all of the Black sororities.

International Women's Year and Decade

AKA and Delta took part in International Women's Year and Decade. The time span of the decade was marked from 1975 to 1985, with the first International Women's Year conference held in Mexico City in 1975. The goals of the first conference included reducing illiteracy, making birth control information and methods accessible to women, and requesting that development programs take into concern the impact the plans would have on women (Tinker 1975). An article in a 1975 issue of the *Delta* exclaimed that "1975 should be a turning point for all Black women to achieve equal employment opportunity" (Delta Sigma Theta Sorority 1975: 5).

The 1977 International Women's Year Conference was held in Houston, Texas. Prior to the conference, there were preparatory conferences held in each state to elect delegates for the conference (Mattingly and Nare 2014). The Houston conference was attended by over two thousand delegates from around the world. Delegates at the conference discussed ways to combat issues like discrimination in credit and equal employment. They also called for an end to involuntary sterilization and discussed the importance of providing public funding for abortion (Mattingly and Nare 2014).

The national president of AKA, Bernice Sumlin, attended the International Women's Year conferences in Mexico and Houston. According to Sumlin, the events of the conferences were responsible for the creation of the National Women's Agenda, a declaration that she describes as "a dramatic statement of what remains to be accomplished if women are to play a full and equal role in our nation's life." Sumlin contends that "the agenda spells out the goals for equality in politics, education, jobs, access to economic power, childcare, healthcare, housing, media, criminal justice, physical safety, and respect for the woman as an individual" (Alpha Kappa Alpha Sorority, Inc. 1976: 2).

Delta played a large role in the 1985 Decade for Women conference—a conference to assess the work done by the women over the past decade. According to a Winter 1985 issue of the *Delta*, the conference proceedings were grouped under the umbrella of "equality, development, and peace" (9). Delta contributed to the conference by presenting a paper and conducting a workshop addressing the problems facing single mothers worldwide (9). Summing up the conference proceedings, the *Delta* described how being in

Africa brought forth the plight of women in developing nations. They high-lighted some of the issues covered at the conference as:

1. Women who live and struggle in apartheid-torn South Africa.
2. Women from the mono-economies of the West Indies, from the fledgling political economies of Latin America including war-torn Nicaragua.
3. Women in the Middle East concerned about their lives and the quality of their communities in the face of resurging Islamic fundamental-ism and the constant wars and conflicts in the Islamic and Arab worlds.
4. Women from Scandinavia and Native American women from the US speaking for world peace and against the arms race.
5. Women in general addressing problems of hunger, impoverishment, inequality and lack of access to basic resources ranging from food, healthcare, and jobs, to shelter and land. (Delta Sigma Theta Sorority 1985: 13)

In preparation for the conferences, both AKA and Delta sent representative members to learn about the economic and political state of women in Africa. Both sororities regularly kept their members at home up to date about the events of International Women's Year and Decade through their national organs (*Ivy Leaf*, *Delta*).

Throughout the decade, women of the BSM worked closely with women abroad. Parker (1990: 245) explains that trips abroad "enabled the Ameri-can women to participate in a conference on rural health in Kenya and to make contact with other African women's organizations." The groundwork laid by the establishment of international chapters as well as International Women's year created space for women of the BSM to focus on the plight of women in Africa.

Focusing on Africa

A large part of each of the four sororities' international involvement was the work they became involved in in Africa. While they did work in other developing countries, all of the sororities established chapters in African countries and supported political struggles against colonization along with working on humanitarian service projects.

AKA, in a 1985 piece "AKA's Role in Africa," stated, "As Black Afro-American women, our individual and collective progress through the years has helped us to demonstrate our increased awareness of the problems and concerns of the African continent" (Alpha Kappa Alpha Sorority, Inc. 1985: 8). The BSM demonstrated this increased awareness through programs like the AKA-Africare Village Development Program (9). The Africare program began as a project to address hunger in Niger in 1970 following drought and famine, and first addressed issues of food insecurity (Africare 1977). Through AKA's partnership with Africare and the beginning of the Village Development Program in the 1980s, AKA adopted more than twenty-seven African villages; "encouraged awareness of and participation in the nation's affairs, registering more than 350,000 new voters; and established the Alpha Kappa Alpha Educational Advancement foundation in 1981" (Africare 1977).

Another example of the sororities' involvement in Africa included DST's work in Kenya, Durban, Swaziland (now Eswatini), and South Africa. In Kenya, in 1961, DST donated $5,000 to help establish a maternity ward in the Thika Memorial Hospital in Nairobi (Delta Sigma Theta Sorority 1985: 6; Parks and Hernandez 2016: 304). By 1964, the hospital provided medical care and trained nurses and midwives (304). In Durban, DST worked with Training and Resources for Early Education to promote early childhood education (Parks and Hernandez 2016). In Swaziland, they established the Delta House, in Vashti Village, as a home for children who were orphaned due to the HIV/AIDS pandemic. In 1980 DST established the Adelaide Tambo School in Soweto. The purpose of the school was to "provide education to disadvantaged scholars with physical, mental, and learning disabilities from grades 1st–12th" (Delta Sigma Theta Sorority 1983: 4). DST also worked with TransAfrica, a lobbying organization comprised of twenty-four religious, political, civil rights, and labor groups that joined together to address issues in Africa and the Caribbean (Delta Sigma Theta Sorority 1983: 4).

DST also held an anti-apartheid drive in support of the Free South Africa movement. DST made five demands that included the release of thirteen labor leaders who organized a strike and were jailed without trial or charges, the release of political prisoners, that the South African government enter into meaningful and effective negotiation with Black leaders, that the US government enact laws requiring American companies and banks to discontinue all business transactions with South Africa, and that the United States change its policies as they relate to South Africa (Delta Sigma Theta Sorority 1985: 5).

ZPB and SGRho also had ongoing programs in Africa. A May issue of ZPB's Archon featured a piece on their Seed for Fun and Knowledge Project. Through the program games, school supplies, and books were sent to children in Nigeria. The article stated, "We as Zetas need to further our program in Africa to strengthen our bonds of friendship, to lend encouragement to the peoples there in their struggle for freedom and self-government. We need to learn about them to understand in what area we can best serve them" (Zeta Phi Beta Sorority 1960: 10). SGRho hosted a Linens for Africa program that began in 1961. In 1964 the Linens program sent more than four hundred pounds of linen to a mission in South Rhodesia (Sigma Gamma Rho Sorority 1965: 49).

Respectability and Window Dressing

A critical analysis of the BSM's international involvement reveals that the sororities' activism may have implicitly employed the same neoliberal, neocolonial, and patriarchal ideals and practices that the BSM explicitly stated that they wished to resist and overturn. These ideals include the politics of respectability and the use of bourgeois organizing as window dressing. A critical analysis of respectability and bourgeois organizing in regard to BSM activism avoids the pitfall of simply engaging in a "good deeds" narrative (Tindall, Hernandez, and Hughey 2011) about their international activism.

The Politics of Respectability

The politics of respectability "first emerged as a way to counter the images of Black Americans as lazy, shiftless, stupid and immoral in popular culture and the racist pseudosciences of the nineteenth century" (Griffin 2000: 34). It was often used as a way to regulate expressions of sexuality of Black women to combat prevailing archetypes that carried over from enslavement that worked to legitimize sexual violence perpetrated on Black women (Collins 2000). These politics became more important as Black women entered into public spaces, like the women of the BSM did (Harris 2003). As African American women sought to be viewed as equals in public spaces, they were met with considerable challenges: "Having been cast as disreputable, these Black women leaders sought to establish their respectability and through that act lay claim to fair and equal treatment in public life. This 'politics of respectability,' enacted through a specific culture of dissemblance, is a response to the myth of hypersexuality" (Harris-Perry 2011: 61). In their efforts to combat controlling images of them, and to prove that they deserved respect in the public spaces that they newly gained access to, these mostly middle-class women began a moral crusade aimed at improving the image of Black women. They did this by self-defining as moral and well-mannered.

Evelyn Brooks Higginbotham (1993) posits that not only did these women believe that they should exercise manners and morals; they also policed and condemned immoral practice among other Black people (187). Higginbotham contends that these women believed that through rejecting racist discourse and defining themselves, they could undermine prevailing beliefs about their inferiority.

The politics of respectability was also used as a tool for racial uplift (Griffin 2000; Higginbotham 1993; Hine 1994). Through "putting forth the best black self," respectability was used to combat negative images of the Black community at large (Gray 2016). The ideology of respectability within the African American community was also utilized to unify the community by raising moral standards that these women hoped would open up opportunity structures for the Black community. For this reason, the politics of respectability became deeply embedded in the nation building strategies of Black organizations. Respectability also served as a source of stratification within the Black community.

The women of the BSM utilized the politics of respectability in their work both domestically and abroad. They built programs similar to those of the early Black women's club movement, who pushed the importance of being pure, pious, and domestic, while also raising children who would be good citizens (White 1999: 53). For example, in establishing the Cleveland Job Corps Center in 1965, AKA was responding to the idea that the Black family was pathological—a belief that was disseminated in Daniel Patrick Moynihan's *The Negro Family: The Case for National Action* (1964). The Job Corps Center was operated with the specific goal of "making young African American women into competent wives and mothers" (Quadangno and Forbes 1995: 176). The director of the center, Zelma George, described the young women who took part in the corps, saying, "They come bearing labels of failure, dropout, slum-dweller, hard-core welfare case, and others. One of the first jobs of the center . . . is to remove these labels" (*New Amsterdam News* 1967).

Through the establishment of institutions like the Cleveland Job Corps Center, AKA attempted to utilize respectability as a tool for racial uplift. Black sororities' engagement with the politics of respectability is also evident in their activism abroad as they employed some of the same tactics for racial uplift internationally. The sororities established institutions and programs geared toward teaching women and youth skills to make them good citizens.

Bourgeois Organizing and Philanthropy as Window Dressing
In connection with issues caused by their adherence to the politics of respectability, Black sororities engaged in bourgeois organizing for causes that did not do much to help Black women or the Black community at large. E. Franklin Frazier (1957) argues that the service and philanthropy of these organizations is based on gaining recognition and power, while "molding the outlook of the Black bourgeoisie" (94). He contends that the organizations' purposes are self-serving, stating that, "All of the fraternities and sororities attempt to justify their existence on the grounds that they render service to the Negro masses" (95). In this sense, sororities' projects of racial uplift operate under the guise of supporting the Black community while fostering and reproducing the Black middle and upper classes.

Throughout the analyzed time period, a recurring example of the sororities' engagement with bourgeois organizing is the debutante ball. The debutante ball is a long-standing tradition in each of the BSM organizations (Graham 1999). The ball, through introducing young women to society, serves the purpose of reproducing the social standing of middle- and upper-class Black women (Kendall 2002). Each of the sororities' organs reflected this type of organizing. Similarly, the sororities engaged heavily with other social activities like fashion shows and dances. This type of social organizing became such a large part of the sororities' activities that in 1976, the national president of DST wrote a piece for *Ebony* magazine demanding that Greek-letter organizations "stop the dance" and refocus on enhancing Black communities (Benbow 1976).

Black sororities have also been criticized for using philanthropy like window dressing, or making their philanthropic efforts appear more useful than they actually are. This claim is a reason that it is crucial to critically examine their philanthropic work, including their international work. Did planting "friendship trees" address the structural issues affecting women in East Africa in the 1960s? What good are shallow, surface-level, changes? How far does developing a sense of "world-mindedness" and reporting back about travels and tourism abroad go to improve the lives of the people in the places they visited? If the work of Black sororities is simply window dressing, it is difficult to justify the relevance of these organizations both in the past and in the present day.

Remaining consistently conscious of these potential issues, especially when analyzing the national organs of the BSM, is important for complicating the image of these organizations and moving beyond seeing their work as simply a laundry list of good deeds.

Conclusion

This article demonstrates that the BSM transformed from a focus on the domestic civil rights of Black people in the United States into a consideration of human rights on a broad, international scale. Through an examination of the sororities' national organs, the *Ivy Leaf*, the *Delta*, the *Archon*, and the *Aurora*, I have shown that the organizations shifted their focus through varying tactics including an emphasis on members reporting back about their international travels, the establishment of international chapters, working with the United Nations, their work with International Women's Year, and their move toward focusing exclusively on women in Africa. Our research also reveals that while their international involvement is indicative of a shift toward including all Black women in conceptions of human rights, a critical interrogation of their work shows that their activism is enmeshed in the politics of respectability and the use of philanthropic work as window dressing.

The current national conversation on police brutality has brought questions of the relevancy of Black sororities to the forefront. In light of late 2014 statements by AKA and DST urging their members to refrain from wearing paraphernalia at protests against police brutality, people have questioned Black sororities' stances on both human and civil rights. Such actions beg for all to reflect on how BSM organizations, in relation to their histories of civil and human rights engagement, will (or will not) involve themselves in the contemporary quest for full human and citizenship rights, as well as how these organizations may be too entangled in neoliberal, neocolonial, and patriarchal practices. For many, Black sororities should not lose sight of their commitments to human rights, while for others, a disengagement with these issues is part and parcel of their elitist underpinnings. In either case, their legacy—and possibly their survival as relevant and important organizations—shall wax and wane in relation to the extent to which they involve themselves in the contemporary quest for human rights.

Future research on the BSM should turn attention toward how their international involvement has grown contemporarily, paying close attention to the spaces and places to which it has expanded. It would also be worthwhile to examine the sustainability of international programs. If we are to ask questions about BSM social reproduction and window dressing, knowing whether the international programs are sustainable and effective is necessary information in determining how authentic and effective are their commitments to advancing human rights abroad. Additionally, further research on the BSM should continue to remain critical of the work done by these organizations. Only through remaining consistently conscious of their potential for reproducing neoliberal ideals can we avoid advancing simple, "good deeds" narratives about Black sororities.

Aisha A. Upton Azzam is an assistant professor of sociology at Susquehanna University. Her research agenda is centered on race, gender, and social movements. More specifically, Dr. Upton Azzam's work has explored Black women's organizations, Black social movements, and Black feminism. She has published in venues like *Black Feminist Sociology* and *Humanity and Society*.

Notes

This article was inspired by reading the national organs of Black sororities and thinking critically about their international work.

1 Paula Giddings (1988: 6) uses the concept of "Black sorority movement" in defining sororities as social movement organizations and how they "change individuals within them and/or the society." Here, I am not discussing individuals or labeling the organizations social movement organizations, I am discussing internationalism.

Works Cited

Africare. *Africare Annual Report*. 1977. Alpha Kappa Alpha Archives.

Alpha Kappa Alpha Sorority, Inc. 1930. "Report on 1928–1929 Foreign Scholarship." *Ivy Leaf*.

Alpha Kappa Alpha Sorority, Inc. 1958. "Alpha Kappa Alpha Goes Abroad." *Ivy Leaf*.

Alpha Kappa Alpha Sorority, Inc. 1976. "Message from the Supreme Basileus." *Ivy Leaf*.

Alpha Kappa Alpha Sorority, Inc. 2008a. "Centennial Celebration Timeline." www.aka1908.com/centennial.

Alpha Kappa Alpha Sorority, Inc. 2008b. "National Programs." www.aka1908.com/centennial.

Benbow, Lillian. 1976. "It's Time to Stop 'The Dance.'" *Ebony Magazine*, October.

Bracey, John H., Sharon Harley, and August Meier. 2000. "The Ivy Leaf, 1921–1998: A Chronicle and Alpha Kappa Alpha Sorority." In *Black Studies Research Sources*

Microfilms from Major Archival Manuscript Collections, edited by John H. Bracey, Sharon Harley, and August Meier. Bethesda, MD: University Publications of America.

Collier-Thomas, Bettye. 2001. *Sisters in the Struggle: African American Women in the Civil Rights– Black Power Movement*, edited by Bettye Collier-Thomas and V. P. Franklin. New York: New York University Press.

Collins, Patricia Hill. 1998. *Fighting Words: Black Women and the Search for Justice.* Minneapolis: University of Minnesota Press.

Collins, Patricia Hill. 2000. *Black Feminist Thought: Knowledge, Consciousness, and the Politics of Empowerment.* New York: Routledge.

Cooper, Anna Julia. 2017. *A Voice from the South: By a Black Woman of the South.* Chapel Hill: University of North Carolina Press.

Delta Sigma Theta Sorority. 1960. "Write for Civil Rights." *Delta.*

Delta Sigma Theta Sorority. 1962. "The Story of Friendship Trees." *Delta.*

Delta Sigma Theta Sorority. 1975. "International Women's Year." *Delta.*

Delta Sigma Theta Sorority. 1983. "Delta Attends TransAfrica Benefit." *Delta.*

Delta Sigma Theta Sorority. 1985. "Poverty, Illiteracy are Global Concerns at Women's Conference." *Delta.*

Delta Sigma Theta Sorority, Inc. n.d. "International Awareness and Involvement." https://www.deltasigmatheta.org/international.php (accessed December 2014).

Evans, Stephanie Y. 2008. "The Vision of Virtuous Women: The Twenty Pearls of Alpha Kappa Alpha Sorority." In Parks 2008: 41–66.

Frazier, E. Franklin. 1957. *The Black Bourgeoisie.* New York: Free Press Paperbacks.

Gasman, Marybeth. 2011. "Passive Activism: African American Fraternities and Sororities and the Push for Civil Rights." In *Black Greek-Letter Organizations 2.0: New Directions in the Study of African American Fraternities and Sororities*, edited by Matthew W. Hughey and Gregory S. Parks, 47–66. Jackson: University Press of Mississippi.

Giddings, Paula. 1988. *In Search of Sisterhood: Delta Sigma Theta and the Challenge of the Black Sorority Movement.* New York: Morrow.

Gilkes, Cheryl Townsend. 2001. *If It Wasn't for the Women: Black Women's Experience and Womanist Culture in Church and Community.* Ossining, NY: Orbis.

Graham, Lawrence Otis. 1999. *Our Kind of People.* New York: HarperCollins Publishers.

Gray, Herman. 2016. "Introduction: Subject to Respectability." *Souls: A Critical Journal of Black Politics, Culture, and Society* 18, nos. 2–4: 192–200.

Griffin, Farah Jasmine. 2000. "Black Feminists and Du Bois: Respectability, Protection, and Beyond." *Annals of the American Academy of Political and Social* 568: 28–40.

Harris, Jessica. 2008. "Women of Vision, Catalysts for Change: The Founders of Delta Sigma Theta Sorority." In Parks 2008: 75–94.

Harris, Jessica, and Vernon C. Mitchell Jr. 2008. "A Narrative Critique of Black Greek-Letter Organizations and Social Action." In Parks 2008: 143–68.

Harris, Paisley Jane. 2003. "Gatekeeping and Remaking: The Politics of Respectability in African American Women's History and Black Feminism." *Journal of Women's History* 15, no. 1: 212–20.

Harris, Robert L. 2005. "Lobbying Congress for Civil Rights: The American Council on Human Rights." In *African American Fraternities and Sororities: The Legacy and the Vision*, edited by Tamara L. Brown, Gregory S. Parks, and Clarenda M. Phillips. Lexington: The University Press of Kentucky.

Harris-Perry, Melissa V. 2011. *Sister Citizen: Shame, Stereotypes, and Black Women in America*. New Haven: Yale University Press.

Higashida, Cheryl. 2011. *Black Internationalist Feminism: Women Writers of the Black Left, 1945–1995*. Urbana: University of Illinois Press.

Higginbotham, Evelyn Brooks. 1993. *Righteous Discontent: The Women's Movement in the Black Baptist Church 1880–1920*. Cambridge, MA: Harvard University Press.

Hine, Darlene Clark. 1994. *Hine Sight: Black Women and the Re-construction of American History*. New York: Carlson.

Hughey, Matthew W. 2008. "Constitutionally Bound: The Founders of Phi Beta Sigma Fraternity and Zeta Phi Beta Sorority." In Parks 2008: 95–114.

Jones, Jacqueline. 2009. *Labor of Love, Labor of Sorrow: Black Women, Work, and the Family from Slavery to the Present*. New York: Basic.

Kendall, Diana. 2002. *The Power of Good Deeds: Privileged Women and the Social Reproduction of the Upper Class*. Oxford: Rowman & Littlefield.

Mattingly, Doreen J., and Jessica L. Nare. 2014. "'A Rainbow of Women': Diversity and Unity at the 1977 U.S. International Women's Year Conference." *Journal of Women's History* 26, no. 2: 88–112.

McNealey, Earnestine Green. 2006. *Pearls of Service: The Legacy of America's First Black Sorority, Alpha Kappa Alpha*. Chicago: Alpha Kappa Alpha Sorority.

Neumann, Caryn E. 2008. "Black Feminist Thought in Black Sororities." In Parks 2008: 169–86.

New Amsterdam News. 1967. "Alpha Kappa Alpha Defends Job Corps Centers at Congressional Hearing." August 5.

Parker, Marjorie Holloman. 1958. *Alpha Kappa Alpha: 1908–1958*. Washington, DC: Alpha Kappa Alpha Sorority.

Parker, Marjorie Holloman. 1990. *Alpha Kappa Alpha through the Years 1908–1988*. Chicago: Mobium Press.

Parks, Gregory S., ed. 2008. *Black Greek-Letter Organizations in the Twenty-First Century: Our Fight Has Just Begun*. Lexington: The University Press of Kentucky.

Parks, Gregory S., and Marcia Hernandez. 2016. "Fortitude in the Face of Adversity: Delta Sigma Theta's History of Racial Uplift." *Hastings Race and Poverty Law Journal* 13, no. 2: 273–347.

Pruitt, Bernadette, Caryn E. Neumann, and Katrina Hamilton. 2008. "Seven School-Teachers Challenge the Klan: The Founders of Sigma Gamma Rho Sorority." In Parks 2008: 125–41.

Quadangno, Jill, and Catherine Forbes. 1995. "The Welfare State and the Cultural Reproduction of Gender: Making Good Girls and Boys in the Job Corps." *Social Problems* 42: 171–90.

Roberts, Laura Morgan, and Lynn Perry Wooten. 2008. "Exploring Black Greek-Letter Organizations through a Positive Organizing Lens." In Parks 2008: 273–88.

Scott, Anne Firor. 1990. "Most Invisible of All: Black Women's Voluntary Associations." *Journal of Southern History* 56, no. 1: 3–22.

Sigma Gamma Rho Sorority. 1949. "At Home in Germany." *Aurora* 19, no 1: 4–5.

Sigma Gamma Rho Sorority. 1955. "European Trip Enjoyed by Soror Camille Murphy." *Aurora* 24, no. 3: 6.

Sigma Gamma Rho Sorority. 1965. "Linen for Africa." *Aurora* 34, no 1.

Springer, Kimberly. 2005. *Living for the Revolution: Black Feminist Organizations, 1968–1980.* Durham, NC: Duke University Press.

Tindall, Natalie, Marcia D. Hernandez, and Matthew W. Hughey. 2011. "'Doing a Good Job at a Bad Thing': Prevalence and Perpetuation of Stereotypes among Members of Historically Black Sororities." *The Oracle: The Research Journal of the Association of Fraternity Advisors* 6, no. 2: 36–53.

Tinker, Irene. 1975. "International Women's Year." *Science, New Series* 190, no. 4221: 1249.

Washington, Michael H., and Cheryl L. Nuñez. 2005. "Education, Racial Uplift, and the Rise of the Greek-Letter Tradition: The African American Quest for Status in the Early Twentieth Century." In *African American Fraternities and Sororities: The Legacy and the Vision*, edited by Tamara L. Brown, Gregory S. Parks, and Clarenda M. Phillips. Lexington: The University Press of Kentucky.

Whaley, Deborah Elizabeth. 2010. *Disciplining Women: Alpha Kappa Alpha, Black Counterpublics, and the Cultural Politics of Black Sororities.* New York: State University of New York Press.

White, Deborah Gray. 1999. *Too Heavy a Load: Black Women in Defense of Themselves, 1894–1994.* New York: W. W. Norton.

Zeta Phi Beta Sorority. 1957. "Director Seeks New Support." *Archon* (September), 3.

Chia-Hsu Jessica Chang

....

De-naming
Unraveling the Sex-Skin and Gender-Mask Technologies in the Colonial Naming Structure

Abstract: This article analyzes how the colonial naming structure creates and sustains what it means to be human and nonhuman in coloniality. It begins with a preliminary reading of Sylvia Wynter's interpretation of Frantz Fanon's "white mask" as a cultural technology, where the modern human's names lie. The author argues that the "colored skin," where the dehumanizing names are marked, is the other cultural technology inseparable from the white mask in constituting the colonial naming structure. By understanding skin technology as external to the embodied self, the author investigates how the modern idea of sex also functions as skin technology. The politics of women of color are then explored, interpreting the relation between sex and gender as the "sex-skin/gender-mask structure," isomorphic to the Fanonian black-skin/white-mask structure. The article further engages with Naifei Ding's concept of the "feminist knot" to analyze how this structure is reified and reproduced specifically in third-world Taiwan. It concludes with a proposal of "de-naming" as a decolonial methodology to shift away from dehumanizing names that fix a person into their sexed-and-colored skin and toward names that transform their embodied self.

The Colonial Naming Structure and the Skin and Mask Technologies

We, the dehumanized living under colonial humanity, struggle with the colonially given names that wrongly define, ossifyingly fix, and violently erase us. We are socially dissected, amputated, and murdered, sometimes by others, sometimes suicidally, in order to fit into those names of

MERIDIANS · feminism, race, transnationalism   23:2 October 2024
DOI: 10.1215/15366936-11266372 © 2024 Smith College

intended misnaming invented not for us but for the sake of colonizers', imperialists', and modernity embracers' calculation, manipulation, and exploitation. *We, the dehumanized, need new names that do name something new.* The request is not for a new name within teleological modernity but for a transformative journey toward a revitalized self, embracing resilient cosmologies and ancestral memories to embody each present moment.

This article contributes to developing the concept of *the colonial naming structure* and understanding how *gender embedded in racial dehumanization* plays an important role in this structure. Following my preliminary readings of Frantz Fanon and Sylvia Wynter, the subsequent sections will delve into the colonial naming structure's concealed relationship with sex and gender through exploring the politics of women of color in America and the third-world gender politics in Taiwan. I strive to diversify my epistemic reference points by interweaving an intellectual current that includes knowledge from thinkers embodying "the 'third world' consciousness within the first world," as described by Cherrie Moraga (2015: xix), and thinkers located in the geopolitical third world, defying "the Western way of mapping the world" from "the [strategic] point of organic resistance," as expressed by Yingzhen Chen (2005: 536).

Fanon's *Black Skin, White Masks* portrays his psychological struggle as a person in a colonial society where only white individuals are seen as "human" (2008: 2). His black skin becomes ladened with stigmatizing connotations that imprison him within a "zone of nonbeing" (xii, xiii, xv), becoming a "bodily curse" etched onto his skin (xv, 91, 95). Desiring recognition as "human" in colonial society, he is trapped in an unending yearning for another epidermal transformation of a white skin where the name "human" is etched. Ironically, this path never leads to achieving a white skin but condemns him to wear a deceptive white mask, an illusory representation of that coveted white skin. Sylvia Wynter (2001: 53) astutely characterizes the white mask as a "cultural technology":

> Fanon's hypothesis that, in the case of our own culture, Black skins wear white masks, being but a *special case* of the fact that all humans wear *cultural masks* . . . , results in that, although born as biological humans (as human skins), we can experience ourselves as human only through the mediation of the processes of socialization effected by the invented *teckne* or *cultural technology* to which we give the name culture. (emphasis mine)

Wynter's analysis sees the white mask within the black-skin/white-mask structure as a cultural mask that performs normative humanity within colonial society. Viewing the white mask as a cultural technology is significant in highlighting its detachment from a person's physical body. There is a process of strangulating internalization of this technology that a racialized or colonized can never bypass. The external nature of the white mask raises pertinent questions: Who creates this technology? Who possesses it? Who ultimately benefits from this cultural technology? The same answer applies to all three questions: the White colonizers who are claimed to be the only humans, the modern Man, the sole species on Earth to have undergone self-evolution and successfully achieve both civilizational modernity and biological humanness.

Wynter's analysis delves into the historical diachronism of the concept of Man, debunking its seemingly ahistorical status. She exposes how Man "overrepresents [him]self as if it were the human itself," the "present ethnoclass conception of the human," generating an equally ahistorical category comprising "the peoples of African hereditary descent and the peoples who comprise the damned archipelagoes of the Poor, the jobless, the homeless, and the 'underdeveloped'" (2003: 260, 317). Wynter sees the present Man as an evolved second version, originating from the pre-bourgeois and premodern/precolonial Fallen Flesh under Christian institutions. The first version of Man emerged as the bourgeois and modern/colonial Man, acting as a new master created by God, controlling everything in the world referred to as "Nature" (264, 266, 281, 286–88). The transition from the Fallen Flesh to God's secularized advocate retains Christianity but distinguishes the rational Man from their irrational counterparts. The rational Man, as political subject, gains rationality from God but submits to the secular nation-state. In contrast, the "irrational others"—Black Africans, Indigenous peoples in America, and dark-skinned non-Europeans—are seen as closer to animals, lacking God-given rationality, and deemed incapable of forming their own nation-states (288–89, 318). The second version of Man emerged in the nineteenth century and solidified during neoliberal globalization, inheriting the established structural pattern but adopting a Darwinian biocentric discourse. In this version, the white population is considered biologically superior (naturally selected), while Blacks, darker-skinned, and Indigenous peoples in America are seen as biologically inferior (dysselected). These notions of superiority and inferiority are represented ahistorically and supported by material evidence like economic success and failure (breadwinners and the poor) and the developmental status of regions (First World and Third-and-Fourth Worlds; 303–5, 309–11, 313–14, 316–17, 320–21).

I understand this entire evolutionary process of Man as the development of the white mask as a cultural technology that does two tasks. One task is to superiorize and thereby humanize the white bourgeois class first into the alternative-substitutive presence of God and second into the naturally selected species for biological evolution and de facto economic success. The other task is to inferiorize and thereby dehumanize Blacks, the darker-skinned, and Indigenous peoples, first as the "missing link" between rationality and irrationality (in the case of Blacks), savages (in the case of Indigenous peoples), and creatures that exhibit different degrees of irrationality and proximity to animals (in the case of the darker-skinned); and second into the naturally dysselected species that are unable to achieve biological evolution and economic success (266, 301, 303–4). If the "white mask" is a "cultural technology," the term *cultural* denotes the combined influence of cultural and civilizational patterns rooted in Christian rule, the rational/irrational dichotomy, and the genetically selected/dysselected differentiation. The white mask molds a white person into Man in two directions. One direction, in the Foucaultian term, is to mold a person into a modern automaton performing what the name "human" conveys, although the historical diachronism in which the white mask takes root in Wynter's analysis exceeds way back than the Victorian age or the Enlightenment that the Foucaultian term focuses on (Foucault 1995: 137–38). The other direction is to tautologically ensure that the inventors of the white mask, namely the white bourgeois class, retain possession of this cultural technology and continue to benefit from it. In this sense, the Foucaultian disciplinarity can be understood as a *dual process*: one in which a white person becomes disciplined into the notion of Man, and the other in which they justify and enforce discipline as a *disciplinary figure*.

Noteworthily, the concept of "skin" becomes intermingled with the evolutionary trajectory of the white mask during its second transition from the politically rational Man to the biologically and economically selected Man. In the rising and stabilizing biocentric and economically deterministic discourse, the white mask functions differently for a person of color. Even if one puts on the white mask, one is not truly the user or possessor of this technology, but rather becomes possessed and dispossessed by it. This leads to my question: If, as Wynter suggests, nobody can exist in a bare biological body, then what is the significance of colored skin? Taking Wynter's reasoning further, I argue that *colored skin is another cultural technology* that operates alongside the white mask to make the skin-mask structure operative. As a cultural technology, just like the white mask, the colored skin is invented for, possessed by, and benefits the white colonizers. It is not an inherent part of a person of color's body but rather external to it and must be ferociously internalized. Viewing colored skin as a cultural technology helps demystify the modern separation between the biological and the cultural that cloaks the colonial intentions of technology possessors under the seemingly neutral biological discourse using the term *skin*. Thus, the "skin" in the skin-mask relationship is always already *cultural*. This is why Fanon describes his experience as if the White colonizers are peeling his skin off, technologizing it into colored skin inscribed with a dehumanizing name, and wrapping his body with that colored skin in return, "causing a hemorrhage that left congealed black blood all over [his] body" (2008: 92–93). Consequently, the statement "a Black skin wearing a white mask" can be reformulated as "a body wearing a black skin *and* a white mask," a situation of *double application* of the two cultural technologies, one is epidermally coloring, the other is maskingly whitening.[1] While both technological applications are constructs, the colored skin is made into a normative reality with venomous material manifestations and representations, while the white mask is made into an unattainable hallucination.

   Here, a brief note on "white skin" could enhance our thinking. I suggest that white skin functions less as a physically and materially marked idea, unlike black skin, but rather as *an empty category*, akin to a phantomlike cultural technology. This emptiness can be understood in two ways. First, it duplicates the white mask and does not require a distinct physical marker or material evidence. The biocentric and economically deterministic discourse of the second version of Man constructs a new model for the white mask, making it unnecessary to view white skin as a distinct and independent category as it essentially functions as the mask itself. Second, white skin is empty because it manifests itself as an *opposing silhouette* to physically marked blackness and coloredness. It does not require a racial mark of itself, only those of others. For instance, even the white poor in the United States may cling more anguishedly to the idea of white skin than their wealthy counterparts, claiming intrinsic difference from people of color and the chance to be attributed a white mask as long as they occupy the silhouette slot of white skin, an antonym to colored skin. Therefore, we can conclude that the white skin serves as both *a phantomlike cultural technology* and *an empty buffer zone* that reinforces the significance of the white mask while influencing the skin-colorization of others, as reflected by Fanon's unfulfillable longing for epidermalization.

Continuing my investigation of the double technological application faced by people of color, Wynter's (2001: 53) clever term, *special case*, points me to grasp this application as something distinct from Foucaultian disciplinarity. While a white colonizer undergoes molding *once* through the white mask technology to *become human*, as he does not need to overcome any skin issues until he feels bare, a person of color must undergo molding *twice* for (1) *eradicating* her human subjectivity outside modernity by the colored skin technology, as if she can and should only be seen as the colored skin, and (2) *eradicating* her possibility of becoming a human subject in modernity by the white mask technology because the white mask is an unfulfillable hallucination. The Foucaultian disciplinary power, which is a process of *humanization*, does not apply to people of color. Instead, they undergo a process of *dehumanization* through double eradication. Transitioning from the colored-skin/white-mask structure to the body/colored-skin/white-mask structure, we uncover an additional cultural technology: the colored skin, on which the names of the dehumanized are engraved. This revelation exposes the harsh reality that our bodies, within the context of colonial humanity, are reduced to mere skin and do not truly belong to us. The mask technology, the skin technology, and the names engraved on these technologies were not intended for the dehumanized but rather serve as instruments of sadistic manipulation by those who possess them.[2]

To further emphasize, all names within the colonial naming structure fall into two metacategories: the *human metacategory* and the *nonhuman metacategory*. The skin technology that is seemingly "natural," such as colored skins, serves as reified and naturalized borders, reinforcing the hierarchical and mutually exclusive nature of these metacategories. The skin technology is utilized for *border making* and *border maintaining*. Names within the human metacategory are reserved for the colonizers, while the names within the nonhuman metacategory are, as Hortense Spillers (1987: 65) puts it, the colonial "marks" assigned to the oppressed. Once one is marked by her colonially given name(s), one is perceived as permanently immutable, ahistorically reduced, and timelessly fixed in the nonhuman metacategory. To tackle the colonial naming structure, we must *de-name* at least two names: one on the dehumanizing skin and another on the white mask. Increasingly, we are skeptical of names that adhere to the white mask while purporting to be "for everyone," such as universal humanity (clinging to the name of "human" in modernity), Eurocentric feminisms (clinging to the name of "woman" in modernity), and state-led nationalism (which has failed those who are not viewed as proper citizen-subjects). The modern names must be abandoned if they only mean assimilation and reduction. As Alexander Weheliye (2014: 9–10) argues, some posthumanist discourses tend to "reinscribe the human subject (Man) as the personification of the human by insisting that this is the category to be overcome, rarely considering cultural and political formations outside the world of Man that might offer alternative versions of humanity." It would be illogical to say that we are always already posthuman; in fact, we, the colonially dehumanized, have always been nonhuman in colonial humanity. Kelvin Santiago-Valles (2016: 75) reminds us that "the history of actually existing colonialism is still about the world as we know and live it today" and about how racial identities are "continued to be socially produced, embodied, and 'naturalized,'" whereas a "non-colonial age" is achievable only if we painstakingly unsettle "the system of meaning and ideological representation" in coloniality.

Sex Skins Wearing Gender Masks: Are We Caliban's Women?

In this section, I articulate how the colonial naming structure works with what Maria Lugones (2010: 196) refers to as the "coloniality of gender." My politics stands with ongoing philosophization by women- and -queers-of-color thinkers about how gender never functions without race, and vice versa, in understanding folks of color's everyday realities. Gender has always been integral to racial dehumanization and cannot be analyzed in isolation, as doing so overlooks the survival crisis in everyday reality. Instead, we must examine how *gender, embedded in race,* operates at the border between the human and nonhuman metacategories, reproducing and sustaining that very border. My intervention identifies where *skin technology* is reified, naturalized, and clings to our bodies within the coloniality of gender. I contend that this skin technology is *the modern idea of sex.*

   In her groundbreaking theorization of the coloniality of gender, Lugones (2007: 206) shows how the gender system is constructed through the colonial epistemic mapping of the "light side" and "dark side" of colonial humanity. On the light side, two modern human names—"modern

man" and "modern woman"—were created, delineating two dichotomous
social roles. Lugones refers to gender as both "a mark of human" and "a
mark of civilization" (2010: 743). Women are the counterpart of white
bourgeois men, characterized as physically and mentally weak, sexually
passive, and primarily confined to the domestic sphere, where their role is
to give birth to the inheritors of capital and colonial humanity (2007: 202;
2010: 743). Notably, the birth of modern men and modern women coincided with the emergence of the modern idea of sex. Thomas Laqueur
(1992) emphasizes that dimorphic sex, conveying the "incommensurable
difference" (11) between European men and women, was a sociohistorical
invention tailored to "our needs in speaking about it" (149). In the early
European modernity, new names for female sex organs—some had shared
the same names as male organs in the European premodern one-sex model
(e.g., ovaries, which were called testicles), some had never been named
before (e.g., vagina)—emerged (145–61). These new names of female sex
organs began to designate the distinguishable physical qualities to reify
and naturalize European women's modern gender role as reproducers. As
Sylvia Federici (2004: 192) articulates, this aimed to transform European
women into "a being *sui generis*, more carnal and perverted by nature, in
order to turn European women into reproductive work." The way I see it, in
the context of the light side, sex was invented to be *both like gender and
simultaneously separate from it*, akin to *gender's doppelganger*. Gender and sex
create *a perfect circulation*: gender represents the social destiny of sex, while
sex serves as the biological proof of gender.

If one claims that the gender division significantly torments the colonized, one is obliged to question what it is that the colonizers "need"—
borrowing Laqueur's term—to invent sex as a means to "speak about" the
colonized. What implications does the birth of the modern idea of sex hold
for the colonized? On the dark side of colonial humanity, where the colonized dwell, Lugones (2010: 744) stresses that "sex was made to *stand alone*
in the characterization of the colonized" (emphasis mine). It seems that
gender disappears in colonizers' perception of the colonized, but the fact
is that gender has never been needed in describing the colonized, while
sex has. The bodies of colonized females are characterized as lacking
socially gendered femininity because they are not seen as reproducers of
the inheritors of capital and colonial humanity but female animals (2007:
203). In Lugones's terms, they are understood as "not-human-as-not-
woman," while their male peers are seen as "not-human-as-not-man" in
the same logic (2010: 744). Sex was invented for the colonizers to "speak

about" the colonized as not-socialized (read: not-gendered and not-civilized) beings that are different from the colonizers in their nature. The colonizers and colonized are portrayed as fundamentally different species, the former the human, the latter the animal (745). The modern idea of sex, in this sense, serves as a mark of animality and nonhumanity. The way I see it, for the colonized, gender does not represent the social destiny of sex, nor does sex serve as the biological proof of gender. Here, there is no seamless circulation between gender and sex; instead, it is an unfulfillable project of that very circulation, a noxious dream of no real promise.

I propose conceptualizing sex and gender as two cultural technologies that co-constitute a structure *isomorphic* to the colored-skin/white-mask structure. This structure, which I refer to as "the structure of sex-skin/gender-mask," encompasses gender as a normative cultural technology, akin to a human mask within colonial humanity, and functions as a regulatory tool that disciplines white colonizers to embody human subjects. In addition to being disciplined by the gender mask, the white colonizers also serve as the disciplinarians who enforce the gendering disciplinarity—often white bourgeois men and, at times, white bourgeois women. As a cultural technology, the gender mask is an invention and possession of the white colonizers, which they wield to reap its benefits. However, for the colonized and racialized, gender operates differently. Before gender is ever going to discipline them, sex attacks them as *the other cultural technology*, fashioned in the semblance of *sexed skin*, a reified and naturalized material package of stigmatizing meanings, including animality, wilderness, raw materiality, and a deficit in civilization, forcefully enveloping and confining the colonized into a state of nonhumanity. As a cultural technology sharing the isomorphic position with the colored skin in the skin-mask structure, "sex" in the sex-gender relation is also external to a person's body, yet it must be ferociously internalized. With the modern separation between the biological and the cultural demystified, I contend that "sex" in the sex-gender relation is always already *cultural*, carrying and transmitting the colonial intentions of those who possess the technology.

To repeat as to intensify my argument, on the light side of colonial humanity, sex is both like gender and simultaneously separate from it, akin to gender's doppelganger. The relationship between gender and sex creates *a perfect circulation*: gender becomes the social destiny of sex, while sex serves as the biological proof of gender. As a result, white Europeans and their descendants are molded *once* by the disciplinary gender mask to express themselves as human subjects because their sex, similar to the white skin analyzed in the previous section, is essentially an empty category that is always already gendered. Sex serves as an extended expression of gender, similar to how the white skin serves as an extended expression of the white mask. However, on the dark side of colonial humanity, gender is not the social destiny of sex, nor is sex the biological proof of gender. There is *no circulation between gender and sex* here; instead, it becomes an unfinishable project of that very circulation. As a consequence, the colonized and dehumanized are molded *twice* for (1) *eradicating* their human subjectivity outside modernity by the sex skin, as if their bodies cannot be understood without dimorphic sexual difference, and (2) *eradicating* their possibility to become human subjects in modernity by the gender mask, which rebuts them as sexual deviants, always sexually excessive or inadequate, and incapable of evolving into beings with properly gendered sexuality. Both cultural technologies—gender and sex—were invented by the colonizers, possessed by them, and wielded to maintain the border between human and nonhuman. Therefore, it is reasonable to assert that the gender system violates and harms the colonized, but it is illogical to claim that the colonized are inherently gendered. Instead, they are *sexed* in the way that is *repudiated by gender*. Sex operates differently across the border between the human and nonhuman metacategories. Even when discussing the concept of sex, its meanings vary across that border. In the human metacategory, sex is used to reductively perceive white women as reproductive machines, linked to new names invented exclusively for women's bodies. In the nonhuman metacategory, sex is employed to view the colonized as animals with no control over their wild sexuality. Even when a colonized gives birth, she is seen as reproducing in an animalistic way rather than a womanly way. In this sense, the meaning of sex for the colonized is not merely a reduction but something much more complex. It is an *epidermalization*.

The colonial transformation of a colonized from an embodied subject to an animal-machine echoes what Spillers (1987: 67) calls the "pornotrope" of Africans in the Middle Passage. In the pornotroping process, a captive woman's body "reduces to a thing," a "slave vessel" considered as "quantities," a "female flesh ungendered," a raw animal material in a cargo ship with no difference in her social meaning from her African brothers (67). All bodies, whether female or male, are metamorphosed into labor-machines for the colonizers' capital accumulation (67, 68, 72). Spillers describes the

Middle Passage as a confined itinerary of no name, where captives were deprived of their native names but not yet given their new American names (72). I contend that the Middle Passage is an incarcerating time-space where the colonial naming structure was in its birthing process, the sexed-and-colored skin technology was epidermally germinating, and the bodies of the embodied subjects were gradually being deprived of their subjectivity. Pornotrope, therefore, is a *sexing process*, as sex is embedded in racial dehumanization. It is less a process of dispossession of gender but more an *imposition of the dehumanizing modern idea of sex*.

Once the skin technology forms, the gender mask constantly flashes up to harass and punish the sexed person, further hammering the skin technology into her body, reminding her of forced sexual passiveness and physical exploitability. Saidiya Hartman (1997: 80) illustrates how the law's selective recognition of a captive woman in North American slavery sometimes assigned a fake gender agency to merely justify the legal punishment. When the master's rape and physical abuse occurred, the law did not truly consider the captive woman capable of consenting or acting as an agent; instead, it assumed her criminality and responsibility for the master's desire and offense. Hartman describes this situation as "the dual invocation of the slave as property and person" that "wed reciprocity and submission, intimacy and domination, and the legacy of violence and the necessity of protection" (80). The captive woman becomes a "will-less object" or a "chastened agent," passively bearing abuses and liability simultaneously. I interpret this gendered agency as a delusion of the gender mask, shaping rape and physical abuse as acts of reciprocity and intimacy while erasing colonial domination and submission. As Hartman succinctly addresses, "the captive female does not possess gender as much as she is possessed by gender"; the gender mask denies her expression of intention, desire, and sense of the self in the name of gender recognition (100). The colonial system of law, settler state, and slavery masters are the technology users of this mask in the context of gender recognition in front of the law under slavery. The captive woman is rendered a sex-skinned creature misrepresented by the gender mask. Sojourner Truth's (1851) revolutionary interrogation—"Ain't I a Woman?"—also divulges this misrepresentational logic.

Rejecting Eurocentric feminisms invites critical reflection because they have focused on challenging the gender mask but not adequately addressed the sexed skin imposed on the dehumanized. While they do problematize the concept of sex, they fail to grasp that sexed skin is the distorted mirror image of gender mask within the dehumanized context, uncritically labelling the dehumanized as "woman" (read: *female*) based on the dehumanizing sex, and aim to assert a universal and global sisterhood. The discourse of sisterhood imagined in the name of "woman" is called out from the protected locus behind the gender mask—"from the outside," as Lugones (2020: 40) warns us—limiting their understanding of the struggles faced by the colonized. Seen from the outsider's perspective, third-world and colored women are reduced to the colored-sexed skin, like poor little female animals awaiting master's rescue.[3] Or, like the exotic and innocent frozen figures on the picture hanging on the white sisters' walls, as Jo Carrillo (2015: 60–61) writes,

> And when our white sisters
> radical friends see us
> in the flesh
> not as a picture they own,
> they are not quite as sure
> if
> they like us as much.
> We're not as happy as we look
> on
> their
> wall.

To question the colonial naming structure, we must confront the cruel reality that as racially sexed, we have never been included in the modern gender narrative. Instead, we've been made absent in that narrative. Our existence had to disappear in the colonizer's version of the gender story for it to even begin. My reading of Wynter's (1990) critical intervention of the disappeared Caliban's woman corroborates this reality. Wynter problematizes the colonial triangular relation between Prospero, Miranda, and Caliban by seeking the disappeared Caliban's woman (335). Wynter suggests that Caliban's woman is made invisible by the colonizer's ontological denial of her existence. This denial extends not only to Caliban's woman but also to the existence of Caliban's species as a whole. Caliban's woman is deemed unnecessary as his species is believed to be headed for extinction, lacking the potential to possess human Reason, be it Prospero's ideal version or Miranda's flawed one. This species lacks the biological ability to procreate, hindering the species' evolution. An intriguing question arises: are we truly Caliban's women, or even part of Caliban's kind? The understanding of evolution in this sense is *not about gender as much as it is about sex.* The colonizer's view hinders Caliban's species from evolving by presuming the absence of a "female" Caliban as the heterosexual counterpart to the "male" Caliban, which would have initiated evolution. Yet, this notion of female sex is not purely biological but a colonial imposition used to "speak about" the colonized. Enthrallingly, what we observe here is a way to "speak about" female sex *by not speaking about it, by assigning and then erasing it,* as if it is something that should be there but is not—a pathological dearth of Caliban's species. Female, a nonhuman metacategory that sex stands alone to define, is a trap of colonizers' speculation of biological evolution. Drawing such a dangerous conclusion—"Yes, Caliban has his women; we are Caliban's women and, yes, we can certainly mate with him and evolve"—traps us in a premodern box and reinforces the heterosexually determined and heterosexually instinctual pattern of life. To reject being colonizers' Caliban, we must also reject being Caliban's women. Neither Caliban nor women nor female is our name.

Gender-Making One's Precolonial Past, Sex-Skinning Others' (Post)colonial Present

Continuing my intervention on the sex skin and gender mask, this section examines how the colonizer's cultural technologies and the colonial naming structure impact the gender politics of third-world state feminists. I explore how the term *woman,* embodying skin and mask technologies, integrates into third-world state feminists' self-perception. Ding Naifei's critique of state feminism in Taiwan offers me a compelling perspective to elaborate on my concerns. Approaching state feminism in late and post–Cold War Taiwan as a third-world experience, I maintain a critical distance from economic determinism in defining *third world.* Taiwan's status as a US ally and its reputation as an "economic success" and "Asian Tiger" of capitalist modernity from the 1970s to the present in the international order often excludes it from the societal and political imagination of the "third world," erasing local resistances and engagements with third-world liberatory consciousness. I view *third world* not as a passively assigned colonial identity but as a decolonial and coalitional identity actively chosen to understand oneself in the global racial order and raise critical consciousness with one's people. The "third world" identity empowers us to perceive different layers of material realities and logics of thinking hidden under economically deterministic discourse. My analysis, in conversation with Ding, is epistemically situated within the sphere of the "third world" for self-transformation, aligning with Chen Kuan-Hsing's (2010: 212, 223) call in *Asia as Method* to shift "points of reference" toward the third-world and other Asian subjects.

State feminism in Taiwan emerged in the 1970s and 1980s and reached maturity in the 1990s during a period when the pro-US Chinese nationalist party (Kuomintang) lost its state sovereignty in the inter-state system The party's authoritarian rule weakened alongside the lifting of martial law in 1987, coinciding with the transitioning—instead of dissolving—of the Cold War binary structure. During the Cold War era, the Chinese nationalist party justified its authoritarian rule by collaborating with the US-led capitalization and militarization in transpacific Asia. This collaboration aimed to compete with Chinese communists for representing the modern Chinese nation-state in the inter-state order. Success in this competition required wearing the white mask, symbolizing acceptance by Western imperialists as a modern Chinese entity capable of handling and suppressing local dissidents. Dissidents in Taiwan, including left-wingers, Indigenous groups, and nativists, suffered political purges that deprived them of freedom of speech and social movements. Despite the end of authoritarian rule in the late 1980s and early 1990s, the desire to wear the white mask and pursue modernity persisted, with many dissidents engaging in mask-wearing efforts more intensely than the Chinese nationalists. While postcolonial Taiwanese identity evolved with prominent expressions of freedom of speech and social movements, critical examination of the desire for the white mask remains lacking. Those who engage in and endorse this pursuit are whom I refer to as "modernity's embracers."

One of the primary aims of modernity's embracers is to include educated and elite women, as well as middle- and upper-class housewives, in electoral and representative politics. The result of this project was enabling selected women to enter state-led political spheres while simultaneously subordinating women's movements to the postauthoritarian nation-state (Liu 2015: 60). The emergence of state feminism signifies that gender-based feminism has started parting its way from the marginalized groups (61). While gender-based feminism embraces the colonial notion of universal womanhood and largely aligns with the state-led institutional and legal reformations, domestic workers (particularly migrant women from Southeast Asian countries), licensed sex workers, and individuals who challenge normative, heterosexual, and reproductive standards of sex and sexuality have been muted and represented as abnormal (61). What, then, is the psychological structure of state feminism in relation to the endless longing for recognition in the imperialist-led inter-state system and its own Taiwanese local colonial imaginary?[4]

Ding Naifei (2002) coins the term *feminist knot* to describe state feminists' psychological impasse of being haunted by "a sense of historical shame" (455) manifested by their third-world others—domestic workers and licensed sex workers. This hard-to-unknot impasse confines state feminists to focus solely on their subordinate status as "women" without questioning the coloniality of gender contested by domestic workers and sex workers. State feminists adopt the Eurocentric feminists' perspective, viewing domestic workers and sex workers as "not-yet (feminist) subjects" from the backward third world, needing to be civilized and rescued but not considered eligible to join feminist movements (463–64). The feminist movements only welcome modern citizen-subjects who are properly gendered, meaning that one can express one's sense of self through the gender mask. The state feminists thus believe that they can occupy the "house"— the metaphorically normative space provided and sanctioned by the nation-state—as the "host" of an "organic body-politic that is the pre-existing 'natural' totality" and distinguishably separate their "parasites" from themselves (Ding 2000: 309–10). The segregation of improper others from the proper feminist subjects is created and delineated by the reimagination and reinterpretation of Chinese precolonial social roles within the colonial logic. On the one hand, state feminists identify themselves with the *postcolonial* positionality of "modern good women" (*xiandai haonuren*) that inherits the positionality of household mistresses/first wives (*liangjia funu/ yuanpei*) from *precolonial* time (Ding 2002: 463). On the other hand, sex workers and domestic workers are relegated to the *postcolonial* positionality of baseness and promiscuity that inherits the positionality of bondmaid-concubines (*biqie*) and lascivious women (*yinfu*) from *precolonial* time (460).

The historical shame emerges in two convoluted ways, and each is grasped as a threat. The first threat originates from the reimagination and reinterpretation of the local precolonial past, where bondmaid-concubines and lascivious women appear to menace the standing of household mistresses/first wives within their families (463). Extending this logic, domestic workers and sex workers in postcolonial Taiwan pose a menace to the "modern good women's" standings in their households. The specific representations of marginalized subjects "cannot be simply condemned as feudal residues of a disavowed and simplified past," rather, they are "reinvention[s]" in its timely connection to the late and post–Cold War social and political tensions (Ding 2007: 222). Unlike the precolonial bondmaid-concubines and lascivious women, state feminists argue that modern occupations are the result of personal choices, reflecting a person's morality. This perspective sugarcoats the neoliberal structural inequalities at play (Ding 2010b: 103). In this view, if someone engages in a job considered despicable, she is seen as embracing the immorality associated with precolonial bondmaid-concubines and lascivious women. *If I were you, I would be ashamed of myself; I succeeded in becoming a modern good woman through personal choice and hard work, so I am qualified to declare your shamefulness; you should feel ashamed, shouldn't you?* Neoliberal structural inequalities are replaced and erased by the measurement of morality, supported by the reimagined concept of concubinage from the local historical past (Ding 2010a).[5]

The second threat arises from state feminists internalizing the colonial sense of time, viewing domestic workers and sex workers as embodiments of their own third-world cultural past, which they sought to detach from, following evolutionist and teleological linearity. Such an imagined shameful past is crystalized in the image of "third-world women" that are pitiful and waiting for their modern sisters' rescue, a construct largely propagated by Eurocentric feminists. As state feminists aspire to be reborn anew in the postcolonial nation-state, they must eliminate their imagined backward sense of self, as represented by domestic workers and sex workers, by establishing a totally incompatible differentiation between themselves and these workers and excluding them from public feminist discussions. In other words, one must validate one's modern identity by *forging a premodern identity for others*. In this sense, the second kind of threat that domestic workers and sex workers pose to state feminists is internal to state feminists' *postcolonial identity building*.

These two convoluted threats give rise to state feminists' sense of historical shame, forming the basis for the specific reproduction of the sex-skin/gender-mask structure. The psychological impasse seen in state feminists' postcolonial identity building is not merely a residue of a precolonial sentiment; rather, it is *a colonial psychology* that seeks to justify the coloniality of gender through intentionally (mis)represented and fragmented precolonial sociality. Two presumptions underlie this context: (1) Taiwanese society is *different* from Western societies, and (2) Taiwanese society can be *as modern as* Western societies. Regarding the first presumption, the precolonial social roles, including bondmaid-concubines, lascivious women, and household mistresses/first wives, are reinterpreted and reimagined as *the sexed roles in the modern definition of sex* and are unquestionably accepted as local traditions. Even though these precolonial social roles are considered "traditional" and immutable, they are understood as universal biological facts. The major function of the first presumption is to indicate that if the shameful sentiment is passed onto us in the present from our "tradition," it is, then, undoubtedly a sentiment that is coherent with our nature and, therefore, unquestionable.

Regarding the second presumption, the *sexed roles* of the precolonial time must be transferred into modernity anew. However, not all sexed roles are qualified for a modernizing transference; only those deemed *suitable* for civilizational evolution are chosen. The ones considered unsuitable must gradually fade away in modernity. This is where the *gender mask* comes into play. Intriguingly, the gender mask is not directly placed onto the bodies of postcolonial state feminists but must first be applied to the bodies of household mistresses/first wives in the precolonial time to mold them into *"protomodern women,"* as if they were always destined for a journey of modernizing transference. The protomodern woman is a *protogendered role* that is not just *sexed* but also *somewhat gendered, yet not fully,* and is therefore selected to be transferred into modernity. Bondmaid-concubines and lascivious women in the premodern time were only sexed and remain only sexed in their postcolonial inheritors (domestic workers and sex workers). What is tricky here is that these marginalized workers in the postcolonial present are actually the real targets of the colonially imposed sex skin technology. Indeed, state feminists' process of *masking* themselves as "modern good women" is juxtaposed with domestic workers' and sex workers' *epidermal becoming* of sexed-yet-not-gendered nonhuman females. While the former kind of becoming looks forward to the future, the latter kind of becoming is trapped in the past. Domestic workers and sex workers are coerced into embodying the "sin of third-world premodernity" that state feminists seek to distance themselves from, solidifying the asymmetry between the two groups in the postcolonial present. The concept of white skin resurfaces here, as state feminists delineate the boundaries of the category "protomodern women"—a gendered and white-skinned construct imagined as a pre-mask entity. They occupy this defined space to both assert their oppositional identity to the sexed-yet-not-gendered others and to rationalize their apparent gender mask within the late and post–Cold War neoliberal society. Similar to the concept of white skin, "protomodern women" is an empty and elusive category, a mere silhouette. Ding (2010b: 86) emphasizes that those confined within the bound of "modern good women" feel more ashamed about the alleged premodernity sin compared to the marginalized workers. In my view, it is because they are the ones who internalize this sin and project it onto their sexed counterparts.

Moreover, I suggest that the colonial psychology of the feminist knot happens when the "modern" weirdly yet justifiably marries the "traditional." It is made rational in the state-led modernizing logic that "tradition," which is actually more of a fragmented misrepresentation than a sociohistorical reality, can be a tool to be used to justify the modern gender structure and its attached shameful sentiments, while the modern gender structure can be a tool to be used to decide what parts of "tradition" are high-minded and transferrable to modernity and what parts should be dysselected. Modernization, in this sense, is detoxification, a process of selecting and dysselecting that resonates with Wynter's biocentric selection/dysselection. The more perfectly the selected good "traditions" match modernity, the more distanced state feminists can stay from third-world backwardness, and, in consequence, the more state feminists are fitting into the name of "modern good woman." So, through this detoxification, the sex-skin/gender-mask structure is transplanted in the way in which it reconfigures the imaginary of precolonial society but actually aims at building and concretizing the colonial humanity in the postcolonial present. The gender-masking of household mistresses/first wives in the precolonial time enables the sex-skinning of domestic workers and sex workers in the postcolonial present.

Coda: De-naming

The bodies shaped by the sexed skin technology and the names engraved on those skins do not truly belong to us. I am not suggesting that we do not have diverse sexual and reproductive expressions based on our distinct characteristics. As a matter of fact, these expressions have been and may continue to be not dimorphic or dichotomous. Rather, I am trying to see how "sex" in its sociohistorical functions, as a mirrored image of gender, wrongly contains our bodies and kills our potential. I am also trying to see the sexed interpretation of our body as not just a reduction based on physical materiality but, more complicatedly, an epistemological imposition and addition hidden by the discourse of physical materiality. One has to ignore the sexing skin technology in order to speak about sex as just a biological fact, even if one is arguing against gender. If the colored skin cannot be just the biological-colored skin but always already *opposes* the white mask, then sex, in a similar fashion, cannot be just sex, but always already *opposes* gender. Understanding sex as a cultural technology offers us a departure from the sexed physical materiality in coloniality toward the physical possibilities outside the designated difference of sex. The bodies on the outside can question, think, create, and can certainly live not as someone else's dichotomous counterpart or someone else's uncultured version. The sex-skin/gender-mask structure, therefore, can be rephrased as the body/ sex-skin/gender-mask structure to bring our lively and resistant *bodies* into our emancipatory vision and open a path for understanding our bodies without the dehumanizing skins. It is a process of "strip[ping] down through layers" of colonial skins that have been epidermally enveloping our bodies, as Spillers remarks (1987: 65), and incessantly exploring our bodies' decolonial potentials.

Fanon (2008) critically questions the dehumanizing reality through his embodied corporeality, deliberately separating himself from the technologized skin, as seen in his self-reflection: "Here are the fragments put together by another me" (89). The body split from the reified skin technology is not an object "in opposition to what [the colonizers] call the soul" but an embodied subject that questions, thinks, and creates, and can move outside the colonial naming structure (106). When it does not "stay in line," it can actively create unnatural sparkles—"unnatural" in the sense of not aligning with the colonizer's law of nature, "unnatural" as it cleverly befuddles the colonizers. It can move away from colonial humanity and reject the colonially given name(s) because asking for an egalitarian stance under modern names is not its purpose (14). To repeat the demand of the dehumanized, *we need new names that do name something new*, I emphasize that it is voiced out by the embodied subjects that skin technology is unable to eliminate. It is a call from the misnamed souls who strive for genuine *rehumanization* that regenerates, remembers, and rekindles the resisting names they have been carrying and at the same time designs and plays with new names and new elements. Rehumanization undertakes the *de-naming* process to resist dehumanizing labels imposed by skin technologies and reject universalized names associated with mask technologies. The "de-" in "de-naming" seeks decoloniality that uproots colonial meanings that sentence us to symbolic death.

. . . .

Chia-Hsu Jessica Chang is a doctoral candidate in comparative literature at Binghamton University, State University of New York. Her academic praxis stands at the intersection of decolonial feminism, third-world feminism, and the politics of women and queers of color, critical race and ethnic studies, and translation and communication studies in transpacific Asia and North America. Her current research explores the role of decolonial translators, who create communicative resistance and communal knowledge through the strategic utilization of their untranslatability. She is the winner of the 2023 National Women's Studies Association Women of Color Caucus—*Frontiers* Student Essay Award.

Notes

1   See Maria Lugones's (2020: 31) description of the "double denial" of a person's humanity.

2   To draw a conclusive picture, the colonial naming structure follows a series of steps: (1) Dividing beings into distinct groups using dichotomous logic. (2) Reifying and naturalizing concepts through the visualization of colored skin, creating skin technology. (3) Perceiving individuals within each group in a predetermined and reductionist manner. (4) Erasing sociohistorical relationships between coexisting groups and enforcing a linear narrative. (5) Imprinting colonial names onto the skin technology. My conclusive picture aligns with the insights of Fernando Coronil, Stephen J. Gould, and Anibal Quijano. See Coronil (1996: 56, 57); Gould (1996: 27, 53); and Quijano (2000: 549, 551–53, 556).

3   Sylvia Wynter writes that the female circumcision in Africa which conveys a symbolic birth for local people is misinterpreted by the Eurocentric feminists as genital mutilation with the premise that patriarchy, or male sexual control, is a universal phenomenon. Under this premise, African women automatically fall into the submissive position attached to the "woman" category which has ever just taken the white women into consideration and, thereby, needs to be rescued. Likewise, Chandra Mohanty indicates that the image of the "average Third World woman" is constructed based on her being interpreted as having a feminine gender and therefore must be sexually constrained, and also her being "third-world" and therefore must be uncivilized. This double-element image of "woman" and "third world" is, Mohanty argues, made to contrast with the image of Western women that are educated, freer in making decisions, and have the power to control their own bodies. See Wynter 1997; and Mohanty 2003: 22.

4   I am fully aware of the dynamic shifts in state feminism in Taiwan over the past two decades, particularly the influence they have had on the rise of gender-based representational politics of LGBT+ people that do not necessarily create space for the exploration and interpretation of nonbinary and non-performative queer praxes, and may even restrain them. The analysis in this article lays the foundation for my future research on these dynamic shifts.

5   Viewing the roles of white-collar elites and housewives as "personal choices" raises concerns, just as it does with sex workers and migrant domestic workers. Jini Kim Watson's insights reveal the challenges faced by Taiwanese women striving for a balance between modern career pursuits and traditional values. Watson's analysis exposes the difficulties in fitting into the modern domestic space, highlighting the impossibility of fully embodying the gender mask. See Watson 2011: 153, 155–56.

Works Cited

Carrillo, Jo. 2015. "And When You Leave, Take Your Pictures with You." In *This Bridge Called My Back*, edited by Cherrie Moraga and Gloria Anzaldua, 60–61. Albany, NY: SUNY Press.

Chen, Kuan-Hsing. 2010. *Asia as Method: Toward Deimperialization*. Durham, NC: Duke University Press.

Chen, Yingzhen. 2005. "What the 'Third World' Means to Me." *Inter-Asia Cultural Studies* 6, no. 4: 535–40.

Coronil, Fernando. 1996. "Beyond Occidentalism: Toward Nonimperial Geohistorical Categories." *Cultural Anthropology* 11, no. 1: 51–87.

Ding, Naifei. 2000. "Prostitutes, Parasites, and the House of State Feminism." *Inter-Asia Cultural Studies* 1, no. 2: 305–18.

Ding, Naifei. 2002. "Feminist Knots: Sex and Domestic Work in the Shadow of the Bondmaid- Concubine." *Inter-Asia Cultural Studies* 3, no. 3: 449–67.

Ding, Naifei. 2007. "Wife-In-Monogamy and 'The Exaltation of Concubines.'" *Interventions* 9, no. 2: 219–37.

Ding, Naifei. 2010a. "Imagined Concubinage." *positions: east asia cultures critique* 18, no. 2: 321–49.

Ding, Naifei. 2010b. 看/不見疊影: 家務與性工作中的婢妾身形 ("Seeing Double: Domestic and Sex Work in the Shade of the Bondmaid-Concubine"). In 超克'現代': 台社後/殖民讀本（下冊）(*Overcoming the Modern: Taishe Reader in Post/colonial Studies* [Vol. 2]), edited by Kuan-Hsing Chen, 85–114. Taipei: Tonsan.

Fanon, Frantz. 2008. *Black Skin, White Masks*. Translated by Richard Philcox. New York: Grove Press.

Federici, Silvia. 2004. *Caliban and the Witch: Women, the Body, and Primitive Accumulation*. Brooklyn: Autonomedia.

Foucault, Michel. 1995. *Discipline and Punish*. Translated by Alan Sheridan. New York: Random House.

Gould, Stephen J. 1996. *The Mismeasure of Man*. New York: W. W. Norton.

Hartman, Saidiya. 1997. *Scenes of Subjection: Terror, Slavery, and Self-Making in Nineteenth-Century America*. New York: Oxford University Press.

Laqueur, Thomas. 1992. *Making Sex: Body and Gender from the Greeks to Freud*. Cambridge, MA: Harvard University Press.

Liu, Petrus. 2015. *Queer Marxism in Two Chinas*. Durham, NC: Duke University Press.

Lugones, Maria. 2007. "Heterosexualism and the Colonial/Modern Gender System." *Hypatia* 22, no. 1: 186–209.

Lugones, Maria. 2010. "Toward a Decolonial Feminism." *Hypatia* 25, no. 4: 742–59.

Lugones, Maria. 2020. "Gender and Universality in Colonial Methodology." *Critical Philosophy of Race* 8, nos. 1–2: 25–47.

Mohanty, Chandra. 2003. *Feminism without Borders: Decolonizing Theory, Practicing Solidarity*. Durham, NC: Duke University Press.

Moraga, Cherrie. 2015. "Catching Fire: Preface to the Fourth Edition." In *This Bridge Called My Back: Writings by Radical Women of Color*, edited by Cherrie Moraga and Gloria Anzaldua. Albany: State University of New York Press.

Quijano, Anibal. 2000. "Coloniality of Power, Eurocentrism, and Latin America." *Nepantla: Views from South* 1, no. 3: 533–80.

Santiago-Valles, Kelvin. 2016. "Trying to Pin Myself in History: Race, Sex, and Colonialism." *Border/Lines* 29/30: 72–77.

Spillers, Hortense. 1987. "Mama's Baby, Papa's Maybe: An American Grammar Book." *Diacritics* 17, no. 2: 64–81.

Watson, Jini Kim. 2011. *The New Asian City: Three-Dimensional Fictions of Space and Urban Form*. Minneapolis: University of Minnesota Press.

Weheliye, Alexander. 2014. *Habeas Viscus: Racializing Assemblages, Biopolitics, and Black Feminist Theories of the Human*. Durham, NC: Duke University Press.

Wynter, Sylvia. 1990. "Afterword: Beyond Miranda's Meanings: Un/silencing the 'Demonic Ground' of Caliban's 'Woman.'" In *Out of the Kumbla: Caribbean Women and Literature*, edited by Carole Boyce Davies and Elaine Savory Fido. Trenton, NJ: Africa World Press.

Wynter, Sylvia. 1997. "'Genital Mutilation' or 'Symbolic Birth?' Female Circumcision, Lost Origins, and the Aculturalism of Feminism/Western Thought." *Case Western Reserve Law Review* 47, no. 2.

Wynter, Sylvia. 2001. "Towards the Sociogenic Principle: Fanon, Identity, the Puzzle of Conscious Experience, and What It Is like to Be 'Black.'" In *National Identities and Socio-Political Changes in Latin America*, edited by Antonio Gomez-Moriana and Mercedes Duran-Cogan, 30–66. New York: Routledge.

Wynter, Sylvia. 2003. "Unsettling the Coloniality of Being/Power/Truth/Freedom: Towards the Human, after Man, Its Overrepresentation—An Argument." *New Centennial Review* 3, no. 3: 257–337.

Aurora Santiago Ortiz

....

Colectiva Feminista en Construcción
Building a Transnational Feminist Pedagogy

Abstract: Colectiva Feminista en Construcción (La Cole) is a Black feminist political organization that emerged in 2014 in San Juan, Puerto Rico. This article discusses the ways La Cole's public discourse around sexism, racism, and homophobia in the archipelago is articulated through the collective's presence at marches, demonstrations, and on social media. While core membership is small, La Cole has been able to convene collaborators and supporters to organize against the imposition of neoliberal economic and public policies that negatively impact the most dispossessed populations in Puerto Rico, namely Black, poor, queer, and trans women. La Cole has constructed a transnational intersectional feminist pedagogy as a means of political education both within the organization itself and more broadly in Puerto Rico's public sphere. The organization's pedagogical strategies include the rewriting of Christmas songs and *plenas*, an Afro Puerto Rican musical genre, and their Radical Feminist School, a political education space open to nonmembers. Through these pedagogical interventions La Cole simultaneously calls attention to the ways state and structural gender-based violence and femicides, housing precarity, and austerity measures affect the most marginalized sectors of the archipelago while carving out their identity as a decolonial Black feminist political organization.

Introduction

I arrived at the Sagrado Corazón train station parking lot in Santurce, Puerto Rico, early in the morning of March 8, 2018. The sun's first rays cut through the night sky as I got out of the car and saw at least twenty people clad in purple shirts that read "Anti-patriarcal, feminista, lesbiana, trans,

MERIDIANS · feminism, race, transnationalism 23:2 October 2024
DOI: 10.1215/15366936-11266396 © 2024 Smith College

caribeña, latinoamericana."[1] I was there to observe and take part in an
International Working Women's Day demonstration led by Colectiva
Feminista en Construcción (La Cole), a Black feminist political organization mainly based in San Juan, Puerto Rico. We were waiting for two
busses to take us to the Capitol building for a demonstration. Before we left
one of the founders and spokespeople of La Cole, Shariana Ferrer Núñez,
addressed the heterogenous group, composed of mostly women and
femmes of diverse ages, some of whom identified as Afro Puerto Rican.
Shariana discussed logistics with the participants regarding who would be
in the thick of the demonstration's direct action and who would flank the
group and provide backup support. Not having taken part in the logistical
planning of the demonstration, I oscillated between being a participant in
the action and an observer, and after asking the logistics committee where
I should go, I was finally placed with the second group that would not be at
the frontlines of the direct action.

Police flanked our school bus to El Capitolio (Capitol building). A few
women commented on this being more of a surveillance tactic than protection. At El Capitolio, there were already demonstrators waiting. The
groups dispersed to different entrances. I followed one of the groups to a
side entrance where Shariana approached a security guard. She requested
to meet with the pro-statehood senate president Thomas Rivera Schatz.
The guard told her he was not available. We waited in the foyer by the metal
detector until it became evident that no one was going to meet us. On
Shariana's signal, everyone sat down. Suddenly and unexpectedly, I was in
the middle of a sit-in, or an "ethnographic zone of emergency" (Juris 2008:
187, citing Feldman 1995). I remained standing, documenting the events as
they unfolded.[2] La Cole blocked staffers and other employees from entering, and the security guards became more and more agitated. One of the
guards started to physically block and push some of the demonstrators,
including a woman in her sixties.

Eventually, we were allowed into a large meeting room. Feminists
chanted and unfurled a purple banner that stated "Construyamos Otra
Vida" (Let's Build Another Life), a phrase that has been a fixture in La Cole's
various campaigns. They demanded that Rivera Schatz sit down with
them and discuss their document containing more than one hundred and
fifty-three demands, including access to universal health care, access to
medical care for incarcerated women, and guaranteed free medical treatment for trans and intersex people. La Cole's document also called for

reparations, particularly for Black and nonwhite women subjected to birth control and sterilization experiments from the 1950s onward and the elimination of abortion in Puerto Rico's penal code. In terms of public education, La Cole demanded the democratization of schooling, an audit of the public university debt, and the elimination of any austerity measures that entailed school closures or budget cuts. La Cole also called for the creation and implementation of an anti-racist curriculum incorporating a gender perspective inclusive of neurodiversity. These are just some of the demands included in the document that detail proposals and solutions to the archipelago's social, economic, and political crisis.[3]

The sit-in received news coverage, and, eventually, some legislative officials agreed to hear La Cole out. A meeting with a representative from the pro-independence party was scheduled for the following Wednesday; however, the representative was from a minority party that wields very little influence on Puerto Rico's legislative body. During the meeting, the representative listened to La Cole's demands, yet to date none have been addressed.[4] Despite this lack of action, La Cole has had an enormous impact in transforming multiple discourses in Puerto Rico's public sphere.

I began conducting ethnographic fieldwork of La Colectiva Feminista en Construcción in March 2018 when I participated in and observed the International Women's Day strike, attended the Women's Day march (known as 8M), and interviewed five members of La Cole—Shariana Ferrer Núñez, Vanesa Contreras, Sara, Cristina, and Rita.[5] I attended an organizational meeting at the union headquarters of a public corporation as well as a follow-up meeting with a pro-independence party representative at his office in the capitolio the week after the 8M protest. Because I have a personal and political stake in the goals of the organization, I decided to subsequently continue my involvement with La Cole as a participant and collaborator, as well as engaged ethnographer. I participated in their 2019 8M demonstration against the Puerto Rican and foreign banking sector, denouncing their role in Puerto Rico's debt crisis. My participation in La Cole's demonstrations and marches continues as a student of several of their Radical Feminist Schools, which I later discuss. Besides drawing from my own participation in actions and protests, I engage with La Cole's own archive of written and audiovisual materials that are available on their social media and website.

In this article, I trace the origins of La Cole in the context of Puerto Rican feminisms and discuss their pedagogical work within the broader cartographies of feminist struggle in Puerto Rico. I then outline the organization's protest repertoires and political education work, which include rewriting *plenas* and Christmas songs with lyrics denouncing sexist violence, before highlighting the organization's transnational dialogue with other feminist movements in Latin America. The combination of these elements illustrates the two main arguments I put forth in this article. The first is that La Cole signals a rupture in Puerto Rican protest politics by embodying, practicing, and disseminating an intersectional feminist pedagogy anchored in a decolonial feminist praxis. Echoing M. Jacqui Alexander (2015), I locate the pedagogical at the margins, as a methodology that seeks to "destabilize existing practices of knowing and thus cross the fictive boundaries of exclusion and marginalization" (7). La Cole has been able to carve out an explicitly anti-racist, anti-homophobic, anti-transphobic, and feminist discourse that is seldom heard in Puerto Rico's public sphere. Their public pedagogy around sexism, racism, and homophobia in Puerto Rico is articulated at rallies, marches, demonstrations, and on social media, as well as through their political education initiatives. In this sense, La Cole's double pedagogy operates on two levels: internally, as part of its members' political education and development, and externally, by reshaping Puerto Rico's public sphere (Phillips and Cole 2013).

La Cole's actions focus on agitation, education, and organization.[6] Throughout the years, they have a robust archive of political education materials including bulletins, campaigns, and *manifiestas*. Their protest repertoires have also uniquely shaped anti-racist feminist militant organizing by shifting the protest terrain of Puerto Rico through song and performance, including the use of traditional Puerto Rican folkloric music such as *plenas*, a musical genre with African roots. These strategies draw from and are influenced by Black, Indigenous, popular, communitarian, and autonomous feminist movements in other parts of Latin America as well as Black feminist thought in the United States and southern cone (Collins 2000; Gago, Malo, and Cavallero 2020; Curiel Pichardo 2014; Espinosa Miñoso 2016).

The second point I expand on is that La Cole intentionally situates itself in an assemblage of Latin American feminist movements oriented toward the Global South (including the South in the North), rather than toward white US-based and European movements. This assemblage allows for the building of "coalitions and solidarities across borders" (Mohanty 2003: 226) by producing a transnational dialogue with other Latin American countries, where social media and travel facilitate feminist activist networks with shared strategies, campaigns, and tactics. Although feminist demands are shared by other movements around the globe, La Cole's mobilization strategies are framed within Puerto Rico's particular local context and directed toward the political, economic, cultural, and colonial crises Puerto Ricans face.

Last, I write as a brown Puerto Rican feminist who has a stake in La Cole and whose claims are represented by the organization. While I am not a member of the organization, I am a collaborator. I attend their demonstrations when I am in the archipelago; I promote their campaigns and work on social media and participate in some of their ongoing projects. Their work is designed to be shared widely and to create spaces for conversation, both in person and virtually.[7]

La Cole's core membership ranges from about five to ten people and includes Afro Puerto Rican as well as non-Black feminists. However, the organization collaborates with a wide network of anti-colonial, anti-racist, and feminist organizations. They convene and attract feminists of all ages, class backgrounds, genders, races, and sexualities at their demonstrations. La Cole's demonstrations and direct actions have been featured in Puerto Rican national newspapers such as *El nuevo día*[8] and US outlets such as *Teen Vogue*.[9] One of the founders of La Cole, Shariana Ferrer Núñez, has been invited to speak on television shows that feature politicians, political scientists, and commentators.[10] While not everyone agrees with La Cole's platform, protest tactics, or message, their impact on Puerto Rico's public and political life has been undeniable.

Building La Colectiva Feminista en Construcción

La Colectiva Feminista en Construcción emerged in 2014 when women from socialist and student organizations came together because they felt gender was not being foregrounded in their organizing spaces. Feminist activists Shariana Ferrer Núñez and Vanesa Contreras, among other women, decided to create intentional spaces for feminists to organize. Shariana notes, "The idea began to create a space; we were having political differences . . . so we decided to make our own, instead of being fragmented in different spaces."[11] Shariana was participating in another feminist organization, Movimiento Amplio de Mujeres de Puerto Rico (Women's Ample Movement in Puerto Rico, or MAM), and was also active in the student movement at the University of Puerto Rico during a pivotal time of resistance against austerity measures which resulted in two major strikes in 2010–11. The strikes protested tuition hikes and budget cuts that affected the most economically vulnerable students at the archipelago's only public institution. Vanesa was also active in the student movement in Spain as well as Puerto Rico, and previously participated in other socialist organizations.[12]

A group of women began meeting at Vanesa's home to talk about the issues and projects that concerned them. Shariana, Vanesa, and other feminists decided to create an intersectional space: a feminist, anticapitalist, anti-racist, and queer space that ran counter to white, bourgeois feminism in Puerto Rico. It was a space under construction, hence the name Colectiva Feminista en Construcción. Vanesa explained the construction aspect of the collective, describing it as "a group of feminists building something, and the first thing we put out was 'La Manifiesta' (the Manifest).[13] The writing of that document took about six months. We divided the topics, then discussed them and held an assembly to approve the document."[14]

"La Manifiesta" outlines La Cole's political position as an explicitly intersectional feminist organization, one that "recognizes that the different manifestations of oppression, sexism, cis-sexist misogyny, racism, xenophobia, and capitalism are all interrelated."[15] This stance echoes Kimberlé Crenshaw's (1990: 1244) conceptualization of intersectionality, which "explor[es] the various ways in which race and gender intersect in shaping structural, political, and representational aspects of violence against women of color." La Cole's attention to intersectionality is also influenced by the Combahee River Collective (CRC). The CRC's paradigm-shifting "Statement" is central in La Cole's work, vision, and discursive practice. The organization takes as its point of departure Black feminism, although not all the members and collaborators of La Cole identify as Black or Afrodescendant.[16] La Cole follows the CRC's stance on identity politics as stemming from the personal experiences of Black women by "focusing upon [their] own oppression" (Combahee River Collective 1982, n.p.). In their 2020 "Anti-racist Manifesto," La Cole states that "given these hierarchies of power that sustain the racial state, we reaffirm, together with the Black feminists who have gone before us—that the liberation of Black women will be the end of all oppressions, the end of the racial state in all its manifestations and all its articulations with different structures of power."[17]

In addition to the Combahee River Collective, La Cole cites the Movement for Black Lives, the Ejército Zapatista de Liberación Nacional, the Black Panthers, and the Young Lords as influential in their political and community organizing work, recognizing the legacies of the Black radical tradition and the anti-imperial and anti-colonial activism and community work of these organizations.[18] These legacies are anchored, much like some of the mid- to late-twentieth-century feminist activists I discuss below, in a vision of decolonization for all oppressed people in the world.

Cartographies of Feminist Struggle in Puerto Rico

The work of La Cole does not exist in a vacuum. It's situated within a longer history of anti-colonial, anti-capitalist, and anti-racist feminist activism on the archipelago and Puerto Rican diaspora. This brief overview serves to map the groundbreaking work of Puerto Rican feminists in the twentieth century and to bridge their activism to La Cole. Although Cole does not consider itself to be a continuation of previous Puerto Rican feminist groups, many of the demands of earlier feminists are still relevant and central to La Cole's work as well.

The 1970s saw the advent of feminist organizations in Puerto Rico that were successful in garnering legal victories that amplified the rights of women. It was not until 1972 that women could not be discriminated against in the workforce based on their gender (Azize Vargas 1987). In 1976, legislation was approved that allowed women to co-administer their finances in marriage; another law granted women greater rights in divorce proceedings and custody disputes. Abortion was legalized in 1980, following *Pueblo v. Duarte*, which incorporated the *Roe v. Wade* ruling. However, the Puerto Rican government did not immediately accept the ruling and many doctors refused to perform abortions (Crespo Kebler 2001).

Feminist organizations and activisms in these years focused on the division of labor and sought legal recourse to expand women's rights in marriage and in the workforce. During the 1970s and 1980s, much of the Puerto Rican feminist movement also addressed domestic violence. However, some feminists began to critique the issue of "double militancy," where they felt pulled in diverging directions: forced to choose between political organizations that sought independence for Puerto Rico or feminist organizations that sought gender equality (Torres Martinez 2004). Torres Martinez (2004) notes that "feminist discourses were primarily heterosexual" (109) in these decades, with few organizations explicitly addressing LGBTQIA+ rights. In terms of the intersections of race and gender, "few people spoke about the need to bring together discussions about the prejudices against women and racism" (Rivera Lassén 2016: 59).

Lawyer, activist, poet, and politician Ana Irma Rivera Lassén is a key figure of anti-racist, lesbian, and feminist organizing in Puerto Rico. Rivera Lassén was coeditor of *Tacón de la chancleta*, a feminist newspaper that ran in the 1970s. It featured women's reproductive rights and participation in the workforce and included a transnational element of women's struggles in the Caribbean, Latin America, and worldwide.[19] Describing her experiences as a Black lesbian in Puerto Rico, Rivera Lassén (2016) points to the tensions and difficulties around discussions of race and lesbophobia (and their intersections) in feminist organizations. Racism was portrayed "as a personal issue, not as an agenda of the organization" (59–60).

Rivera Lassén (2016: 64), drawing from Kimberlé Crenshaw (2001), emphasized the need for intersectional analyses "in discussions of discrimination against Afro-women," and since "the so-called 'second wave' of feminisms, the critiques for the need to recognize these intersections have been a constant, a tension, a challenge, and an agenda always in construction."

Many Afro Puerto Rican feminists, including Rivera Lassén, participated in the creation of the Network of Afro-Caribbean and Afro-Latin American Women, which later included those in the diaspora, and in the 1990s Black and Afrodescendant organizations that emerged in Puerto Rico. These organizations have been largely ignored because "they lack official [institutional] support and visibility," according to María Ramos Rosado, cofounder of the Union de Mujeres Puertorriqueñas Negras (Union of Black Puerto Rican Women [cited in Lavoy Zoungbo 2011: n.p.]). That erasure is part of the ongoing project of coloniality, which operates "through the naturalization of racial and social hierarchies that . . . subalternize and obliterate the knowledge, experiences and ways of life of those who are thus dominated and exploited" in Puerto Rico, the Caribbean, and Latin America (Gómez-Quintero 2010: 89).

In Puerto Rico, like other places in the Caribbean, colonialism, homophobia, transphobia, and misogyny have rendered LGBTQIA+ issues contentious and difficult to navigate (Saunders 2009, 2012; Negrón-Muntaner 2018; Espinosa Miñoso 2021). Since the Spanish invasion and subsequent U.S. control over Puerto Rico, the colonial matrix of power has created relations of domination and subordination that privilege cis men, heterosexuals, and white/light skinned Puerto Ricans (Ostolaza Bey 1989; Quijano 2000; Lugones 2010; Godreau 2015; Lloréns 2021; Curiel 2022). As a conservative society steeped in cultural Christianity, sexuality and queerness are seen as a taboo. De jure separation of church and state exists, yet religious groups exert influence over legislation. For instance, prayer circles are not infrequent in government buildings, including the judicial branch.[20] However, religious interests have not always prevailed. *Lawrence v. Texas* was already legally binding three days earlier in Puerto Rico than in the United States. The landmark court case ended the prohibition of what was then considered sodomy. Marriage equality became legal in Puerto Rico due to the Puerto Rican legal system's obligation to adopt Supreme Court decisions (La Fountain-Stokes 2018). Transgender people are also, as of April 2018, allowed to legally change their name on their birth certificate to reflect their gender (or as it is still referred to in Puerto Rico, sex) identity.[21]

Although La Cole is the only militant Black feminist political organization in Puerto Rico, there are other anti-racist feminist organizations active in Puerto Rico such as Taller Salud and Colectivo Ilé. Taller Salud, a feminist health and reproductive rights organization, started in 1979 in the historically Afro Puerto Rican town of Loíza in the northeastern coast of the archipelago. It was founded by two women who returned to the archipelago after living in New York and fighting against mass sterilization of Latin American women, including Puerto Rican women. Some of Taller Salud's initiatives include community mobilization to eradicate poverty and violence, strengthening community leadership, and gender violence prevention initiatives (LeBrón 2019).[22] Founded in 1991 in Northampton, Massachusetts, before moving to Puerto Rico in 1997, Colectivo Ilé is a decolonial feminist organization that focuses on anti-racist education and awareness through workshops and campaigns, one of them being "África en mi piel, África en mi ser" (Africa on my skin, Africa in my being [Franco-Ortiz 2018; Reinat Pumarejo 2018]). The campaign focused on educating the population in Puerto Rico about embracing their Blackness, particularly in the census. Colectivo Ilé also recognizes the imbrication of racism, sexism, classism, and homophobia in Puerto Rican society. Like La Cole, these organizations are central to feminist, anti-racist, and anti-colonial organizing writ large in Puerto Rico; they too are part of broader infrastructures of resistance that enact decolonial futures in the present through anti-racist pedagogies, practices, and activism.

La Cole's Double Pedagogy

La Cole's political work overlaps with that of the late twentieth-century Puerto Rican feminists on issues such as reproductive rights, abortion access, and denouncing corruption in the Puerto Rican government. However, La Cole takes a decidedly anti-institutional stance and seeks to "construct another life" entirely.[23] It is through this construction that an intersectional feminist pedagogy emerges, one that is connected to other transnational feminist struggles. I evoke M. Jacqui Alexander's (2006) notion of the pedagogical, as a transgressive, disruptive, and displacing practice that can "make different conversations and solidarities possible" (22).

La Cole's pedagogy functions twofold: internally through their Escuela Feminista Radical (Radical Feminist School, RFS hereafter) and meetings; and externally through mobilizations and actions that transmit anti-racist, anti-capitalist, feminist messages through repurposed songs and chants that are catchy and easily remembered. This double pedagogy confronts the state, demanding it fulfill its mandate toward those who are treated as nonhuman and disposable (Black femme bodies), but it also seeks to create another world outside of coloniality and colonialism by "plot[ting] a course towards collective self-determination" (Alexander 2006: 18). This is accomplished through protest and activist modalities in addition to popular educational strategies that foster political subjectivity through a Black feminist epistemology capable of linking multiple, intersecting forms of oppression with living in a colony (Saunders 2009).

Catherine Walsh (2018) connects M. Jacqui Alexander's notion of the pedagogical to the decolonial, by linking the pedagogical to "the work of decolonial praxis . . . grounded in peoples' realities, subjectivities, and struggles" (88). La Cole's pedagogy directly pursues Puerto Rico's decolonization from US occupation while also disrupting Puerto Rico's nation-building projects centered around discourses of mestizaje (Dávila 1997). These discourses are due in large part to the "myth of Puerto Rican identity from the building blocks of the racial triad" under a unifying Hispanic, Occidentalist narrative (1997: 61).[24] Puerto Rican cultural institutions have continued to disseminate the myth of racial harmony through discourses of racial blending, privileging traditions rooted in Spain, casting indigeneity as a thing of the past, and positioning Blackness as devoid of Black people. Puerto Rican anthropologist Isar Godreau (2015: 26) writes to this point, positing that "narratives about benevolent slavery, Hispanicity, and race mixture are also strategically deployed . . . as discursive tactics that attempt to whiten the majority while making blackness palatable for celebratory displays of national identity."

Anti-Black racism is not unique to Puerto Rico (Paschel 2016). For instance, in Brazil, the state institutionalized Black culture through events such as Carnaval while systemically disadvantaging Black folks, particularly Black women, by situating them on "the lower rungs of Brazil's socioeconomic ladder" (Paschel 2016: 39). In Colombia, the nation-building project excluded Black people from national discourse, viewing mestizaje as Indigenous and European mixture only (Paschel 2016). These discourses locate Puerto Rico within Latin American forms of racial categorization. In other words, racism and anti-Blackness are folded into the myth of the "great family," thus minimizing Blackness and exalting a mestizo culture that foregrounds Spanish and Native elements (Rivero 2005: 13; Godreau 2015).

La Cole views capitalism and colonialism as the root causes of precarity, calling attention to how women and femmes have been affected by manifestations of state forms of violence tied to neoliberal policies and legislation. These policies have resulted in massive layoffs in the public sector, the privatization of public corporations as well as schools, and budget cuts to pensions and Puerto Rico's public university. La Cole has continuously called for the end of public/private alliances, the cancellation of Puerto Rico's debt (considered by many to be illegal), and the overturning of austerity measures such as the Labor Reform Law, among others. The Labor Reform Law allows employers to cut workers' hours, slash benefits such as health care, and extend probationary periods.[25]

Their pedagogical and practical work is in direct opposition to precarity. Precarity, as Judith Butler (2015) formulates it, "designates that politically induced condition in which certain populations suffer from failing social and economic networks of support more than others, and become differentially exposed to injury, violence, and death" (33). Yet precarity is felt differently by different subjects. Therefore, La Cole is specific about who they make demands on behalf of and claims for—that is, the most precarious: Black, trans, poor, femme, and lesbians who are enveloped in necropolitics and are at a higher risk of dying at the hands of partners or ex-partners, some of them police. These are the bodies that have always been precarious and bear the brunt of state and institutional violence.

Through their strategies, La Cole simultaneously raises public awareness of their platform and carves out their identity as a Black feminist political organization. The organization seeks to render visible the oppressions that stem from the state and hold them responsible by creating proposals that will have long-term macropolitical impact. At an internal organizational level, members participate in political education initiatives such as *portavocía*, or spokesperson development, so that anyone in the organization can speak to the media or the public about La Cole's activism, demonstrations, and demands.[26]

Although La Cole operates with a small core membership, they create spaces for other feminists to discuss issues that are relevant to women and femmes. "Every political victory," Shariana notes, "is possible because there is an organization and an articulation behind it, a strategy." Education is central to this idea of forming political subjects who are aware of both the historical material conditions of colonial oppression in Puerto Rico and the broader cartographies of globalization, racial capitalism, and imperialism.

La Cole's Radical Feminist School

To strengthen the political education and activist formation of the core membership as well as their collaborators and allies, La Cole started a Radical Feminist School. The curriculum is based on issues discussed at meetings and those outlined in "La Manifiesta." Past RFS curricula include texts on the Martinique and Guadeloupe general strike, the Haitian Revolution, the revolution in Granada, and US social movements. The RFS incorporates an explicitly intersectional perspective that includes Black feminisms, Marxism, decolonial, and Afro-Caribbean feminisms, among other theoretical strands. The RFS is open to anyone and everyone. The last in-person RFS I attended was held in October–November 2019. There have been three subsequent sessions that met virtually due to the Covid-19 pandemic in 2020 and 2021 before returning to in-person meetings in 2022.

The RFS in October and November 2019 focused on Black feminisms and decolonial methodologies. Combahee River Collective member Demita Frazier and decolonial scholar Nelson Maldonado-Torres were invited to discuss their work and exchange ideas with those in attendance. Attendees also read the work of decolonial and Black feminist scholars and activists across the hemisphere. Folks from grassroots organizations attended, as did other activists and academics. It was a racial, socioeconomic, and age-diverse space, all of which rendered visible issues of access, including the challenges mothers experience in terms of the time that political organizing demands. The group discussed topics such as cancel culture and the need for tools to work through conflict in feminist spaces.

La Cole's identification as Black feminists, though Shariana is one of two core members who identify as Black in the collective,[27] has more to do with a conscious anti-racist, decolonial feminist praxis that centers Black women and femmes' experiences than with the racial identification of the whole organization per se. These tensions were discussed in the RFS, along with Puerto Rico's complex racial dynamics which have been the historically a site of contentious debate. In Puerto Rico and Latin America, for example, the term *Afrodescendant* has been increasingly used as a self-identifier for people who are non-Black, yet do not identify as white either. This definition departs from that of decolonial feminist Ochy Curiel (2002), who uses the term interchangeably with *Black*, noting that *Afrodescendant* indexes a relationship to the historical processes of slavery and colonialism.

Plenas and Christmas Songs as a Public Pedagogical Tool

Plenas originated in San Antón, a historically Black community in the town of Ponce, Puerto Rico (Godreau 2015). Plena songs are interactive, using a call-and-response structure, and lyrics may depict current events or be used as a tool to protest government injustices (Godreau 2015; Howard 2019). La Cole's use of plenas is intended "to be more accessible towards the public" by making political content "catchier," as Cristina mentioned in an interview.[28] They also call attention to issues such as gender violence and dispossession, while inviting passersby and newcomers to get acquainted with the organization. One such chant, directed toward misogynist men, was,

> ¡Macharrán, macharrán, conmigo no te equivoques!
> ¡Candela te vamo' a dar, no me mires, no me toques!
> (Misogynist, misogynist, don't get it wrong with me!
> We're gonna give you fire, don't look at me, don't touch me!)[29]

This song was also directed toward Hector O'Neill, former mayor of the city of Guaynabo. In 2017, La Cole led a successful pressure campaign calling for the resignation of O'Neill, who was accused of multiple sexual assaults, some by his former staff.[30] A video of Shariana confronting O'Neill about his misogynist behavior and sexual abuse at a San Juan restaurant went viral on social media.[31] La Cole also staged a citizen's arrest against O'Neill in public spaces to capture the attention of passersby and "interrupt the impunity of a government official . . . who would not face the same fate as impoverished or working-class men, especially [B]lack men or men racialized as nonwhite, with similar charges" (Zambrana 2021: 105).

La Cole aims to impact public opinion and public policy and to render visible a reality from the perspective of women and femmes by fore-grounding issues of race, gender, and class by exposing how these are threaded together.[32] On March 8, 2019, I attended La Cole's Feminist Embargo in the Caribbean's largest mall, Plaza las Américas. La Cole and a group of collaborators went to various banks in the mall, where employees closed their rolling doors as we stood outside chanting and holding signs that read "Embargo Feminista" and "Nosotras ante la deuda" (Us [women and femmes] against the debt). The demonstration "denounced the role of banking in the housing and debt crises" in Puerto Rico (Zambrana 2021: 107). We marched around the mall, disrupting business as usual for shop-pers and establishments alike. The protest flipped the script on the concept of foreclosure and instead placed the responsibility on those that dispos-sess and evict. Further, La Cole "pointed out that evictions impact women disproportionately, especially [B]lack women and women racialized as nonwhite" (Zambrana 2021: 107). Protesters brought flyers and bulletins denouncing the unelected Fiscal Control Board imposed by the US Con-gress. This Junta, as many call the board, oversees Puerto Rico's finances and has imposed austerity measures that include closing more than four hundred schools in the archipelago.[33] The "Black Feminist Friday" (a nod to Black feminism) demonstration used Christmas songs, because, in Sara's words, people already have those songs in their head. La Cole sang the traditional Christmas song "El jolgorio" using tongue-in-cheek lyrics to denounce La Junta's nefarious effects on poor women:

Esa Junta está
Esa Junta está
Bien por la maceta
Vamos a luchar
Venga lo que venga
. . .
Las mujeres pobres
Las mujeres pobres
Robando chuletas

Mientras el gobierno

Cocina pobreza

Vamos a luchar

Venga lo que venga

(This Junta is, this Junta is, over the top, we are going to fight,
   come what may)

(Poor women, poor women, stealing pork chops, while the
   government cooks poverty, we are going to fight, come
   what may).[34]

A shorter plena was performed by La Cole during their "Fogueo feminista," a musical agitation demonstration that took place on January 21, 2017, during the biggest yearly carnival in Puerto Rico, the Fiestas de la Calle San Sebastián.[35] The plena, which La Cole cites as a decolonization tool, centered abortion access in its lyrics: "Santa María, no te dejes engañar/El aborto es un derecho/el aborto es legal" (Saint Mary, don't be fooled. Abortion is a right, abortion is legal). Another plena was their version of the popular plena "Cortaron a Elena": "Cortaron a Elena/Cortaron a Elena/ Cortaron a Elena cuando el aborto era illegal" (They cut Elena/They cut Elena/They cut Elena when abortion was illegal).[36] La Cole described the event as an "exercise in denunciation" as well as collective resistance.[37] While the crowds went up the cobblestone streets of Old San Juan to join the festivities, members and collaborators of La Cole distributed condoms and sang what they called "rearticulated" songs to share their message.[38]

These examples draw into relief how La Cole's campaigns and performances serve multiple purposes: they function as a vehicle to raise awareness for the general population and create possibilities for networks of solidarities that function as resistance and, as Judith Butler (2018) writes, form, "new sources of support, articulating a new movement to overcome colonial rule" (17). They also constitute a praxis of resistance toward the state, which acts as an accomplice to private capital, embodying a decolonial praxis that places front and center the demands of those the state has marked as disposable: poor, Black women and femmes (Zambrana 2021).

La Cole in Transnational Dialogue with Feminist Movements

The fight against multiple systems of oppression such as colonialism, patriarchy, capitalism, and anti-Black violence is a transnational struggle.[39] Alexander and Mohanty (1997: xix) conceptualize the transnational as a lens to "think about women in similar contexts across the world, in *different* geographical spaces," while attending to their specific local conditions. Yet the transnational is also "an understanding of unequal relationships among and between peoples" framed within and "in relation to an analysis of economic, political, and ideological processes which foreground operations of race and capitalism" (xix). La Cole understands itself as part of the larger context of anti-racist, anti-capitalist struggles in Latin America and collaborates with feminist groups from Central America, South America, and the Caribbean. Shariana notes, "In a certain way, we are creating these networks and these transnational articulations on a regional [Caribbean] level and also trying to catalyze it on an international level."[40]

La Cole has been attentive to feminist organizing in other countries and is part of La Internacional Feminista, a coalition of popular feminist movements that began in Latin America. As a representative of La Cole, Shariana has participated in activist meetings in Bolivia, Brazil, and Uruguay. The International Women's Day march and demonstration on March 8 were part of a larger coordination within La Internacional Feminista, with several organizations from different countries holding their own demonstrations that highlighted their own local contexts and demands.

Through her experiences and collaboration with other feminists in Latin America, Shariana has been able to share and receive material on mobilization strategies. She gave the example of some *compañeras* in Brazil who organized the Women's Spring,[41] which served as inspiration for La Cole's Feminist Spring. La Cole then organized a Feminist Tide on May Day 2017. Comrades from Panamá contacted La Cole and mentioned that they wanted to carry out a Feminist Spring, and in response La Cole gave them materials to support their campaign.

La Cole has also studied social movements in other countries and territories. The 2009 general strikes in the French overseas territories of Guadeloupe and Martinique served as a guide to La Cole's anti-colonial organizing work. The general strike began in Guadeloupe in January, prompted by union leaders, and later expanded to include a coalition of activists, artists, and civil society actors (Bonilla 2015: 151). Days later, in the nearby island of Martinique, protesters took to the streets to protest the high cost of living and the neocolonial conditions they experience (Maddox 2015). Although ultimately the strikes did not create a radical shift in the structural conditions for those living in these French Antilles, they provided a concrete example of what successful organizing *processes* could look like in the Caribbean. While many were disappointed with the outcome, Puerto

Rican anthropologist Yarimar Bonilla (2015: 173) notes that, in the case of Guadeloupe, the general strike "fostered feelings of empowerment, exposed them to the pleasures of collective action, stirred their desire for alternative models of community and political action, and emboldened their search for small-scale forms of ordinary change."

La Cole's formulation of strategies also emerges from direct exchanges with other comrades in Latin America. By utilizing strategies such as the *cacerolazo* (a mobilization tactic that began in South America),[42] La Cole mobilizes the domestic into the public sphere and remains in dialogue with broader Latin American feminist movements. For example, the strike that La Cole organized on March 8, 2017, was part of a larger global International Working Women's Day campaign. La Cole is connected to a transnational feminist activist network that shares ideas, tactics, and strategies for mobilization through social media and other virtual means while also organizing in their own localities. The "Construyamos Otra Vida" was partially inspired by a campaign against the dictatorship in Chile. Uruguay passed three laws that La Cole cites as influential to their work: the decriminalization of abortion, the legalization of marijuana, and marriage equality for gay and lesbian partners. In South American countries such as Argentina, feminists went on strike on March 8, 2017, declaring "¡Ni una más! Vivas nos queremos!" (Not one more, we want each other alive!) to protest gender-based violence and femicides (Gago 2018). La Cole has also incorporated this slogan in their protests, as well as the phrase "Si nosotras paramos, el país se detiene" (If we strike, the country stands still). Economic, social, cultural, and political claims converged on March 8, as Shariana explains: "We strike for health, we strike against the Fiscal Control Board, we strike against the labor reform law, WE STRIKE BECAUSE WE DEMAND A LIFE WITH DIGNITY."[43]

In 2017, La Cole began a campaign titled "¡Abortemos el sistema, construyamos otra vida!"[44] as part of the International Safe Abortion Day/Día Internacional de la Despenalización del Aborto. Although not as successful as other campaigns, due in large part to the recent passing of Hurricane María, La Cole carried out activities such as facilitating healing circles in affected communities and occupying and converting an abandoned house into a community center in Río Piedras.[45] In September 2018, La Cole led a pressure campaign to protest the proposal of P950, a Senate bill that would heavily restrict abortion access and place a forty-eight-hour waiting period on those seeking an abortion. The bill also created twelve criminal offenses related to abortion, banned abortion after twenty weeks, and placed restrictions on people under twenty-one seeking abortions. The project was supported by senators known to be religious fundamentalists. On September 28, 2018, La Cole mobilized to protest the bill and wore green bandanas in solidarity with the Argentinian vote to decriminalize abortion.[46] During public hearings, La Cole was denied access and forcefully taken out of the room.[47] Ultimately, the bill did not pass, and Governor Ricardo Rosselló said he would not sign a bill that limited women's rights.[48]

La Cole's transnational connections with other anti-racist, decolonial, and radical feminist organizations across the hemisphere, together with their incessant organizing and political education work in the archipelago, articulate the possibilities for a decolonial praxis of solidarity across borders (Mohanty 2003). This praxis recognizes common struggles as well as differences in the local and specific contexts of these struggles. A powerful manifestation of these linkages was seen in the 2021 RFS held virtually due to the COVID-19 pandemic. Although the pandemic exacerbated the precarious conditions of the most vulnerable in the archipelago, this virtual space allowed feminists of all ages and corners of the globe to participate. A total of 329 people from 14 Latin American countries signed up for the RFS, their biggest turnout yet.

The Feminist Plantón, State of Emergency, and #RickyRenuncia

On November 23, 2018, La Cole carried out a feminist plantón, or sit-in, in front of the governor's mansion, La Fortaleza. They demanded that Governor Rosselló declare a state of emergency via executive order to address the alarming number of femicides in Puerto Rico—twenty-three women at that time with others still under investigation. Around that time, eighty-two police officers were being investigated for gender violence in Puerto Rico.[49] Their own executive order addressed gender violence and called on agency directors to create concrete plans to address the emergency and assign funds for educational campaigns.[50] Members of La Cole spent two nights in front of the governor's mansion, holding concerts, children's activities, and workshops to educate the public about gender-based violence. Tourists took photos of themselves in front of La Fortaleza, with the protest in the background, seemingly oblivious or apathetic to the sit-in.

Rosselló did not meet with members of La Cole; instead, the Procuradora de la Mujer (women's advocate) sat down with two members of La Cole. Nothing came of it. At one point, the protest became tense when police officers started struggling with demonstrators by pulling a barricade away and using pepper spray; one plain clothes officer used his baton on protesters. These events were recorded on social media so that those not physically present could share, repost, and call international attention to the situation.

La Cole continued to call for the declaration of a state of emergency regarding the alarming number of femicides in Puerto Rico, even after the ousting of Governor Ricardo Rosselló.[51] Rosselló's unelected successor, Wanda Vázquez Garced, also refused to declare a state of emergency, even after meeting on repeated occasions with members of La Cole. La Cole continued to hold demonstrations and campaigns pushing for a plan to address gender violence in the archipelago. On January 24, 2021, newly elected pro-statehood Governor Pedro Pierluisi finally signed an executive order declaring a state of emergency.[52] However, the lack of implementation of the executive order led La Cole to stage another plantón, on May 3, 2021. They demanded to know "¿Dónde está el estado de emergencia?" (Where is the state of emergency?). The sit-in launched a week of intense protests convened by La Cole all over the archipelago, many of which were decentralized and organized by young feminists.[53]

Along with activism around gender violence and trans/femicides in the archipelago, La Cole has led the shift in anti-colonial and radical organizing. In the past few years, various queer and self-described intersectional groups have emerged, such as Espicy Nipples, Editorial Casa Cuna, and La Sombrilla Cuir. These groups have very active presences on social media, where they merge educational campaigns about queer and trans issues with art and workshops through an anti-racist and transfeminist lens. During the first months of the COVID-19 pandemic, feminist pantries were established in different towns around the main island. Some of the members of these organizations are collaborators of La Cole as well. La Cole's impact continues to reverberate in all corners of the archipelago.

Conclusion

La Cole's protest repertoires represent a rupture in the Puerto Rican activist landscape. The organization has shifted protest politics through the resignification and adaptation of popular and folkloric music into protest chants and songs, yet their pedagogical intervention goes beyond this. Their tactics and ways of mobilizing are "a different way of doing politics" (Phillips and Cole 2013: 13), a way that the government is forced to look at, to answer and contend with, even if they refuse to acquiesce to La Cole's demands. La Cole joins the anti-globalization and feminist movements across the Global South in creating "new discursive and political conditions of possibility" (Juris 2012: 273). Whether through legislation restricting abortion access and marriage equality or limiting education with a gender perspective, conservative and Christian fundamentalist lawmakers in Puerto Rico have "abandoned to precarity or left to die through systematic negligence" the most vulnerable sectors of the population (Butler 2015: 81). La Cole continues to work for those very sectors: those that are displaced, dispossessed, and harmed by colonial necropolitics.

Although La Cole has impacted Puerto Rico's political landscape, the organization, and Shariana in particular, are targets of a mostly conservative, anti-Black, and homophobic set of detractors. For instance, in the comments section in online news articles about La Cole—as well as the group's Facebook page which details their activism and demonstrations— many people denounce, insult, and demean the organization and its members. Insults about body shape and size, Blackness, and queerness are particularly hurled at Shariana. These opinions mirror much of Puerto Rican society, which has yet to face its own legacies of racism, homophobia, and patriarchy perpetuated through colonialism and coloniality.

Due to and despite its colonial status, it is important to locate Puerto Rico within Latin American feminist assemblages that push against colonial legacies of modernity such as racism, heterosexism, and capitalism. La Cole's members are actively forging a decolonial praxis through the construction of another life by embodying "cultures of dissent," at the margins, through collective practices (Alexander and Mohanty 1997). Perhaps more than other anti-colonial or radical organizations of recent times, La Cole has impacted Puerto Rico's national politics. Although they are in contentious opposition to the government, "their goal is not to replace the state but to construct an alternative society" (Verdesoto 1986: 187). In addition to demanding "basic needs," La Cole seeks to confront the state by shaping national discourse around gender violence as well as the effects of colonial austerity measures on poor, Black (cis and trans) women, and femmes.

Through their pedagogy and activism, La Cole continues to fight for the lives of those that the state renders invisible or those that the state exposes to premature death. As Vanesa and Shariana mentioned, La Cole has nothing to lose, because Puerto Rico is already in social, financial, and political collapse. By taking on la colonia, la Junta, y el patriarcado, La Cole shows us the urgency, possibility, and reality of building another life, collectively.

Aurora Santiago Ortiz is an assistant professor of gender and women's studies and Chicane/Latine studies at the University of Wisconsin–Madison. Her research focuses on decolonial and anti-racist feminisms; community-based, participatory action research; and critical methodologies.

Notes

1   "Antipatriarchal, feminist, lesbian, trans, Caribbean, Latin American." Adapted from the Bolivian feminist band Las Conchudas' song "Las Pibas Chongas." Their version does not have trans included. https://www.youtube.com/watch?v=1UFZ3Axd8Kg.

2   I was hesitant whether to join the protest and sit down or continue photographing the events. I chose the latter, to bear witness to the events, and record state officials. I thought that having the footage could be useful in case any of the feminists were arrested. There is a known history of the police using excessive and repressive force against protestors. See LeBrón 2019.

3   Two years prior, on June 30, 2016, President Barack Obama signed the Puerto Rico Oversight, Management, and Economic Stability Act (PROMESA or promise, by its initials, taken to be a highly cynical gesture), in response to the Puerto Rican government's inability to repay its debt to bondholders. PROMESA designated an unelected Fiscal Oversight and Management Board (FOMB), whose members are designated by US Congress to restructure Puerto Rico's debt, which is approximately $129.2 billion. The FOMB dictated the increase of the cost of potable water and electricity, as well as budget cuts to the archipelago's only public higher education institution, the University of Puerto Rico, among other measures.

4   In a follow-up interview on December 6, 2018, Shariana confirmed this.

5   Ferrer Núñez and Contreras are cofounders of La Cole and because they are the most visible figures in La Cole, I did not use pseudonyms with them. I did so with the rest of the members of La Cole. As of late 2019, Contreras exited La Cole. Sara, Cristina, and Rita are pseudonyms.

6   Interview, Sara, March 2018.

7   This article was written in 2018–19 and submitted in 2020. I have subsequently included some of La Cole's later activism and work during the revision process.

8   https://www.elnuevodia.com/noticias/locales/notas/la-colectiva-feminista-reclama-pronta-accion-del-comite-pare-contra-la-violencia-de-genero/.

9   https://www.teenvogue.com/story/la-colectiva-feminista-en-construccion-is-helping-puerto-rico-recover-from-hurricane-maria.

10   See Pelota Dura, https://www.facebook.com/UnivisionPuertoRico/videos/284444922201343/.

11   Interview, March 15, 2018.

12   Interview, March 15, 2018.

13   "La Manifesta," https://es.scribd.com/document/263057948/La-Manifiesta-Colectiva-Feminista-en-Construccion.

14 Interview, March 15, 2018.
15 *La Manifiesta*, https://es.scribd.com/document/263057948/La-Manifiesta
    -Colectiva-Feminista-en-Construccion.
16 https://www.colectivafeminista.org/quienes-somos.
17 https://www.latinorebels.com/2020/06/07/antiracistmanifesto/.
18 https://www.colectivafeminista.org/nuestras-referentes.
19 *Tacón de la Chancleta—Año Internacional de la Mujer* 1, no. 4, Mayo–Junio 1975.
20 https://www.elvocero.com/gobierno/van-los-d-as-de-ayuno-y-de-oraci-n
    /article_6d73cafb-fd4e-544d-8ba1-cb1d513cc3c8.html.
21 metro.pr/pr/noticias/2018/07/16/personas-trans-podran-cambiar-genero-
    certificados-nacimiento.html.
22 https://www.english.tallersalud.com/iniciatives.
23 Shariana, personal communication, February 6, 2020.
24 The racial triad is Taíno, African, Spanish.
25 Ley 4 del 26 de enero de 2017, www.lexjuris.com/LexLex/Leyes2017/lexl2017004
    .pdf.
26 Interview, Sara, March 2018.
27 This was in 2020.
28 Cristina, Interview, March 2018.
29 https://www.metro.pr/pr/noticias/2018/03/08/protestan-las-mujeres-capitolio
    .html.
30 In late 2021, O'Neill pled guilty to sexual harassment in the workforce, gender
    violence, and violating the Governmental Ethics Code. However, many of the
    charges against O'Neill were dropped. https://www.elnuevodia.com/noticias
    /tribunales/notas/hector-oneill-se-declara-culpable-en-caso-por-violencia-de
    -genero-y-hostigamiento-sexual/.
31 https://www.primerahora.com/noticias/gobierno-politica/nota/activista
    queincrepoaoneillhacellamadoanocallar-1226988/.
32 Sara (pseud.) is no longer a member of La Cole.
33 https://www.primerahora.com/noticias/gobierno-politica/nota/revel
    anelusoqueseleestadandoa204escuelascerradas-1314821/.
34 The original "El jolgorio" is written by Alfonso Vélez.
35 The event date also coincided with the Women's March in the US, as the Face-
    book description of the event noted.
36 https://dialogo.upr.edu/suena-la-plena-en-el-fogueo-feminista/.
37 https://www.facebook.com/events/1416874811658511/.
38 https://www.facebook.com/events/1416874811658511/.
39 Personal communication with Shariana, December 2018.
40 Shariana, interview, March 15, 2018.
41 Women and femmes took to the streets of Brazil to protest a bill that would
    limit women's access to abortion in the case of rape: http://www.elnuevoherald
    .com/noticias/mundo/america-latina/article44766003.html.
42 Consisting of banging pots and pans to call attention as a form of protest.
43 https://fb.watch/teiqG_p8bU/?mibextid=w8EBqM.

44 Let's abort the system! Let's build another life!

45 https://www.teenvogue.com/story/la-colectiva-feminista-en-construccion-is
    -helping-puerto-rico-recover-from-hurricane-maria.

46 https://www.publico.es/internacional/legalizacion-aborto-panuelos-verdes
    -continuan-lucha-argentina-pesar-opresion-iglesia-muerte-abortos
    -clandestinos.html.

47 https://www.telemundo51.com/noticias/puerto-rico/Con-golpes-y-empujones
    -termina-manifestacion-en-vista-de-aborto-492528541.html.

48 https://www.elnuevodia.com/noticias/politica/nota/rossellovuelveaexpresar
    seencontradelcontroversialproyectosobreelaborto-2445671/.

49 https://www.elnuevodia.com/noticias/seguridad/nota/investigana82policiaspor
    violenciadegenero-2465972/?fbclid=IwAR0QEmpCdUN0Bwx1hR56O24oho
    FeBHaLhHevHZ-2hdQWAQJsR6tb4jIB4qc.

50 https://www.facebook.com/Colectiva.Feminista.PR/videos/268776747174314/.

51 After more than two weeks of sustained protests as a result of leaked Telegram
    chats where Rosselló and a group of his cabinet members and advisors wrote
    homophobic, fatphobic, and misogynist statements about public figures and pri-
    vate citizens, including Shariana. The chats showed how Hurricane María's dead
    were also used as publicity pawns by the Puerto Rican government. After suffering
    through months without electricity and water, enduring school closings and wide-
    spread government corruption, the people of Puerto Rico had had enough. The
    protests marked a shift in Puerto Rico's protest landscape, as Puerto Rican flags
    with pride colors as well as trans pride flags were front and center at the demon-
    strations. Drag balls were held as a form of protest, and feminist groups, includ-
    ing La Cole, were present. This was an uprising that centered on identity politics,
    rather than Puerto Rico's ongoing debate about its political status and future.

52 https://www.fortaleza.pr.gov/content/gobernador-declara-estado-de
    -emergencia-por-violencia-de-g-nero.

53 https://nacla.org/puerto-rico-state-emergency-femicides.

Works Cited

Alexander, M. Jacqui. 2006. *Pedagogies of Crossing: Meditations on Feminism, Sexual Politics,
    Memory, and the Sacred.* Durham, NC: Duke University Press.

Alexander, M. Jacqui, and Chandra Talpade Mohanty. 1997. "Introduction: Genealo-
    gies, Legacies, Movements." In *Feminist Genealogies, Colonial Legacies, and Democratic
    Futures,* xiii–xlii. New York: Routledge.

Azize Vargas, Yamila, ed. 1987. *La mujer en Puerto Rico: Ensayos de investigación.* San Juan,
    PR: Huracán.

Bonilla, Yarimar. 2015. *Non-sovereign Futures: French Caribbean Politics in the Wake of Disen-
    chantment.* Chicago: University of Chicago Press.

Butler, Judith. 2015. *Notes toward a Performative Theory of Assembly.* Cambridge, MA: Har-
    vard University Press.

Collins, Patricia Hill. 2000. *Black Feminist Thought: Knowledge, Consciousness, and the Poli-
    tics of Empowerment.* New York: Routledge.

Combahee River Collective. 1982. *A Black Feminist Statement.* Boston. https://we.riseup
.net/assets/43875/versions/1/combahee%25252oriver.pdf.

Crenshaw, Kimberlé. 1990. "Mapping the Margins: Intersectionality, Identity Politics, and Violence against Women of Color." *Stanford Law Review* 43, no. 6:
1241–79.

Crenshaw, Kimberlé. 2001. "The Intersectionality of Race and Gender Discrimination." In *Race, Ethnicity, Gender, and Human Rights in America: A New Paradigm for Activism*, edited by Celiany Romany. Puerto Rico: American University; Universidad Interamericana de Puerto Rico.

Crespo Kebler, Elizabeth. 2001. "Ciudadanía y nación: Debates sobre los derechos reproductivos en Puerto Rico." *Revista de ciencias sociales-Nueva Época* 10: 57–84.

Curiel, Ochy. 2002. "Identidades esencialistas o construcción de identidades políticas: El dilemma de las feministas negras." *Otras miradas* 2: 96–113.

Curiel Pichardo, Ochy. 2014. "Construyendo metodologías feministas desde el feminismo decolonial." In *Otras formas de (re)conocer: Reflexiones, herramientas, y aplicaciones desde la investigación feminista*, edited by Irantzu Mendia Azku, Marta Luxán, Matxalen Legarreta, Gloria Guzmán, Iker Zirion, and Jokin Azpiazu Carballo, 45–60. Universidad del País Vasco: Hegoa.

Dávila, Arlene M. 1997. *Sponsored Identities: Cultural Politics in Puerto Rico.* Philadelphia: Temple University Press.

Espinosa Miñoso, Yuderkys. 2016. "De por qué es necesario a feminismo decolonial: Diferenciación, dominación co-constitutiva de la modernidad occidental y el fin de la política de identidad." *Solar* 12, no. 1: 141–71.

Espinosa Miñoso, Yuderkys. 2021. "And the One Doesn't Stir without the Other: Decoloniality, Anti-racism, and Feminism." *Women's Studies Quarterly* 49: 100–116.

Feldman, Allen. 1995. "On Cultural Anesthesia." *American Ethnologist* 21, no. 2: 404–18.

Franco-Ortiz, Mariluz. 2018. "Intersecciones en el trabajo antirracista con mujeres desde el Colectivo ilé en PR." In ¡*Negro, negra!: Afirmación y resistencia. Memorias del Primer Congreso de la Afrodescendencia en Puerto Rico*, edited by Afrodescendencia en Puerto Rico. Río Piedras, PR: UPR Río Piedras.

Gago, Verónica. 2018. "La tierra tiembla." *Critical Times* 1, no. 1.

Gago, Verónica, Marta Malo, and Luci Cavallero. 2020. *La internacional feminista. Luchas en los territorios.* Madrid: Traficantes de Sueños.

Godreau, Isar. 2015. *Scripts of Blackness: Race, Cultural Nationalism, and US Colonialism in Puerto Rico.* Urbana: University of Illinois Press.

Gómez-Quintero, Juan David. 2010. "La colonialidad del ser y del saber: La mitologización del desarrollo en América Latina." *El ágora USB* 10, no. 1: 87–105.

Howard, Karen. 2019. "Puerto Rican Plena: The Power of a Song." *General Music Today* 32, no. 2: 36–39.

Juris, Jeffrey. 2008. *Networking Futures: The Movements against Corporate Globalization.* Durham, NC: Duke University Press.

Juris, Jeffrey. 2012. "Reflections on #Occupy Everywhere: Social Media, Public Space, and Emerging Logics of Aggregation." *American Ethnologist* 39, no. 2: 259–79.

La Fountain-Stokes, Lawrence. 2018. "Recent Developments in Queer Puerto Rican History, Politics, and Culture." *Centro: Journal of the Center for Puerto Rican Studies* 30, no. 2: 502–40.

Lavoy Zoungbo, Victorien, ed. 2011. "Maria Ramos Rosado: Catedrática Universidad de Puerto Rico, Recinto de Río Piedras (Porto Rico)." In *Bartolomé de las Casas: Face à l'esclavage des Noir-e-s en Amériques/Caraïbes. L'aberration du onzième remède (1516)*. Perpignan, France: Presses universitaires de Perpignan.

LeBrón, Marisol. 2019. *Policing Life and Death: Race, Violence, and Resistance in Puerto Rico*. Oakland: University of California Press.

Lloréns, Hilda. 2021. *Making Livable Worlds: Afro-Puerto Rican Women Building Environmental Justice*. Seattle: University of Washington Press.

Lugones, María. 2010. "Toward a Decolonial Feminism." *Hypatia* 25, no. 4: 742–59.

Maddox, Camee. 2015. "'Yes We Can! Down with Colonization!' Race, Gender, and the 2009 General Strike in Martinique." *Transforming Anthropology* 23, no. 2: 90–103.

Mohanty, Chandra T. 2003. *Feminism without Borders: Decolonizing Theory, Practicing Solidarity*. Durham, NC: Duke University Press.

Negrón-Muntaner, Frances. 2018. "'Can You Imagine?' Puerto Rican Lesbian Activisms, 1972–1991." *Centro: Journal of the Center for Puerto Rican Studies* 30, no. 2: 348–77.

Ostolaza Bey, Margarita. 1989. *Política sexual en Puerto Rico*. San Juan, PR: Huracán.

Paschel, Tianna S. 2016. *Becoming Black Political Subjects: Movements and Ethno-racial Rights in Colombia and Brazil*. Princeton, NJ: Princeton University Press.

Phillips, Lynne, and Sally Cole. 2013. *Contesting Publics: Feminism, Activism, Ethnography*. London: Pluto Press.

Quijano, Anibal. 2000. "Coloniality of Power and Eurocentrism in Latin America." *International Sociology* 15, no. 2: 215–32.

Reinat Pumarejo, María. 2018. "Colectivo Ilé. África en mi piel, África en mi ser: Forjando metodologías antirracistas y descolonizadoras." In *¡Negro, Negra!: Afirmación y resistencia. Memorias del Primer Congreso de la Afrodescendencia en Puerto Rico*, edited by Afrodescendencia en Puerto Rico. Río Piedras, PR: UPR Río Piedras.

Rivera Lassén, Ana Irma. 2016. "Afrodescendant Women: A Race and Gender Intersectional Spiderweb." Translated by Manuela Borzone and Alexander Ponomareff. *Meridians* 14, no. 2: 56–70.

Rivero, Yeidy M. 2005. *Tuning Out Blackness: Race and Nation in the History of Puerto Rican Television*. Durham, NC: Duke University Press.

Saunders, Tanya L. 2009. "La Lucha Mujerista: Krudas CUBENSI and Black Feminist Sexual Politics in Cuba." *Caribbean Review of Gender Studies*, November. http://sta.uwi.edu/crgs/november2009/journals/CRGS%20Las%20Krudas.pdf.

Saunders, Tanya L. 2012. "Black Thoughts, Black Activism: Cuban Underground Hip Hop and Afro-Latino Countercultures of Modernity." *Latin American Perspectives* 39, no. 2: 42–60.

Torres Martinez, Lizandra. 2004. *Retos de la autonomía: Micro historias feministas*. San Juan, PR: Gaviota.

Verdesoto Custode, Luis. 1986. "Los movimientos sociales y la crisis de democracia en Ecuador." In *Los Movimientos sociales ante la crisis*, edited by Fernando G. Calderón. Buenos Aires: Universidad de las Naciones Unidas.

Walsh, Catherine. 2018. "The Decolonial For: Resurgences, Shifts, and Movements." In *On Decoloniality: Concepts, Analytics, Praxis*, edited by Catherine Walsh and Walter Mignolo, 15–32. Durham, NC: Duke University Press.

Zambrana, Rocío. 2021. *Colonial Debts: The Case of Puerto Rico*. Durham, NC: Duke University Press.

Umayyah Cable

. . . .

Coming Out for Community, Coming Out for the Cause

Queer Arab American Activism in the 1990s

Abstract: This article focuses on the life experience and political activism of Palestinian American lesbian activist Huda Jadallah as a representative example of how lesbian, gay, bisexual, and transgender (LGBT/queer) Arab Americans came out to both queer communities and Arab American communities in the 1980s and 1990s. The author argues that this dual outness was utilized as a strategy through which to accomplish three interrelated aims: to build a queer Arab American community, utilize that community as a starting point from which to challenge anti-Arab racism within queer communities, and challenge homophobia in Arab American communities. Based on an oral history interview with Jadallah, in conjunction with analysis of Jadallah's personal ephemera collection, this article takes a queer archiving methodological approach to consider how outness as strategy may also be utilized with regard to queer Arab American archiving and history.

On June 8, 1989, approximately eighty women gathered at the Women's Building in the heart of San Francisco's Mission District to attend a community forum, "The Palestinian Uprising and the Lesbian Community: An Evening for Lesbians about Palestine" (Jadallah 1990: 5). Cosponsored by the activist groups Lesbians in Solidarity with the Palestinian People (LISPP) and the Arab Lesbian Network (ALN), the forum was hosted by ALN founder Huda Jadallah and another Bay Area feminist activist (ALN and LISPP 1989b). According to the flyer that advertised the event (see fig. 1), the forum set out to cover four interrelated issues: "the roots of the

MERIDIANS · feminism, race, transnationalism 23:2 October 2024
DOI: 10.1215/15366936-11266340 © 2024 Smith College

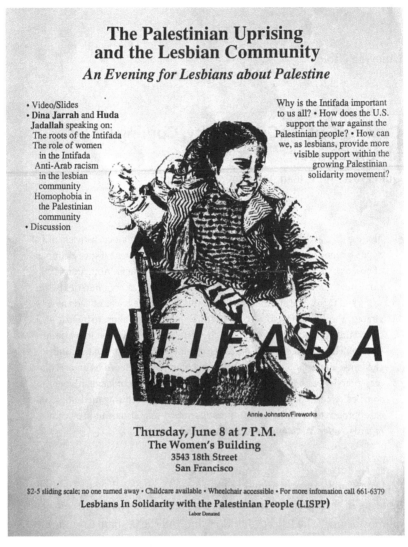

The Palestinian Uprising
and the Lesbian Community

An Evening for Lesbians about Palestine

• Video/Slides
• **Dina Jarrah** and **Huda
Jadallah** speaking on:
The roots of the Intifada
The role of women
in the Intifada
Anti-Arab racism
in the lesbian
community
Homophobia in
the Palestinian
community
• Discussion

Why is the Intifada important
to us all? • How does the U.S.
support the war against the
Palestinian people? • How can
we, as lesbians, provide more
visible support within the
growing Palestinian
solidarity movement?

INTIFADA

Annie Johnston/Fireworks

Thursday, June 8 at 7 P.M.
The Women's Building
3543 18th Street
San Francisco

$2-5 sliding scale; no one turned away • Childcare available • Wheelchair accessible • For more infomation call 661-6379
Lesbians In Solidarity with the Palestinian People (LISPP)
Labor Donated

Figure 1. Flyer advertising "The Palestinian Uprising and the Lesbian Community" event. June 8, 1989.

intifada, the role of women in the intifada, anti-Arab racism in the lesbian community, [and] homophobia in the Palestinian community." The flyer features an artist's rendering of a young girl with the word intifada printed across the lower portion of the image. The girl's face expresses a wincing grin and furrowed brow of concentration as she stretches her arm behind her, poised to throw a stone. Her body language is represented as open, active, and determined. In the background, an elderly woman looks on with mouth agape and the suggestion of an outstretched arm, perhaps offering simultaneous encouragement and concern for the girl's safety. Or perhaps she too wields a stone.

Posted on telephone poles and bulletin boards in coffee shops, groceries, and bookstores throughout the Mission and Castro neighborhoods, the flyer served to hail two ostensibly distinct yet overlapping communities: lesbians and Arab Americans. The Castro and Mission neighborhoods have served as important sites for both lesbian and Arab American communities. The Women's Building in the Mission served as a community space for feminist and lesbian activism, while in both the Castro and Mission neighborhoods an established community of Arab American small business owners made these neighborhoods socially and economically significant for the Arab American community (Rafkin 2012). Although directed specifically toward the lesbian community, the forum's topic of Palestine would certainly have caught the attention of Arab American community members who frequented local businesses.

The flyer thus served a dual educational purpose: to represent and relate the topic of Palestine for the wider lesbian community while also signaling lesbians as potential allies—and making Arab lesbian existence visible— to the wider Arab American community. For non-Arab lesbians reading the flyer who did not know the meaning of the word *intifada*, the image provided visual cues indicating it as a form of uprising that is inherently feminist in nature by representing an image of Palestinian feminist resistance to the US-backed Israeli occupation, which contradicted deeply entrenched Orientalist stereotypes about Arab women as tragically oppressed and in need of rescue through the machinations of US imperialism (Jarmakani 2008: 9–12). For Arab Americans reading the flyer, it signaled both the existence of organized lesbian solidarity with the Palestinian liberation cause, while simultaneously indexing the existence of Arab lesbians. Put another way, this simple flyer performed the dual work of outing Palestine and Palestinians to the lesbian community as relevant to intersectional feminist politics and lesbian of color activism, while also outing Arab lesbian existence to the Arab American community in a way that demonstrated the potential for further development of Palestine solidarity throughout the broader queer community.

In addition to the visual elements, the flyer's text posed a series of rhetorical questions geared toward the event's potential lesbian audience:

"Why is the Intifada important to us all? How does the US support the war against the Palestinian people? How can we, as lesbians, provide more visible support within the growing Palestinian solidarity movement?" By grammatically posing the questions from the perspective of non-Arab lesbians situated in the US, the flyer rhetorically implicated potential attendees within the matrix of issues that the forum sought to address.

This flyer and the event it promoted offers an example of how lesbian, gay, bisexual, and transgender (LGBT, referred to as *queer* from here on) Arab American activists mobilized coming out, on multiple identity registers, as a strategy in the service of community building and social justice activism. For lesbian Arab Americans like Jadallah, this strategy of coming out was not limited to sexuality and its accompanying cultural politics, it also meant coming out as Palestinian, along with accompanying cultural politics, Palestine solidarity included. From the late 1980s through the early 1990s, Jadallah and others strategically deployed this outness in order to accomplish three interrelated goals: 1) to formally organize a queer Arab American community and social life, in order to 2) challenge Arab invisibility and anti-Arab racism (Jarmakani 2015: 122) within the broader queer community, and 3) challenge homophobia and lesbian erasure within the Arab American community.[1] This was a dual outing process, and it involved coming out of two closets: the closet of compulsory heterosexuality and the closet of compulsory Zionism.

Radical Biography, Archival Outness, Archiving Outness

Before delving into analysis, it is necessary to explain the archival context of this flyer, its methodological significance in terms of queer Arab American archiving, and the role of radical biography in queer Arab American history. This article is based on my interview with Jadallah in conjunction with analysis of Jadallah's personal ephemera collection, aforementioned flyer included. Jadallah's life experience as a Palestinian American lesbian and her activism within the San Francisco queer and Arab American communities serves as a representative (but by no means comprehensive) example of some of the social activities, as well as political strategies and goals, among queer Arab Americans during the 1980s and 1990s. This flyer serves as both a record of some of those strategies and goals, and it is also an artifact of queer Arab American outness.

Jadallah was born in San Francisco in 1964 and raised in the Bay Area after her parents had emigrated from Ramallah, Palestine, in the early

1960s. Her family's primary social network was that of an extended Arab, mostly Palestinian immigrant community. Like many Palestinian families in the region at the time, Jadallah's parents owned a corner store. She recalls that much casual socializing among the community took place in Palestinian-owned corner stores and groceries throughout the Bay, of which there were numerous in the Mission and Castro districts: it was not uncommon to just hang out in the stores of family friends and relatives. This social and economic network endowed Jadallah with a strong sense of Palestinian identity. Jadallah came to consciousness about her sexuality in her first year of college, wherein she began to identify as bisexual; after coming out and engaging more visibly in political activism in the 1980s, Jadallah made a deliberate choice to identify as lesbian for political reasons. After graduate school, she worked for United Against Violence, an openly LGBT-focused nonprofit organization, wherein she served as an advocate for victims of gay bashing. Although she had been out within the queer community for some time, the aforementioned lesbian forum on Palestine and her desire to cross-pollinate queer activism and Palestine solidarity activism was the catalyst for Jadallah's coming out to her family and by extension the larger Arab community.

My focus on Jadallah's story is partially a consequence of certain archival limitations. It is also partially an intentional effort to tell an *out* queer Arab American history, or put another way, a history of queer Arab American outness. These limitations and intentions raise four important methodological questions: How do we address outness with regard to queer Arab American subjectivity, a group that has largely rejected the outness paradigm as colonialist in nature and which requires and reifies certain racial, class, and gender privileges? How does one conduct historical, archival research of queer Arab American social life and political activism that occurred during a moment in time that could arguably be described as a "threshold" period, or a moment of organized emergence from the closet? How does one conduct this research when faced with a dearth of officially out (i.e., specifically cataloged as LGBT/queer) archival materials? And lastly, what is the "stuff" of out queer Arab American history and how do we collect, manage, and store those materials?

The field of Arab American studies is experiencing a moment of methodological intervention regarding the aforementioned questions, and which radically transforms the very methodological premises of the field itself. Charlotte Karem Albrecht and Mejdulene B. Shomali provide two distinct yet related queer analytical tools by which to undertake queer Arab American studies in ethically and intellectually nuanced ways. Thanks to Karem Albrecht, the existence and social lives of Arab Americans who engaged in same-sex—or even merely non-heteronormative—sexual and romantic relationships in the early twentieth century, long before the advent of contemporary sexual identity-based social movements, is a given. In *Possible Histories: Arab Americans and the Queer Ecology of Peddling*, Karem Albrecht's (2023: 4) method of "historically grounded imagining" offers ways to approach Arab American archival material (previously assumed to be heteronormative) and conduct reparative reading of that material, thereby weaving the lives queer Arab Americans back into the fabric of early Arab American history. Through this analytic, Karem Albrecht reminds us that queerness is always a possibility in archival research. In *Between Banat: Queer Arab Critique and Transnational Arab Archives*, Shomali (2023: 6) provides an analytic of "queer Arab critique" as a method and reading practice attuned to revealing queer Arab subjectivity and through which to "make and unmake queer Arab archives." In dealing with texts and materials both expressly labeled as or produced by those who openly identify as queer and those absent of openly queer identification, queer Arab critique accounts for the ambivalence toward LGBT identity categories while simultaneously identifying the possibilities of queerness even in the absence of outness. With these methodological interventions in mind, I analyze Jadallah's ephemera material in the service of archiving queer Arab outness, while respecting the ambivalence of all the unnamed actors present in these materials, and leaving open the possibility for those same actors to resurface elsewhere, archivally speaking, through historically grounded imagining and queer Arab critique.

Although highly specific, the importance of this focus and these materials is indicative of a queer archival methodology. Queer historicizing originated through the intentional amassing of otherwise overlooked materials, by way of paranoid or reparative reading (Sedgewick 2003) of seemingly heteronormative materials, or, as has become increasingly common, by literally placing private materials into public, institutional containers such as libraries and archives. Feminist and queer of color scholars argue that how we conceive of what an archive is and does must go "beyond a repository or storage of information and documents or a legitimizing instrument of power" and instead embrace the idea of an archive as "a space for dwelling and a quotidian site for marginalized subjects"

(Manalansan 2014: 94). In this sense, scholarship on queer archival methodology that emphasizes the historical import of ephemera informs my analysis of Jadallah's materials. For José Esteban Muñoz (1996: 6), ephemera functions as a kind of anti-evidence, in part because overt evidence of outness exposes queers to very real threats of violence. As such "instead of being clearly available as visible evidence, queerness has instead existed as innuendo, gossip, fleeting moments, and performances that are meant to be interacted with by those within its epistemological sphere—while evaporating at the touch of those who would eliminate queer possibility" (10). In *An Archive of Feelings*, Ann Cvetkovich (2003: 242) emphasizes how *ephemera* is a "term used by archivists and librarians to describe occasional publications and paper documents, material objects and items that fall into the *miscellaneous* category when being cataloged" (emphasis mine). The word *miscellaneous* itself denotes something of "mixed composition or character," and when in reference to a person, such as a writer or archivist, means "many-sided, non-specialist" (OED 2002). Something of a queer category in and of itself, Cvetkovich (2003: 243) argues that "in insisting on the value of marginal and ephemeral materials, the collectors of gay and lesbian archives propose that affects—associated with nostalgia, personal memory, fantasy and trauma—make a document significant." As a miscellaneous category, "ephemera" is, in many ways, a euphemism for "mess," and what is "mess" if not an untenably mixed composition; the visual, emotional, or organizational equivalent of nonspecialization; an object, pile, or person with many, often chaotic, sides.[2] It is this "mess, clutter, and muddled entanglements," argues Martin Manalansan, which, writing in the context of queer immigrant households, makes up "the 'stuff' of queerness, historical memory, aberrant desires, and the archive" (2014: 94). In this sense, Jadallah's personal collection of ephemera is significant because it is charged with the nostalgia and personal memory of her firsthand experience of the events and practices documented within the materials themselves, and because they are the literal "stuff" of her coming out as lesbian in the context of her life within an extended Arab American community.

Yet Jadallah's ephemera did not resemble mess or clutter in the way Manalansan describes. Her small collection of ephemera is labeled, it is organized, it lives tidily in a folder within a large file cabinet in her home office. I view her careful treatment of these materials less as a sign of pedantism and more as a sign of how she values herself, the respect she holds for her own history, and the bittersweet knowledge that if she doesn't archive these materials, who will? But there is more to Jadallah's careful collecting of these materials. When I asked if she would consider donating these materials to the GLBT Historical Society or ONE National Archives so that it could become part of official archival holdings and therefore part of the larger, out record of queer Arab American history, she revealed her true, most telling motivation for this stewardship. This file folder and its contents are not about preserving her ego, but rather she views this material as a kind of heirloom to pass on to her children in her eventual absence. She archives because she knows that there will be a time when her children will want to know who their mother was before they arrived on the scene, and she may very well not be around to tell them. Who was their mother before she became their mother? These materials, she hopes, will tell them: she existed, outly, as both Palestinian and lesbian at a time when it was difficult to be either, let alone both.

Jadallah's desire to retain her archival material speaks to Shomali's insistence on the ambivalence inherent to queer Arab archiving, namely on "the right of refusal and defiance and the right to privacy," things which are so "often denied Arab subjects, particularly in an Orientalist colonial project, which demands unveiling and discovery" (2023: 20). In this way, Jadallah's reluctance to institutionalize her materials prompts an additional methodological possibility. It reminds us that for every piece of out queer Arab American archival material found within an institutional archive, there is likely abundant ephemera stored within private filing cabinets, strewn about cluttered desks, stuffed in boxes, or hiding in the back of someone's literal closet. While the absence of these materials within institutional archives poses challenges for future scholars who must grapple with a "source deficit" (Pederson quoted in Edleberg 2015: 208; Marshall, Murphy, and Tortorici 2015: 6), it also poses an imperative for current scholars: we must talk to our elders before they are gone. My fascination with this period and thirst for knowledge indeed arises from my own sense of isolation as an out, queer Arab American youth in the 1990s. As such, oral history interviewing functions here not simply as an auxiliary method of documenting a life experience in the words of those who lived it, but also as a critical mode for accessing (with consent) private archival holdings and the transfer of "archival material from generation to generation" (Pederson quoted in Edleberg 2015: 208). That access, in the case of my interview with Jadallah, came in the way of invitation, through my invitation to interview her and in turn her inviting me into her home.

And with these invitations came the opportunity to cultivate intergenerational queer Arab kinship. In this way, queer archival methodology is crucial not only to the preserving and writing of queer Arab American history and presence, but in the cultivation and strengthening of a sense of extended queer Arab American community. Building queer Arab American community, as I will explore later in this article, was one of the central goals of utilizing outness as strategy. Likewise, archiving outness therefore operates with this same community-building goal in mind.

To that end, queer Arab Americans established a series of local collectives in numerous cities across the US throughout the late 1980s and 1990s in order to establish spaces for queer Arab American community and social life, and as was the case in the Bay Area, to undertake anti-imperial, anti-colonial, and other forms of social justice activism. Jadallah's story exemplifies how these groups employed a number of strategies, including intersectional feminist consciousness raising events such as the one previously mentioned hosted by LISPP and ALN, and increasing visibility through visual culture and engagements with the queer press. All together, these activities promoted greater levels of visibility and outspokenness on behalf of queer identities and cultural politics, which meant that queer Arab Americans were also becoming more visible to broader Arab American communities, and as was the case with Jadallah, necessitated a confrontation with homophobia within Arab leftist activism (Naber 2012: 52–59). As Jadallah's story illuminates, queer Arab American activism served triple duty: to challenge and dismantle anti-Arab racism and compulsory Zionism within the LGBT left, to challenge compulsory heterosexuality and disarm homophobia within the Arab American left, and to build a sense of community and social space for queer Arab Americans.

Coming Out as Strategy

From the group's founding, Jadallah had conceived of ALN and the work it performed as political in nature. For example, Jadallah recalled an incident in the late 1980s which served as a catalyst for her lesbian organizing in the service of Palestine solidarity activism. Leftist Arab American groups had organized a protest at the Israeli consulate in San Francisco, and Jadallah attended with a sign that prominently read "Arab Lesbians for a Free Palestine." She recalls a number of "straight Arab lefty men being really mad at me . . . acting like I was a traitor, and telling me I was hurting the cause. . . . and I remember telling one young man 'you know, 10% of San Francisco's population is going to be looking at my sign, not yours, and

giving a shit about what I have to say . . . If it's not a free Palestine for lesbians, then it's not a free Palestine for me" (Cable interview with Jadallah,
July 17, 2017). Although this anecdote relays a moment of conflict, moments
like these provided critical opportunities to reshape the Arab American
left's conception of what the liberation of Palestine should entail and
who that liberation was for. What Jadallah describes here is an example
of how she strategically utilized outness to subvert the politics of cultural
authenticity, which Naber argues constructs gender and sexual transgressions as a threat to Arab American identity, cultural politics, and activism
(2012: 93, 101). In this example, Jadallah's outness as lesbian is condemned
as irrelevant and harmful to the greater goal of generating solidarity
for the Palestinian liberation cause, with the hope of forcing her back into
the closet, thereby controlling her behavior. However, her reference to the
National Gay Task Force's then widely touted claim that 10 percent of the
US population was gay (Spiegelhalter 2015) deflates the notion that her
outness harms Palestine solidarity or liberation efforts by suggesting that
the very fact of her outness would be enough to pique the political interests
of any fellow queers who witnessed her sign. For the "Arab lefty men" who
confronted Jadallah, her outness was viewed as a liability, something
potentially damaging to the greater cause of Palestinian liberation. Homophobia was thereby justified as serving a greater cause. For Jadallah, outness posed an opportunity to expand both the network of Palestine solidarity activism, in this case to members of the queer community, and to expand
the parameters of the Palestinian liberation cause itself.

   This incident offers an example of how Jadallah leveraged coming out as
a distinct strategy to expand the Palestine liberation movement, both literally in terms of the number of people in support of the movement, and
figuratively in terms of how that liberation was itself to be conceived and
achieved. Yet, in Jadallah's words: "It was a lonely battle. It's a lonely process when you're the one forging that path . . . I was the only one holding a
[queer] sign." The loneliness of being one of the few out queer Arabs within
Arab leftist activism is also what motivated Jadallah to more formally organize the queer Arab community through the establishment of groups like
the Arab Lesbian Network.

Coming Out to Each Other: Building Community

The establishment of queer Arab American social groups worked in the service of both building queer Arab American community and as a foundation

from which to conduct certain forms of out queer Arab American activism. Numerous groups formed during the 1990s and into the new millennium to provide social support for queer Arab Americans who felt alienated by anti-Arab racism within broader LGBT social circles and homophobia within the Arab American community. Such groups included the Arab Lesbian Network (ALN) in the San Francisco Bay Area; the Lesbian Arab Network (LAN) in New York City; the Gay and Lesbian Arabic Society (GLAS) in Washington, DC, Los Angeles, and New York City; Karama: The New England Lavender Society in Boston; Gays and Lesbians of Arab-American Descent-Ohio (GLAADO); and Southwest Asian and North African Bay Area Queers (SWANABAQ) also in the San Francisco Bay Area (Jadallah 2004: 76–78). While some of these groups were solely Arab-identified, others groups such as SWANABAQ, Karama, and GLAADO welcomed a broader contingent of ethnic identities such as Armenian and Assyrian identities, as well as from those who ethnically or nationally identify from non-Arab nations in the Southwest Asia and North Africa regions, such Turkey and Iran.

First among these groups was ALN, founded by Jadallah in the San Francisco Bay Area in May 1989 (Jadallah 2004: 76). Sometimes referred to as *al akhawat* ("the sisters" in Arabic), ALN later changed its name to Arab Lesbian and Bisexual Women's Network (I refer to both iterations of the group as ALBN from here on), and also produced a mixed-gender splinter group, the Arab Lesbian, Gay, and Bisexual Network (ALGBN). To aid in broadening ALBN membership, an advertisement was placed in a San Francisco newspaper (ALN "For Immediate Release" 1990). Although primarily operational in the San Francisco Bay Area, the group "boasts members nationwide" who were active in various feminist, Arab American, and lesbian and gay movements across the country. A draft of the ALGBN's statement of purpose lists the group's five interrelated goals:

1. Celebrating the Richness and Diversity of Our Arab Heritage
2. Challenging myths and stereotypes about Arabs.
3. Working for Arabs' rights internationally and we are an anti-Zionist group.
4. Working to increase the visibility of Arab lesbians, gays, and bisexuals within the Arab community and in the lesbian, gay, and bisexual community.
5. Working to provide a safe community for Arab lesbians, gays, and bisexuals.

The group functioned first and foremost to "provide social, cultural, personal, political and spiritual support for Arab Lesbians, Gays, and Bisexuals of all ages" (ALGBN n.d.). In terms of the ALBN, the organizers conceived of *Arab* as a term that "encompasses people who racially, ethnically, or culturally identify with the Arab world," and specified its inclusivity and welcoming of Arab women born in diaspora, or who were of mixed heritage, as well as those who identified as part of ethnic minority groups that are often situated within Arab nations, such as Armenians and Assyrians. The group held monthly potluck dinners, sometimes in conjunction with the co-ed splinter group, to gather in "celebrating the richness of diversity of our Arab heritage" and "share herstories, art, politics, culture, [and] lots of laughs" (ALBN n.d.).

In addition to these regular social gatherings, ALBN also served as a wellspring of Arab American activism. Members overlapped and collaborated with other leftist groups in the Bay Area, such as LISPP and Lesbians and Gays Against Imperialism (LAGAI), to work toward some of the group's stated goals, namely to make queer Arab existence visible to the Arab American community and to educate local queer communities about how and why Arab American cultural politics were relevant to queer cultural politics. The event held at the Women's Building in June of 1989 offers a fruitful example how this work took shape. With the flyer for the lesbian forum on Palestine posted throughout the Mission and Castro neighborhoods, it certainly would have caught the attention of the Arab American community. This was both exciting and anxiety producing for Jadallah, who was very aware that members of the tightly knit Arab American community in which she was raised would see the flyer. Jadallah had already been active in the Bay Area's Arab American leftist movement, particularly around the issue of Palestine. But it was her desire to do more specific Palestine-related outreach with the queer community which prompted her dual coming out. Forging queer-Palestinian solidarities "was work I wanted to do, and I knew if there were signs posted in San Francisco that Arabs my mom knew were going to see it. I felt like I had to tell my mom before someone else told her. That's what motivated me to come out to her, it was political work, actually" (Cable interview with Jadallah, July 17, 2017). In coming out as Palestinian to the lesbian community, Jadallah aimed to leverage her lesbian identity in order to advance Palestine solidarity politics within the lesbian community. Her plans to participate in the LISPP forum and the visibility of the flyers throughout San Francisco is in turn what prompted her to come out as lesbian to her family. Her dual outness here was strategic, but not without ambivalence.

Lesbian Forum on Palestine

In her speech at the lesbian forum, Jadallah explained the tenuous positionality of Arab American lesbians, particularly those of Palestinian descent, and the resultant ambivalence she and other Arab lesbians felt toward the privileging of outness. In Jadallah's own words, coming out was a dual process, one she spoke candidly about in terms of her own experience as a Palestinian American lesbian:

> As I was struggling to come out, I realized that I belonged to two communities which are very isolated from each other. . . . The lesbians were encouraging me to come out, but I often felt no understanding from them of the pain involved with the anticipated rejection from Palestinians. Also, Palestinian lesbians are invisible lesbians of color. Where other lesbians of color have built communities, we remain in isolation from each other. We also are isolated from other lesbians of color, who know little, if anything about Palestinians—about who we are, about our struggle, and who sometimes feed into negative stereotypes. The hardest thing for me has been the realization that lesbian sisters knew so little about Palestine. (Jadallah 1990: 5)

Jadallah outlined several key issues that contributed to Arab lesbian experiences of social and political isolation which complicated her relation to outness. First, Jadallah implies that the "coming out" paradigm fails to accommodate the intersectional conditions of Arab lesbian existence. The pressure Jadallah experienced from non-Arab lesbians to come out about her sexuality revealed to her an ignorance about Arab American culture in general, and the Palestinian condition more specifically. Although many people, regardless of relative privilege, risk familial or social rejection and disownership in the process of coming out, as a Palestinian in diaspora, the stakes of that potential rejection and disownership are compounded by the fact that the Israeli occupation of Palestine already compromises the diasporic Palestinian social fabric. For Palestinians and Arab Americans more broadly, Arab cultural connectivity was always already vulnerable to fragmentation due to the conditions of war and occupation in Arab homelands and their effects on diasporic communities (Naber 2012: 74). Under such pressures, Jadallah herself would go on to write in an academic publication about how Arab diasporic communities attempted to "regulate sexuality through welcoming or denying belonging and membership in the imagined Arab American community." In such a context, Jadallah writes, women "are understood to be the conveyors of culture," and are therefore particularly subject to social control and fears of disconnectivity: "sexual transgression could result in a range of responses including familial or community ties being severed" (Jadallah 2004: 76). Jadallah's speech emphasized how high stakes the process of coming out could be for Arab lesbians in particular. A negative coming out reception did not just hold the prospect of private, interfamilial conflict, it held the potential for ostracization from the Arab community and extended family. Coming out as lesbian potentially meant Arab social death.

Fears of this potential social death among her family and Arab community weighed heavily under what Jadallah explained as a sense of invisibility she experienced within queer community in attempting to negotiate both a lack of understanding and outright anti-Arab racism. This positionality is akin to what Amira Jarmakani refers to as "the politics of invisibility" wherein within the US context, Arab women are perceived as silenced and oppressed victims under the conditions of Arab heteropatriarchy, rendering Arab women, and feminist subjectivity in particular, simultaneously invisible and hypervisible (Jarmakani 2011: 234). In specifically referring to Palestinian lesbians as "invisible lesbians of color," Jadallah invoked the precarious and ambivalent position of Arab subjectivity in the US as historically occupying a position of racial "inbetweenness" (Gualtieri 2009). For Palestinians in particular, that racial ambivalence, in conjunction with the politics of invisibility, at times gives way to outright erasure, perhaps best exemplified through the infamy of former Israeli prime minister Golda Meir's assertion in a 1969 Sunday *New York Times* article that "there were no such thing as Palestinians . . . they do not exist."

Another way to understand the odd coupling of anti-Arab racism and invisibility of which Jadallah spoke is through the concept of compulsory Zionism. I have written elsewhere on how compulsory Zionism produces hegemonic support for the state of Israel in the US context in ways that "naturalize and privilege Israel, subjugate Palestinian existence, and micromanage the politics of solidarity within transnational leftist social justice movements" (Cable 2022: 67). In mirroring the concept of "compulsory heterosexuality," which Adrienne Rich famously argued functions to invisibilize lesbian existence, compulsory Zionism likewise functions to invisibilize Palestinian existence. Through the framing of compulsory Zionism, Arab American cultural politics in solidarity with Palestine renders Arab American subjectivity less in terms of racial otherness and more in terms of "political queerness." Because of this relative position of political queerness, Arab Americans (and Palestinians in particular) experience moments of having to "come out" as Arab. For Jadallah, the utter dearth of knowledge about Arab American culture and Palestine among lesbians, both white and of color, was both a function of Arab racial formation and an indicator of how anti-Arab racism often manifests in the US as compulsory Zionism. What Jadallah was ultimately getting at here is that in the confluence of this invisibility, misunderstandings, and worries over social death, queer Arab Americans experienced a profound sense of isolation, both from each other and from their respective queer and Arab American communities. This isolation, and the resultant need for a sense of community and unconditional acceptance was imperative enough for queer Arab Americans to come out to each other.

Jadallah concluded her speech by appealing to a shared sense of lesbian feminist of color political investment by invoking the words of Audre Lorde: "As lesbians who experience oppression everyday, we must work towards ending the oppression of all people." Jadallah's speech from the lesbian forum on Palestine offers a starting point from which to understand some of the motivations, goals, and methods of queer Arab American community building and political activism of the 1990s. The speech that evening was reprinted in several outlets of the leftist lesbian and gay press, namely the nationally circulating *OUT!* (later known as *UltraViolet*) published by the Bay Area–based LAGAI, and the *Gay Community News* based out of Boston, as well as the newsletter for another newly formed group, the Gay and Lesbian Arabic Society (GLAS) based in Washington, DC. The circulation of Jadallah's speech in the LGBT press marked the beginning of more outward-facing Arab American engagements with queer publics and increased visibility.

Out in Public: Visibility through Photography

Some of that increased visibility amidst queer publics took shape through "marches, protests, educational forums, and conferences" (Jadallah 2004: 77), but also through engagements with photography. As a medium of both visual art and scientific documentation, traditional photography is imbued with what Tom Gunning refers to as the medium's "truth claim," meaning that the photograph itself indexes the truth of its subject's existence (Gunning 2004: 39–40). With regard to the question of locating queer Arab Americans within institutional archives and preservation of queer Arab American archival material, photographs emerge as indices of outness.

For example, one item in Jadallah's ephemera collection consists of a wall calendar, "A Celebration of Colors: A Women of Color Calendar, 1990," for which Jadallah posed as a model (fig. 2). The month of May features a black-and-white photograph of a youthful Jadallah kneeling down on the rocky bank of a creek, a Palestinian *keffiyeh* around her neck. Jadallah faces the camera, her eyes cast in shadow from the high contrast of a bright California day. Her hair is dark, curly, and worn short in what can best be described as a very nineties-era lesbian haircut. She smiles for the camera, indeed for the would-be viewer, a smile of confidence and openness. A brief quotation is featured just below the photograph, encapsulating Jadallah's social and political ethos: "As a Palestinian lesbian, it is important to me to build bridges between the Palestinian and lesbian communities, educating lesbians about the Palestinian struggle and Palestinians about lesbian and gay rights" ("Celebration of Colors" 1990). Facing the viewer with her inviting smile, she touches the water as if to say: we are apart, different, yet connected. Like an electric current flowing through water, we touch and affect one another, electrifying each other's lives and struggles. We generate power collectively. Let us build bridges together.

In another photographic example, this time located in the Bancroft Library Archive, ALBN's existence and public participation within the larger Bay Area queer community was visually documented by Bay Area lesbian photographer Cathy Cade. ALBN's participation in San Francisco's International Lesbian and Gay Freedom Day Parade (now known as the LGBT Pride Parade) in 1990 is captured in Cade's contact sheets.[3] A series of eight photographs show a line of nine women walking down the middle of Market Street in downtown San Francisco (fig. 3). They carry a hand-painted banner with Arabic script prominently featured on the upper portion; it reads "الأخوات" ("*al akhawat*," Arabic for "the sisters"), followed by "Arab Lesbian Bisexual Women's Network." Two connected women's symbols grace the banner's lower righthand corner, while a set of dark, almond-shaped eyes partially encircled by what likely is a rainbow-themed veil look outward to the crowd from the upper left corner. The two women flanking either side of the banner wear light linen tunics and gauzy white head dresses. Another loosely veiled woman walking amidst the group is

May

1990

As a Palestinian lesbian, it is important to me to build bridges
between the Palestinian and lesbian communities,
educating lesbians about the Palestinian struggle and
Palestinians about lesbians and gay rights.

-HUDA JADALLAH

SUN	MON	TUE	WED	THU	FRI	SAT
		1	2	3	4 ASCENCION DAY	5
6	7	8	9	10	11	12
13	14	15	16	17	18	19 ARM FORCES DAY
20	21 VICTORIA DAY CANADA	22	23	24	25	26
27	28	29	30 MEMORIAL DAY	31		

Figure 2. Huda Jadallah featured in "A Celebration of Colors: A Women of Color Calendar, 1990."

Figure 3. Cathy Cade's photographic contact sheet featuring images from the Gay Freedom Day Parade, San Francisco, CA, ca. 1990.

engaged in an animated conversation, her arm draped over a companion's shoulder. Smiling, the listener leans her ear toward her veiled friend, perhaps straining to hear over the DJ, drums, chants, and cheers that are so common at LGBT pride parades.

The contact sheet shows that ALBN had been placed in the parade line in a section brimming with groups mobilized by and for women of color. Based on the images immediately preceding and following the ALBN images, it would appear that the African American Lesbian and Gay Agenda for Unity and the Asian/Pacific Lesbians contingencies marched adjacent to the ALBN contingent. Through its participation in the Freedom Day Parade, ALBN was actively practicing four out of its five goals of celebrating the richness and diversity of Arab heritage, challenging myths and stereotypes about Arabs, increasing the visibility of Arab lesbians and bisexuals within the broader queer community, and creating a safe community for Arab lesbians, gays, and bisexuals. In this act of marching in the parade, those visible in Cade's photographs were and are out, if not to family or friends, then at least in the sense of being out in public, out to the documentary eye of Cade's camera, and now therefore out in the Bancroft Library Archive.

Through Cvetkovich's understanding of ephemera, I read these fleeting photographs and their placements within Cade's larger project of queer visibility and documentation as nostalgic artifacts and indices of the kind of labor undertaken by women like Jadallah and groups such as ALBN to make queer Arab American existence, and indeed *community*, visible. Surely not all of the participants in the ALBN marching contingent agreed on the interrelated politics of visibility, outness, and privacy, and undoubtedly not all those pictured were out to their Arab American families or their extended Arab American community. Still, their willingness to march and be subject to the potentiality of being documented at such a march indicates that there was at least some level of investment in public visibility as a form of outness, if not for an Arab American crowd, then certainly for a queer one.

Out in the Press

Marching and modeling aside, ALBN's visibility politics did not end with the physical parading or display of queer Arab American bodies in public spaces or photography. The group also sought to increase Arab visibility through engagements with the queer press. They did so by sending press releases and letters to the editors of several Bay Area LGBT newspapers to challenge the subtle and overt forms of anti-Arab racism and compulsory Zionism that manifested in what we would now consider to be pinkwashing articles.[4]

In another example from Jadallah's personal archive, a 1989 newspaper clipping from the *San Francisco Bay Times* offers an example of how nonchalantly anti-Arab racism and compulsory Zionism circulated within the LGBT press. The article, titled "Building Lesbian/Gay Pride in Israel," featured an extended interview with Hadar Namir, an Israeli lesbian and gay rights activist and founder of the Society for the Protection of Personal Rights (SPPR) in Israel. In the interview, Namir expounds on the various social and institutionalized forms of oppression levied against gay and lesbian Israelis, ranging from laws against homosexuality, orthodox religious ideology, discrimination within the Israeli military, and the particulars of the AIDS crisis in Israel. Namir touted SPPR as strictly "non-political" and yet "for gay politics only" (Appleman 1989). She justified this nonpolitical/gay politics–only edict by asserting SPPR's exceptionalism within the Israeli context: "We have members from the right wing, the left wing and from the middle. . . . We are the only group to deal with gay and lesbian issues so we have to give space to everybody, no matter what his political ideas." When asked whether there are Palestinian members, Namir professed that while there are indeed Palestinian members, she nonetheless harbors a "deep sorrow" for the lack of Arab participation in terms of formal, registered membership. The reason for such a dearth, Namir asserted, is that "they're more oppressed than even Jewish society oppresses gays and lesbians." She clarified that she was specifically "speaking of gay Arab men," because she "[doesn't] even know of one Arab lesbian," before continuing her erasure of Arab feminism and the rhetorical annihilation of Arab lesbians: "There are maybe ten women who declare themselves feminist in Arab society. It's very difficult for them."

ALN (and by extension Jadallah) and LISPP were quick to draft a coauthored reply to the Namir interview, which the San Francisco Bay Times published in the December 1989 issue (ALN and LISPP 1989a). The letter extensively critiqued Namir's omission of the larger context of the Israeli occupation and the violent oppression of the Palestinian people—including gay and lesbian Palestinians—under that occupation. Since Namir's organization operated on the assumption that shared gay or lesbian identity was enough to create political solidarity, the ALN/LISPP members began their letter by making clear that as a coalition of Arab and Jewish lesbians, Namir "represents a political perspective we cannot share" and that "by isolating the gay rights issue, Namir portrays an Israeli society that doesn't exist" (ALN and LISPP 1989a).

The ALN/LISPP letter provided a critical rundown of the casual bigotry lurking beneath Namir's optimistic picture of Israeli activism. For example, the ALN/LISPP letter shattered Namir's presumption that participation "at all levels of the army, performing very well" should be a barometer of gay and lesbian equality within Israel. The ALN/LISPP letter was quick to point out: "this is the same Israeli army that inflicts terror in the occupied territories . . . it does not make us proud to have gays and lesbians 'performing very well' in the Israeli army; in fact, it horrifies us." The letter moved on to dissect Namir's claims about Israel's healthcare for all people by noting that Palestinians who work in Israel and pay taxes toward that healthcare are excluded from receiving the benefits. While gay Israelis may have better access to healthcare amidst the AIDS crisis, those benefits are reaped through the simultaneous exploitation of Palestinian labor and exclusion of the Palestinian body politic.

Yet the real blow to Namir's credibility came through the revelation of her staggeringly short-sighted and prejudicial beliefs about Arab society.

The ALN/LISPP letter contends that "along with misrepresenting Israeli society, Namir distorts Arab/Palestinian society as well" by peddling a "shocking and racist untruth" about the presence, or lack thereof, of feminism within Arab society:

> That Namir "doesn't even know of one Arab lesbian" is hardly surprising, given the politics she exhibits. That Arab lesbians exist is a given; that they would not particularly feel supported by Namir and her organization which "gives space to everyone, no matter what his political ideas," is also a given. Why would Arab or Palestinian lesbians want to be in an organization with "members from the right wing"; in Israel this represents people who would like to kick all Arabs out of the country. (ALN and LISPP 1989a)

After a concise, point-by-point analysis of Namir's interview, ALN and LISPP provided a succinct suggestion for how SPPR could indeed live up to the bridge-building goals touted in the interview: "Without an understanding and acknowledgment of" the points outlined in their letter, "the lesbian and gay struggle is weakened. Namir says that her organization 'may provide a bridge for Arab and Jewish society.' This bridge can only be built when the organization takes a stand for Palestinian rights" (ALN and LISPP 1989a). In this moment, Arab lesbians introduced Namir to not *one* but a whole *community* of Arab lesbians, while simultaneously disproving Namir's claims of Arab lesbian nonexistence.

But queer Arab American outness in the press did not merely take shape through confrontations in the letters to the editor section. Indeed, queer Arab Americans leveraged outness as a communication strategy to convey the affective experience of being Arab within a US society dominated by anti-Arab racism. In an article authored by LAGAI activist Kate Raphael (1991) titled "Arab Lesbians, Gays Speak Out" in the *San Francisco Sentinel*, queer Arab Americans spoke openly about the social and political predicaments they faced within US society. In the article, an anonymous gay Palestinian man offered an analogy through which to understand his experiences of being subjected to virulent anti-Arab racism and choosing whether or not to expose or conceal his Arab identity: "being Arab here is like being gay. People assume you're not. They think they can say *anything*" (Raphael 1991). His statement offers an additional instance of queer Arab Americans' engagement with the LGBT press in the early 1990s in order to challenge the anti-Arab racism within their queer communities.

But his anonymity also speaks to the malleable nature of outness as strategy. With his anonymous comment, this queer Palestinian man simultaneously speaks *out* while maintaining his privacy. Through the mediation of the press, queer Arab Americans could accommodate their own ambivalence toward the outness paradigm while simultaneously using outspokenness to communicate their concerns to the larger queer community about Arab invisibility and anti-Arab sentiment. Here, outness is at once definitive enough to prove existence and malleable enough to accommodate privacy. Outness is strategic, meaning that there is a nuance to when and how it is deployed or withheld. It is not a zero-sum game. Much like ephemera, outness is miscellaneous, something that is of mixed composition or character, something potentially messy, but also surprisingly mundane.[5]

Conclusion

The ephemera analyzed in this article serves as an archive of queer Arab American existence, experiences, and outness. Through a focus on Jadallah's life experience and ALBN's social and political activities, this article offers—to borrow a photographic metaphor—a historical contact sheet of queer Arab American life in the San Francisco Bay Area from the 1980s and 1990s. The dearth and inaccessibility of archival materials on queer Arab American social life, cultural activities, and political activism from this period makes it all the more important to document and honor this history. Such documentation also serves to recognize the role that outness (in its various intentional, malleable, nuanced, and even anonymous ways) has played in the service of queer Arab American activism and community building.

My emphasis on outness in this article and, relatedly, my desire to amass an out queer Arab American archive is in some ways out of place (pun intended) with regard to the discourses critical of outness and visibility within queer Arab American cultural productions, activism, and studies. Outness, the overdetermination of "coming out," and the attendant assumptions around public visibility's relation to liberation, have, and for good reason, been regarded with suspicion within queer of color communities, especially within queer Arab American circles. That said, I pursue the outness line of argumentation because I cannot ignore the fact that within some of the material examined in this article and in looking back at her experiences, Jadallah herself discusses her own history and experience by using the language of outness. Likewise, I cannot ignore the fact that ALBN marched in the Gay Freedom Day Parade, and how that public display of visibility is now stored and available to the public within an institutional archive, ostensibly rendering those pictured as "out."

Still, many obstacles remain in seeking to archive out queer Arab American life and political activism. To begin, institutional LGBT archives simply have a dearth of material specifically identified and cataloged as "Arab American" (and related keywords and phrases). Likewise, despite abundant holdings of material on Arab student activism during the 1980s and 1990s, university archives are similarly lacking in Arab American material sub-cataloged as "LGBT" or "queer." Although queer Arab Americans were out and both socially and politically active around this same time, the little archival holdings that exist in these institutional archives are often sparse, containing only a few items. Other times, as is the case of Feminist Arab American Network records at the Schlessinger Library at Harvard University, material marked specifically as "lesbian," "gay," "LGBT," and the like are often closed to the public until several decades into the future, likely to respect the privacy of any still-living individuals who may appear or be named in the material.[6] The suggestion here is that the availability of this material is contingent upon death. In death, outness takes on a kind of reverence. It becomes something reserved for ancestors, not for living kin. The skeleton of queer Arab American ancestry emerges out of the closet only upon crossing the threshold of death. Perhaps when we as kin (whether in the role of student or scholar or archivist) seek out these materials, we do so to pay our respects.

In conceptualizing the uses of outness as a strategy in the service of community building and activism, my hope for the future of queer Arab American archiving is twofold. First, I hope that in rethinking it as strategy, some of the ambivalence surrounding outness will give way to political imperative. Instead of being haunted by ambivalence and liability, outness will be recognized as strategic in the service of greater causes. As such, reader, please consider queer Arab American archiving one of those causes. My second hope is that in this rethinking of outness, queer Arab American elders and other guardians of queer Arab American ephemera who dutifully maintain our historical records in private collections will consider donating such material to institutional archives with the express intention of cataloging those materials as LGBT or queer. Because if we don't archive these materials, who will?

Umayyah Cable (they/them) is an assistant professor in the departments of American Culture and Film, Television, and Media, and a core faculty member in the Arab and Muslim American Studies Program at the University of Michigan, Ann Arbor.

Notes

1   I take Amira Jarmakani's (2015: 122) understand of Arab racialization "a partial, diffuse and porous cateroy, shot through with the residual constructions of ethnicity, sexuality, culture, and civilization."

2   Many thanks to Amira Jarmakani for pointing out the definition of miscellaneous and encouraging a greater engagement with it here.

3   Lesbian photographer Cathy Cade's contact sheets—which contain hundreds of thousands of images ranging from the quotidian to the spectacular—are now housed at the Bancroft Library archive at the University of California, Berkeley.

4   Pinkwashing is "a deliberate strategy to conceal the continuing violations of Palestinians' human rights behind an image of modernity signified by Israeli gay life" (Schulman 2011).

5   Regarding outness as mundane: when asked how her mother reacted to her coming out as lesbian, Jadallah stated, "Oh, she was fine with it."

6   Records of the Feminist Arab-American Network are housed at Harvard University's Schlessinger Library, including a folder titled "Membership list, Arab-American Lesbian and Gay Network." This folder remains locked until January 1, 2040. For anyone interested in pursuing research on queer Arab American history, it is worthwhile following up on this folder.

Works Cited

ALN (Arab Lesbian Network). 1990. "For Immediate Release." March 24. Private archive of Huda Jadallah.

ALN and LISPP (Arab Lesbian Network and Lesbians in Solidarity with the Palestinian People). 1989a. "The Intifada and Israeli Lesbians and Gays." San Francisco Bay Times. Private archive of Huda Jadallah.

ALN and LISPP (Arab Lesbian Network and Lesbians in Solidarity with the Palestinian People). 1989b. "The Palestinian Uprising and the Lesbian Community: An Evening for Lesbians about Palestine." June 8. Private archive of Huda Jadallah.

ALBN (Arab Lesbian and Bisexual Women's Network). n.d. "Arab Lesbian/Bisexual Women's Network الأخوات" flyer. Private archive of Huda Jadallah.

ALGBN (Arab Lesbian, Gay, and Bisexual Network). n.d. "Statement of Purpose." Private archive of Huda Jadallah.

Appleman, Rose. 1989. "Building Lesbian/Gay Pride in Israel: An Interview with Lesbian Activist Hadar Namir." San Francisco Bay Times, October. Private archive of Huda Jadallah.

Cable, Umayyah. 2022 "Compulsory Zionism and Palestinian Existence: A Genealogy." *Journal of Palestine Studies* 51, no. 2: 66–71.

"A Celebration of Colors: A Women of Color Calendar, 1990." 1990. Private archive of Huda Jadallah.

Cvetkovich, Ann. 2003. *An Archive of Feelings: Trauma, Sexuality, and Lesbian Public Cultures.* Durham, NC: Duke University Press.

Gualtieri, Sarah. 2009. *Between Arab and White: Race and Ethnicity in the Early Syrian American Diaspora.* Oakland: University of California Press.

Gunning, Tom. 2004. "PLENARY SESSION II. Digital Aesthetics. What's the Point of an Index? or, Faking Photographs." *Nordicom Review* 25, nos. 1–2: 39–49.

Jadallah, Huda. 1990. "Lesbians and Palestine." *Gay Community News*, February 11.

Jadallah, Huda. 2004. "Arab Americans." In *Encyclopedia of Lesbian, Gay, Bisexual and Transgender History in America*, edited by Marc Stein, 76–78. Vol. 1. Detroit, MI: Charles Scribner's Sons. Gale eBooks. https://link.gale.com/apps/doc/CX3403600040/GVRL?u=umuser&sid=GVRL&xid=266cf39b.

Jadallah, Huda. 2011. "Reflections of a Genderqueer Palestinian American Lesbian Mother." In *Arab and American Feminisms: Gender, Violence, and Belonging*, edited by Rabab Abdulhadi, Evelyn Alsultany, and Nadine Naber. Syracuse, NY: Syracuse University Press.

Jarmakani, Amira. 2008. *Imagining Arab Womanhood: The Cultural Mythology of Veils, Harems, and Belly Dancers in the U.S.* New York: Palgrave Macmillan.

Jarmakani, Amira. 2011. "Arab American Feminisms: Mobilizing the Politics of Invisibility." In *Arab and Arab American Feminisms: Gender, Violence, and Belonging*, edited by Rabab Abdulhadi, Evelyn Alsultany, and Nadine Naber. Syracuse, NY: Syracuse University Press.

Jarmakani, Amira. 2015. *An Imperialist Love Story: Desert Romances and the War on Terror.* New York: New York University Press.

Karem Albrecht, Charlotte. 2023. *Possible Histories: Arab Americans and the QueerEcology of Peddling.* Oakland, CA: University of California Press.

Manalansan, Martin F. IV. 2014. "The 'Stuff' of Archives: Mess, Migration, and Queer Lives." *Radical History Review* 2014, no. 120 : 94–107.

Muñoz, José Esteban. 1996. "Ephemera as Evidence: Introductory Notes to Queer Acts." *Women and Performance: A Journal of Feminist Theory* 8, no. 2: 5–16.

Naber, Nadine Christine. 2012. *Arab America: Gender, Cultural Politics, and Activism.* New York: New York University Press.

Raphael, Kate. 1991. "Arab Lesbians, Gays Speak Out." *San Francisco Sentinel*, February.

Schulman, Sarah. 2011. "Israel and 'Pinkwashing.'" *New York Times*, November 22. https://www.nytimes.com/2011/11/23/opinion/pinkwashing-and-israels-use-of-gays-as-a-messaging-tool.html.

Shomali, Mejdulene B. 2023. *Between Banat: Queer Arab Critique and Transnational Arab Archives.* Durham, NC: Duke University Press.

Shreya Parikh

Within and Outside the Black-Maghrebi Binary

A Conversation with Maha Abdelhamid

Abstract: What does it mean to be both Black and Tunisian, Black and Maghrebi, when the two identities are defined as different from each other, and in opposition with each other, in both North Africa and its diaspora? This article is an annotated conversation with Dr. Maha Abdelhamid, a Tunisian Black activist and scholar who has been crucial to the creation of the Black movement in Tunisia and Tunisian diaspora. This conversation examines the construction and negotiation of Tunisian-Black and Maghrebi-Black identities through Abdelhamid's experiences of living in and working against racism in both Tunisia and France. It details Abdelhamid's trajectory in becoming conscious of her Black and African identities, her complex relationship with her Arab identity, her role in building the Black movement in Tunisia after the 2011 revolution, and her arrival in France and experiences of exclusion in both Maghrebi diasporic as well as Black feminist civil society organizations. The interview points to the possible essentialization of Maghrebi and Black as separate identities not only in socio-political discourses that racialize and marginalize these groups, but also among groups challenging Islamophobia or anti-Blackness, leaving those with overlapping identities and racializing experiences outside their scope.

Introduction

What does it mean to be both Black and Tunisian, Black and Maghrebi, when the two identities are defined as different from each other, and in opposition with each other, in both Maghreb (North Africa) and its diaspora?[1] This article is an annotated conversation with Dr. Maha Abdelhamid, a Tunisian

MERIDIANS · feminism, race, transnationalism   23:2 October 2024
DOI: 10.1215/15366936-11266436 © 2024 Smith College

Black activist and scholar who has been crucial to the creation of the Black movement in Tunisia and Tunisian diaspora.[2]

The conversation with Abdelhamid, which forms the core of this article, examines the construction and negotiation of Tunisian-Black and Maghrebi-Black identities through Abdelhamid's experiences of living in and working against racism in both Tunisia and France. It details Abdelhamid's trajectory in becoming conscious of her Black and African identities, both of which are constructed as synonymous and inferior 'other' in the Tunisian social imagination; her complex relationship with her Arab identity; her role in building the Black movement in Tunisia after the 2011 revolution; and her arrival in France and experiences of exclusion in both Maghrebi diasporic as well as Black feminist civil society organizations. The interview points to the possible essentialization of Maghrebi and Black as separate identities not only in sociopolitical discourses that racialize and marginalize these groups, but also among groups challenging Islamophobia or anti-Blackness, leaving those with overlapping identities and racializing experiences outside their scope.

In the pages that follow, I start by providing a brief biography of Abdelhamid. Then, I describe the transnational context that bridges Tunisia and France, and in which Abdelhamid's conversation is located. This is followed by an edited conversation between myself and Abdelhamid that was recorded in November 2021. I end with an epilogue detailing the escalation of anti-Black violence in Tunisia starting in February 2023 and placing it within larger historical and sociopolitical context described by Abdelhamid in the interview.

Introducing Dr. Maha Abdelhamid

Dr. Maha Abdelhamid is a Tunisian Black activist and scholar, and cofounder of multiple anti-racism organizations, including the first anti-racism civil society organization in Tunisia—Association ADAM pour l'Égalité et le Développement (Association ADAM for Equality and Development; ADAM hereafter), created in 2011 after the revolution in the same year.[3]

Abdelhamid grew up in the city of Gabès, around four hundred kilometers (ca. two hundred fifty miles) south of Tunisia's capital Tunis, in a region that is home to a significantly large Black Tunisian population.[4] After obtaining her high school diploma, she moved to Tunis for higher education in the late 1990s. Since 2013, she has been living in France.

Civilian protests broke out across Tunisia following the self-immolation of Mohamed Bouazizi in December 2010, leading the then-president Zine El Abidine Ben Ali to flee the country on January 14, 2011. This moment marked the starting of region-wide protests that came to be described as the Arab Spring revolution. As the country transitioned from authoritarianism to democracy, the appellation of Tunisia as a homogenously "Arab" country came to be challenged by groups that have been minoritized, including Amazigh, Black, and Jewish populations (Pouessel 2012).[5] It was in this context that a group of Black Tunisians, among them Abdelhamid, started ADAM. The contestation of Tunisia's demographic homogeneity also came from scholarship that has flourished since the revolution; Abdelhamid's scholarship is one such example.

After ADAM, Abdelhamid cofounded a civil society organization called La Marche contre le Racisme et pour l'Égalité (The March against Racism and for Equality; The March hereafter) in 2014, and a Black Tunisian women's civil society organization called Voix des Femmes Tunisiennes Noires (VFTN; Voices of Tunisian Black Women) in 2020.[6] The work of these civil society organizations and their members was crucial in the drafting, passage, and implementation of the law criminalizing racial discrimination that was passed in 2018 (Parikh 2021).

Abdelhamid moved to France as a doctoral researcher in geography at the University Paris Nanterre; in 2018, she defended her doctoral thesis titled "Socio-spatial Transformations in the Gabès Oasis (Tunisia): Decline of Agricultural Activities, Informal Urbanization and Environmental Degradation in Zrig (1970s–present)" (Abdelhamid 2018c). Abdelhamid also produced a documentary about Black families in Gabès titled *De Arram à Gabès: Mémoire d'une famille noire* (2012; *From Arram to Gabès: Memory of a Black Family*). At the time of the interview in November 2021, she was working as a social worker in the Greater Paris region. She is an affiliated researcher at the Arab Center for Research and Political Studies (CAREP) where she is working on a project titled "Histories and Experiences of Black Women in North Africa and the Middle East: Dynamics of Intersectionality."[7]

Abdelhamid and I were introduced virtually to each other early in 2020, before I moved to Tunisia to study race and racialization for my dissertation. Her name had come up many times during my exploratory research, including in journalistic interviews as well as through her scholarship on the anti-racism movement and activism in Tunisia (see, e.g., Abdelhamid,

Elfargi, and Elwaer 2017; Abdelhamid 2018a, 2018b). During one of our virtual discussions, Abdelhamid recounted a series of experiences that highlighted a sense of exclusion that she, as a self-identifying Tunisian Black woman, had felt in both Black feminist as well as Maghrebi feminist spaces in France. That became the motivation for an interview where I asked Abdelhamid to expand on her experiences of working against racism in Tunisia and in France, as well as her interpretation of these experiences.

The Transnational Context of the Conversation

Abdelhamid's experiences lie in two interconnected contexts—first, in the context of anti-Black racism in Tunisia, and, second, in the context of Islamophobia and anti-Black racism in France. Both these contexts are connected historically through precolonial trans-Saharan and trans-Mediterranean slavery (Montana 2013; Oualdi 2020; Walz and Cuno 2011), through the French colonization of Tunisia, as well as through postcolonial migration from Tunisia to France that continues today.

As a part of the postindependence nation-building project, the regimes in power discursively constructed North African nation-states as being demographically homogenous (Ltifi 2020). This is reflected in the description of Tunisia as Arab and Muslim in its constitution, as Abdelhamid points out in the interview. At the same time, "Blackness is repeatedly constructed as if it were non-indigenous to North Africa" (Tayeb 2021). Yet, Black populations have been migrating into and/or living in the region since before their colonization; the forced migration of enslaved Black individuals was one among many forms of Black migration (Mrad Dali 2009). Many Black families who live in the region, like Abdelhamid's family, trace their ancestry to enslaved Black families.[8] The stigmatized history of enslavement of the ancestors of *some* Black families plays a key role in the stigmatization of *all* Black Tunisians as well as sub-Saharan migrants in Tunisia; this is reflected in the use of stigmatized Arabic vernacular terms that translate as "servant" or "slave" to refer to any individual racialized as Black.[9]

In Tunisia, dark-skinned Tunisians as well as sub-Saharan migrants are racialized as Black and face anti-Black racism. While there is no census data about the two groups, estimates cited by activists and journalists claim that around 10–15 percent of the population or around 1.5 million Tunisians are Black (King and Rouine 2021). It is estimated that around 30–50,000 sub-Saharan Africans are currently living in Tunisia; most of them are undocumented and face legal, economic, and social precarities because of this status (Parikh 2023a).

Discrimination against Black individuals manifests itself, among other ways, in the form of verbal, physical, and sexual harassment, and there is taboo around racially mixed marriages (Jelassi 2020). One also sees racial inequality in outcomes—for example, the presence of Black Tunisians in positions of political power remains rare, and the proportion of sub-Saharan migrants who receive state-issued work permits is significantly lower compared to that among European migrants in Tunisia (Ben Sedrine 2018).[10]

In France, like in North Africa, the category of "Maghrebi" is politically and socially constructed as synonymous to the categories of Arab and Muslim (Deltombe 2005) and antonymous to the category of Black—as Abdelhamid's experiences reveal. In the diasporic context, it is widely recognized that Maghrebi-origin individuals face Islamophobia (Hajjat and Mohammed 2016). In addition, civil-society groups and scholars have shown that anti-Black racism persists in France (Keaton, Sharpley-Whiting, and Stovall 2012). What type of racism do Black-Maghrebi individuals experience? Do these experiences qualify as Islamophobia or anti-Black racism, or both? The interview with Abdelhamid was motivated by these questions.

In France, anti-Black ideologies are present not only among so-called *français de souche* (translated as native French; terminology employed by right-leaning political groups in France) but also in the North African diaspora (see de Neuville 2021). At the same time, in the context of global Islamophobia, criticizing anti-Blackness present within North Africa and its diaspora can be challenging because any critique of these populations could be instrumentalized against them.[11] In this light, should this critique be made?

Rochelle Terman (2016: 24) argues in favor of a "responsible critique" that allows for multiple critiques to take place simultaneously without prioritizing one. Terman demonstrates that the fear of instrumentalization of gender-based violence in the global Islamophobic context pushes feminist scholarship to criticize any criticism of violence against women in Muslim contexts. According to Terman, this strand of feminist scholarship "obscures a complete understanding of violence against women in Muslim contexts . . . [and] is an expression of a Euro/American experience of Islamophobia post 9/11 that is projected in an ahistorical and politically counterproductive way onto local Muslim and Arab communities" (1). One can extend this criticism to our case as follows: to not critique anti-Blackness present in North Africa and its diaspora would be to "obscure a complete understanding" of anti-Black racism in "Muslim contexts." To refrain from the critique would also result in the margins of the margin bearing the burden of their double marginalization along with the burden of guarding the reputation of the marginalized who oppress them. Furthermore, to refrain from the critique would also imply that we (implicitly) fall into the trap of re-essentializing the figure of the North African "Arab" as a "good Muslim" or "good Arab" in response to the Islamophobic "bad Muslim" or "bad Arab" (Mamdani 2002).

A Conversation with Dr. Maha Abdelhamid

Shreya Parikh: When did you become conscious about being Black?

Maha Abdelhamid: Until I was twenty-two years old, I identified as Tunisian and didn't embrace my Black identity. I became conscious of my Africanity rather late in my life.[12] It happened when I went to university [in Tunis] and met sub-Saharan African students there. The first time I was forced to reflect [about my Africanity] was when a Mauritanian friend asked me a question that shocked me. This was in late 1990s and I must have been a second-year undergraduate student studying history. My Mauritanian friend told me about the history of slavery as well as about Black enslaved people bought and sold by the non-Black folks in Mauritania. Back then, I didn't know that there were Black Mauritanians.[13]

I grew up in a culture [in Tunisia] that has completely cut itself off from Africa. I did not know much about Africa before going to university. I also got to learn about l'*Afrique noire* (Black Africa), which was always hidden in my culture but which has influenced my culture. It became present [to me] at the university.[14]

SP: Did your friend's question push you to ask your family members about their genealogy?

MA: Since I was a child, I had a lot of questions—Why am I Black? Why are the Black people black? We are Black but we live in Tunisia—why? My father used to tell me that our family came from Nubia [i.e., region covered by south Egypt and north Sudan] and I thought, well, Nubians are indeed Black and that may explain why I am Black. I would ask him, "if we arrived here from Nubia, why don't we have a different last name?" I didn't really believe [in my father's story] because my last name—Abdelhamid—is also a last name found among white [Tunisian] families.[15]

In my father's family, they have always refused to speak about slavery. But when I was a child, my [paternal] grandmother would sometimes tell me about this Black woman from whom we descended. She would say, "Your great great-grandfather was the protector of his village, but he was white and he married his slave who was Black and who gave birth to a Black child, and so we have come from this Black child." For men, it wasn't a problem that the women [they married] be enslaved. In our patriarchal society, if the father was born free then his children and grand-children would be born free. I would tell my grandmother, "This is important! Can you give me more details about this?" and everyone would ask me to shut up, because it is shameful. But it isn't shameful! I would like to know this family history.

I started to rethink about this history of slavery and about the African identity of the Black folks in Tunisia when I met my Mauritanian friend, who asked me the question that really disturbed me. And I started to reconcile with this African identity. In Tunisia, they have tried to cut us from this heritage. They have erased all its traces, even in the archives, and so it is hard to find the lineages of my family.

SP: Is this African identity, this "Africanity" as you call it, embraced by other Black Tunisians?

MA: Today, Black Tunisians won't tell you that they have their origins in sub-Saharan Africa! When someone perceives them as African,[16] the Black folks [from Tunisia] will say "I am Tunisian, that's all! I am not African!" Their response reflects an ignorance of history, because Black Tunisians indeed trace their genealogies in sub-Saharan Africa.[17] [In Tunisia,] an "African" represents everything that is negative. And, as Tunisians, we identify as Mediterranean and as Arabo-Muslim rather than as African. This is also the case for the rest of North Africa.[18]

When we started Association ADAM to fight against racism in Tunisia, [other members] refused to speak about the history of slavery because [they said], "Well, this doesn't concern us!" Over time, it was through reading and research that we understood that things are very intersectional and that we cannot fight anti-Black racism without raising the question of slavery. It is because of this history [of slavery] that we face anti-Black racism.[19] It is not possible to analyze our presence [as Black folks] in Tunisia without understanding the history of enslavement of Black folks.

We have a hard time accepting our Africanity and we want to cut ourselves from it in every manner possible. We have these assumptions that we are not like the "Africans," that we are more civilized while the "Africans" are savages who suffer from wars and contagious illnesses. And this is why I say that, if the Tunisians do not recognize themselves as Africans, it is because of the politics [in Tunisia], either directly or indirectly.

The Black movement isn't a movement for the Black folks [alone], but rather it speaks to the entire Tunisian society. After all, our memory is a collective memory! The memory of slavery is not only the memory of the Black folks but also the memory of the non-Black folks and of the whole Tunisian society.

SP: What is your relationship with the Arab identity? Do you feel Arab?

MA: I am Arab by accident because I was born into the Arab culture. For me, the Arab identity is first and foremost linked to the Arabic language. Arabic is a very beautiful and mysterious language. Today, I write better in Arabic and I am more at ease when I write in Arabic compared to when I write in French. To me, "Arab" represents the literary texts with which I grew up, and which I read when I was studying for my high school diploma in literature.

All the books I read as a child and in my adolescence were in Arabic. But there were neither any Black authors nor any Black characters in these books. I didn't ask many questions about their absence [back then], but now I ask these questions because I am conscious of my Black identity. Today, I ask, Why is it that, in [Arabic] literature and writing, the Black individual doesn't exist? Because, Black Arabs doesn't exist as a category in the Middle East as well as in North Africa. Well, at least we have Sudan![20]

SP: But there are other countries (like Chad) that are Arabic-speaking and that are inhabited by Black folks, no?

MA: Yes, there is also Djibouti and Eritrea where people speak Arabic, but are they considered Arab? No![21] Even the Sudanese [Arabic] literature is not integrated into the mainstream Arabic literature corpus. For example, Tayeb Salih's *Season of Migration to the North* is an extraordinary work.[22] One may ask, Why is it not integrated into teaching programs while one finds Najib Mahfouz in the curriculum?[23] A work like *Season of Migration to the North* must be a part of the high school syllabus for Arabic literature classes. But this absence continues because there is a resistance among the Arabs in accepting those who are Black!

Coming back to the question of Arab identity, I am Arab but I think I embrace the Arab identity less and less. The more it rejects me, the more I detach myself from this identity. When I am in Tunis, Tunisians come to me and say, "Oh you are Tunisian? We didn't think you are Tunisian!" What they mean to say is that I do not look Arab.

SP: So, in Tunisia, being Tunisian is associated with being Arab?

MA: Yes! The first article of the Tunisian constitution says, "Tunisia is a Muslim and Arab state."[24] The Black folks are excluded, and the Amazigh folks aren't [represented] there either![25]

SP: You said earlier that you feel more and more detached from this [Arab] identity?

MA: No, not detached! Because I think that [the Arab identity] is something that is a part of me. But I do not embrace it!

My paternal grandfather was an Arabist, a Nasserist, an Arab nationalist.[26] My father wasn't into politics. I used to participate in protests calling for Arab solidarities for Palestine and during the Iraq war. But do the Arabs consider me fully Arab? I think that great Arab leaders like [Tunisian ex-President Habib] Bourguiba and [Egyptian ex-President Gamal] Abdel Nasser have never defended the Black Arab identity. I think that if these presidents and leaders had given some [sociopolitical] place to the Black folks at that time, then the Black folks wouldn't have this [marginalized] place that we have today.

SP: In 2018, a landmark law criminalizing racial discrimination was passed in Tunisia. Black activism played a key role in the passing of this law. Could you tell me about your participation in the making of this law?

MA: Before the closing of the drafting of the Tunisian constitution in 2013, we [at Association ADAM] petitioned for an article that criminalizes discrimination against Black folks.[27] Even though we had enough signatures, our petition was not successful. We had to wait until the events [of 2016] when Ivorian [sic] students faced physical aggression in the center of Tunis city. This coincided with a meeting that was organized in the presence of then–Prime Minister [Youssef] Chahed who declared on that very day that it is imperative to advance the bill criminalizing racism.[28] The Tunisian civil society organizations based in France mobilized support for the bill.

SP: During our earlier conversations, you mentioned that, as a Tunisian Black activist in France, you feel excluded from both Maghrebi feminist and Black feminist spaces here in France. Could you tell me more about that?

MA: I was invited to speak about the Black movement at a women-only conference [in France] organized by Nta Rajel? (translated as "You are a man?" in Arabic), a Maghrebi-diaspora feminist civil society organization. I think this was in 2019! I was the only Black Maghrebi there and so I felt a bit uneasy. The majority of women who were there were Maghrebi women who were born in France, or who arrived here as children and had grown up in France. I was not born in France. So we don't have the same social codes and I was really not at ease. Even though it wasn't said outright, I felt different from the rest who were there. I felt this unease of being in the midst of this group of women who come from the same culture as I do; but they also acquired a second culture which I do not have because I arrived here in France after thirty years [of living in Tunisia]. At the conference, I talked about the challenges of being Black and about the trajectory of the Black movement in Tunisia, and I felt that my presentation didn't interest many. The women in the audience didn't ask me many questions. At the same time, Fatima Ouassak, who spoke after me, got many questions.[29]

It is true that the Muslim Maghrebi women who were at the conference face [Islamophobic] racism here in France. I had hoped that they would empathize with the discrimination we face there [in Maghreb] because of their experience of discrimination in France. Overall, I learned that we [as Black Maghrebis] need to do more work in building the Black movement in our communities in Maghreb, and that we are not yet strong enough to speak about our fight in the immigrant communities. I have also tried to get closer to Black feminist groups [in France]. I would attend their meetings and I had friends there. Folks would tell me "This [work on Black Tunisians] is very interesting," but nothing more than that! I never had anyone approach me and offer to collaborate with me.

The problem is that in the Black feminist spaces I am seen as *Maghrebine* [a Maghrebi woman] and not as a Black woman, and in the Maghrebi feminist spaces I am seen as a Black woman.[30] In the Black spaces, I am labeled as Maghrebi because, culturally, I am Maghrebi and when I speak French, I have a [Tunisian] accent. I don't have the same social and cultural codes as Black women who have lived almost all their lives in France. When I go to the Maghrebi women spaces here in France, I am labeled as Black, and I have to explicitly mention that I am Tunisian in order for them to recognize that I am Maghrebi. For me, this is disturbing and discomforting. So, I no longer try to look for my place, neither among the Maghrebi women, nor among the Black women groups. Slowly, I distanced myself from the two groups. Maybe the obstacles lie in me, but I wish others would make an effort.

SP: Has there been a specific incident that has influenced your decision to distance yourself from both Maghrebi and Black feminist spaces here in France?

MA: No! But you know that there are these feelings, like the feeling of unease, and these feelings certainly are not false, right?

It is true that these women grew up in a different political and cultural context [than I did], and that I would not be able to understand these contexts. But I think that there is no intersectionality in the work of the marginalized feminist groups in France. [In France,] we are living in a society that discriminates against us as North Africans or as Black Africans. But when I see the feminist space at large here in France, the Middle Eastern Arabs—they work alone; the Maghrebis—they work alone; the LGBTQ feminists—they work alone! But to speak about all women together and to try to understand each other? This doesn't exist and this is a problem.

From my experience, I feel that there is a problem of rejection, by feminist groups in France, of the existence of racial discrimination in North

Africa. They have internalized the superiority of the West without their being conscious of it. We are in the [French] society where we, as Maghrebi women and Black African women, are discriminated against. But, at the same time, we can reject someone who does not look like us.[31]

SP: Have you experienced any instances of racism here in France? Do you interpret these instances as Islamophobia or as anti-Black racism?

MA: I am not a veiled woman and I don't think folks realize [that I am Arab and Muslim] before knowing my name. When I walk around in France, I am just a Black woman. So, the racism I face is anti-Black racism. It is also racism against the immigrants because, when I speak, I have a [Tunisian] accent. Of course, there are folks who might discriminate against me because I am Muslim, but this isn't very evident!

SP: Do you think that, in the future, you could build solidarities with these Maghrebi-diasporic and Black feminist groups in France?

MA: For me, it is important that, rather than talking about solidarity with other groups, I orient myself towards the Black folks. We [as Black Maghrebis] are at an early stage of constructing our political identity—our Black identity! The construction of this political identity of the Black folks in the Arab world necessitates a lot of time. There are many internal divisions among the Black [Maghrebi] folks. We have to reunite among ourselves and construct a consciousness of this political identity, whether we are descendants of slaves or whether we arrived here through [other forms of] migrations. Once this identity is clear, we will know better about what to ask of other groups.

Epilogue

The decade that followed the 2011 revolution witnessed the flourishing of civil society organizations, among them organizations that Abdelhamid cofounded in Tunisia. This was a result of a post-revolution rise in legal and political freedoms.[32] At the same time, between 2011 and 2021, the structural inequalities, including the unequal distribution of resources across Tunisia, remained unaddressed by successive governments that came to power. The COVID-19 pandemic lockdowns exposed the

marginalized populations to economic precarity, including loss of employment or other sources of income. It was in this context that Tunisia witnessed country-wide protests during the period marking the ten-year
anniversary of the revolution in early 2021.

Under the rule of President Kais Saied, Tunisia witnessed a coup d'état
on July 25, 2021; the coup resulted in a higher concentration of power in the
hands of Saied. This coup came in the context of increasing use of police
surveillance and control by the Tunisian state to respond to protests as well
as other acts of dissent; the resulting political environment of fear and
distrust has made the work of many civil society actors like Abdelhamid
difficult.[33]

On February 21, 2023, Saied called for urgent security actions to fight
what he described as the threat of "hordes of irregular immigrants from
sub-Saharan Africa" who are changing "the demographic composition of
Tunisia" into "a purely African country with no affiliation with the Arab
and Islamic nations" (Saied cited in Parikh 2023b). His statement provoked
state and civilian-supported violence against anyone who was seen as
"African"—a vernacular term used to refer to sub-Saharan individuals. Yet,
in addition to sub-Saharan migrants, many Black Tunisians were also categorized as "African" and exposed to anti-"African" violence, pointing to
the fact that "African" and being Black are seen as synonymous in the
Tunisian political and social imagination.[34]

Political anti-Black discourses in Tunisia and in France function dialec-
tically. Following Saied's statement, France's far-right politician Éric Zemmour published a tweet in support of the statement, linking the "migratory
surge" in Tunisia to the larger "Great Replacement" theory; the latter is a
conspiracy theory espoused by many far-right nationalists across the world
and proposes that, because of migration, the "native" population will be
replaced by socially less desirable migrants (Zemmour 2023). Zemmour,
who has been at the forefront of the popularization of the Great Replacement theory, is a son of Jewish Algerian immigrants to France. His immigrant and North African origins have not translated into support for
migrants, including those from North Africa.

Like Tunisia, France is also witnessing an increasing state reliance on
police violence, disproportionately exposing young men of immigrant
descent to police harassment, arrests, and killings.[35] The police rely on
perceived ethno-racial background, in addition to age and gender, to make
judgments about the probability that the person in question committed a

crime; those categorized as Arab or Black face a higher probability of police stops and arrests (Gauthier 2015). The unequal distribution of police violence along racial lines has often led to France-wide protests, including in June 2023 to protest the police killing of Nahel, a seventeen-year-old boy of North African origins. These protests bring both North African–origin as well as Black individuals together; it is possible that the conversation on collective experiences of marginalization in France may also open up the question of anti-Blackness in North African diaspora.

Shreya Parikh is a dual PhD in political sociology at Sciences Po Paris and the University of North Carolina at Chapel Hill, and a Bucerius PhD Fellow (2022–24) at Zeit-Stiftung. Her dissertation studies the constructions and contestations of race and racialization in Tunisia through a focus on the racialization of Black Tunisians and sub-Saharan migrants.

Notes

1   In this article, I use the terms *North Africa/n* and *Maghreb/i* interchangeably. Here, *North Africa/Maghreb* refers to the region covered by Morocco, Mauritania, Algeria, Tunisia, and Libya. I am aware that this definition of *North Africa/Maghreb* is contested and that both terms carry different colonial and postcolonial histories and linked sociopolitical imaginations (Hannoum 2021).

2   This article started out as a description of Abdelhamid's biography and our conversation. I added analytical paragraphs and footnotes as the article developed so as to contextualize the conversation. In the end, what I have is a thickly annotated interview that hangs loosely between the descriptive and the analytical genres of writing.

3   In this text, I translate *associations* and *collectives* from French as civil society organizations. In addition, the organization ADAM was formally registered as a civil society organization in Tunisia in 2012. For a detailed history of the emergence of the contemporary Black movement in Tunisia following the revolution in 2011, see Abdelhamid and Hamrouni 2016.

4   In line with Abdelhamid's self-identification as Tunisian first, followed by Black, I describe her as Tunisian Black. *Tunisian Black* is a translation of *tunisienne noire* in French; in French, the terms are conjugated in feminine, an aspect that is lost in its English translation. I use *Black Tunisian* to refer to Tunisian individuals or groups who are racialized as Black and who may or may not self-identify as Black.

5   The political and social constructions of North African nation-states as homogenous have come to be challenged by activists and scholars after the 2011 revolution. For example, Morocco witnessed contestations by marginalized groups, resulting in recognition of Morocco's "Arabic, Amazigh, Hassani,

Saharan, African, Andalusian, Jewish and Mediterranean characteristics" in its new constitution passed in 2011 (Maghraoui 2011: 695).

6   As a part of The March, Abdelhamid co-organized a march against racism over March 18–21, 2014, through the cities of Djerba, Gabès, Sfax, and Tunis. Its goal was to denounce the marginalized conditions of Black folks in Tunisia as well as the racist discourses that are present in public spaces, media, and educational institutions (Abdelhamid 2018b). While both ADAM and The March are inactive presently, VFTN continues to remain active; one of its key activities is to organize online safe-space conversations among Black Tunisian women in and outside Tunisia. For more details, see their Facebook page: https://www.facebook.com/profile.php?id=100067752872324 (accessed June 18, 2023). In addition to these organizations, Association M'nemty was founded by Black Tunisian activist Saadia Mosbah in 2013 with the goal of fighting anti-Black racism; it continues to remain active at the time of the writing of this article.

7   The interview took place in 2021 on a grey November afternoon in Abdelhamid's apartment in Saint-Denis, a suburban town located north of Paris. The recorded conversation was in French, with parts in Tunisian Arabic. I translated the recorded transcripts into English and edited and rearranged them for readability.

8   Slavery was abolished in Tunisia in 1846 by Ahmed Bey who ruled the region between 1837 and 1855. Slavery was reestablished later and then re-abolished in 1890 under the French protectorate (Mrad Dali 2015: 63).

9   Terms like *oussif*, *khadim*, and *abid* are used in Tunisian Arabic to refer to Black folks and can be translated as slave or servant. These terms referring to the status of servitude trace their history to the practice of enslavement of Black individuals in Tunisia. While some Black Tunisians are indeed descendants of ex-enslaved Black individuals, not *all* Black Tunisians share this history (Mrad Dali 2009). Yet it is assumed in the Tunisian social and political imagination that *all* Black Tunisians trace their history to slavery. Furthermore, enslavement of non-Black individuals, including that of European individuals, was also practiced before the nineteenth century in the region covered by modern Tunisia (Montana 2013). Descendants of these individuals do not carry any stigma linked to this history.

10   Many Black Tunisian activists point out the relative absence of Black politicians as well as Black folks in positions of economic or cultural power as evidence for the presence of structural marginalization of Black folks in Tunisia.

11   For example, a presentation of my topic of dissertation research is often interpreted as proof of "Arabs are racist" in France; I study race and racialization in Tunisia.

12   Abdelhamid uses "being Black" and "being African" interchangeably in many places. This is similar to the sociopolitical construction of Blackness both in Tunisia and globally as synonymous to Africanness. In this text, I use Africanity as a translation of *Africanité* (in French); sometimes, this French term is also translated as Africanness.

13 Today, Mauritania's population ethnically comprises around 40 percent Hara-tin (Arabic-speaking descendants of ex-enslaved Black populations), 30 percent Beidane (Arabic-speaking populations of Arabo-Berber descent), and 30 percent sub-Saharan Mauritanians (non-Arabic speaking). While a 2015 law criminalizes it, the practice of slavery continues (Sall 2022).

14 Here, Abdelhamid uses the term *Afrique noire* (Black Africa), which refers to the French colonial division of Africa into Black and white; *Black Africa* refers to sub-Saharan Africa (where everyone is assumed to be homogenously Black) and *White Africa* refers to North Africa (where everyone is assumed to be homogenously white). The terms contain a racial imagery, differentiating the continent based on (presumed) differences in phenotype of its inhabitants. In Francophone vernacular, the term *Afrique noire* continues to be used to refer to sub-Saharan Africa and its people; the term carries a negative connotation. For an example of the colonial usage of the term, see *Le monde* 1960.

15 In Tunisia, certain last names (like Hamrouni and Chouchene) are associated with Black families. Many of these last names point to histories of enslavement of Black populations in Tunisia and carry a negative stigma. For more details on the histories and politics of Black Tunisian last names, see Ltifi 2020.

16 In Tunisia, the term *les africains* (Africans) is used to refer to populations from sub-Saharan Africa alone, and not populations from North Africa. The colonial (and racial) divide between *Afrique blanche* (White Africa) and *Afrique noire* (Black Africa) is reflected in this sociopolitical imagination of the African continent in Tunisia.

17 Some Black Tunisians trace their genealogies to parts of North Africa, like southern Algeria and southern Libya.

18 This statement—that all of North Africa identifies more as Mediterranean and Arabo-Muslim than African remains disputed. During my conversations with Moroccan and Algerian colleagues in Tunisia and France about their African identity, some have pointed out that there is a higher identification with the African continent among their compatriots compared to that which they find among Tunisians. This must not be interpreted to mean that there is lesser degree of anti-Black racism in Morocco and Algeria compared to Tunisia.

19 See note 9.

20 Sudan is an Arabic-speaking country which is a member of the Arab League. In the social imagination of individuals from the so-called Arab region (seen as synonymous to Middle East and North Africa), Sudanese individuals are categorized as Black.

21 Countries that lie at the borders between regions categorized as North Africa and sub-Saharan Africa have Arabic-speaking populations. This includes Chad, Djibouti, Eritrea, Niger, Mali, and Somaliland (among others). Many of them have Arabic as their official language but are not categorized as Arab.

22 Tayeb Salih (1929–2009) was a Sudanese writer whose 1966 novel *Season of Migration to the North* is considered a classic in Arabic literature. The book was originally published in Arabic.

23 Najib Mahfouz (1911–2006) was an Egyptian writer most famous for his work
    The Cairo Trilogy (published in Arabic in 1956–57), which is considered a classic
    in Arabic literature. He received the Nobel Prize in Literature in 1988.

24 According to Abdelhamid, Article 1 of the 2014 Tunisian constitution reads, "El
    tounis dawla muslima w arabia" (Tunisia is a Muslim and Arab state). While Article
    1 of the 2014 constitution only states that Tunisia embraces Islam as its religion
    and Arabic as its language, the Preamble states the commitment of the Repub-
    lic of Tunisia to human values inspired from "our enlightened reformist move-
    ments that are based on the foundations of *our* Islamic-Arab identity" (Republic
    of Tunisia 2014; emphasis mine). After the coup d'état in July 2021, President
    Kais Saied drafted and passed a new constitution in 2022. References to Tunisia
    as an Arab and Muslim state can be found in the Preamble of this new constitu-
    tion. See *Tunisia Coup* 2022.

25 The Amazigh people are the Indigenous people of North Africa. Here, Abdelha-
    mid points to the hegemonic definition of *Arab* that has been imposed by the
    state and adopted in popular discourses about Arabness and Tunisian-ness.

26 A Nasserist is someone who embraces the Pan-Arab ideology as advocated by
    Gamal Abdel Nasser, president of Egypt, 1956–70.

27 This petition became one of the foundations for the bill demanding the crimi-
    nalization of racial discrimination; the bill became a law in Tunisia in October
    2018. For more details about the law, see Fassatoui 2021 and Parikh 2021, 2023c.

28 According to Omar Fassatoui, who was then human rights officer at the Office
    of the United Nations High Commissioner for Human Rights in Tunisia, the
    timeline of the making of the law is as follows: on December 24, 2016, three
    Congolese (and not Ivorian) youth faced violent physical harassment in Tunis;
    on 25 December 2016, civil society groups, which included both sub-Saharan as
    well as Black Tunisian activists, gathered to protest against racial harassment;
    on 26 December 2016, at a preplanned event marking the National Day against
    Racism organized by the UN along with Tunisian civil society organizations,
    then–Prime Minister Youssef Chahed made a last-minute decision to speak in
    support of the bill criminalizing racial discrimination. Notes based on recorded
    interview conducted in March 2021 in Tunis.

29 Fatima Ouassak (1976–present) is a Franco-Moroccan activist living in the
    Greater Paris region. She is known for cofounding the civil society organization
    Front de Mères (Mothers' Front) in 2016 as well as for her 2020 book *La Puissance
    des mères: Pour un nouveau sujet révolutionnaire* (*The Power of Mothers: For a Revolution-
    ary New Subject*; published by La Découverte).

30 Abdelhamid *becomes* Maghrebi in France. In French society, she gets grouped
    together with all immigrant and immigrant-descendent groups from North Africa.
    It is through this categorization by others that Abdelhamid comes to self-identify
    as *Maghrebine*. In Tunisia, while a sense of belonging to the Maghreb region does
    exist (as visible in Tunisian support for the Moroccan football team during the
    World Cup 2022 semi-final match against France), the identification with Magh-
    rebi identity does not take the same shape as it does in the diasporic context.

31 My interpretation of the rejection that Abdelhamid feels in the Maghrebi-diasporic and Black feminist groups in France is that a lot of it comes from differences between Abdelhamid's trajectory and trajectories of those who are members of these groups; as a recent migrant to France from a small town in Tunisia, Abdelhamid has fewer socioeconomic privileges compared to most women in these groups. In addition, sociocultural markers like Tunisian accent when speaking French may also stigmatize Abdelhamid in these groups. Abdelhamid's migrant status in France also makes her stay within and mobility outside France precarious compared to those who have French citizenship.

32 The Freedom House index for Tunisia shifted from "Not free" in 2010 to "Partly free" in 2011.

33 In June 2022, I was detained and interrogated by Tunisian police for a tweet; I was eventually forced to leave the country in January 2023. See Parikh 2023d.

34 While Black Tunisians are exposed to anti-"African" violence, the degree and scale at which they face this violence is less compared to that faced by sub-Saharan nationals.

35 For statistics demonstrating increase in police violence in France, see Déni 2022.

Works Cited

Abdelhamid, Maha. 2018a. "De la libération de la parole raciste à l'émergence d'un mouvement contre le racisme anti-noir." In *Tunisie: Une démocratisation au-dessus de tout soupçon*, edited by Amin Allal and Vincent Geisser, 343–56. Pairs: CNRS.

Abdelhamid, Maha. 2018b. "Les noirs tunisiens après la révolution de 2011—Retour sur les prémices d´un mouvement contre le racisme." *Euromesco Policy Brief 84*. Barcelona: EuroMeSCo.

Abdelhamid, Maha. 2018c. "Les transformations socio-spatiales des oasis de Gabès (Tunisie): Déclin des activités agricoles, urbanisation informelle et dégradation de l'environnement à Zrig, des années 1970 à nos jours." PhD diss., Université Paris Nanterre.

Abdelhamid, Maha, Amel Elfargi, and Moutaa Amin Elwaer. 2017. *Etre noir, ce n'est pas une question de couleur: Rapport d'enquête: les représentations du racisme chez les noirs de Tunisie*. Ariana, Tunisia: Nirvana.

Abdelhamid, Maha, and Mansour Hamrouni. 2016. "L'émergence du mouvement des jeunes Noirs contre le racisme en Tunisie après la révolution du 14 janvier 2011." In *La constitution de la Tunisie: Part 3*, 613–29. Tunisia: UNDP.

Ben Sedrine, Saïd. 2018. *Défis à relever pour un accueil décent de la migration subsaharienne en Tunisie*. Série du projet PROMIG-FES (2017–2020). Tunis: Fondation Friedrich Ebert.

Deltombe, Thomas. 2005. *L'islam imaginaire. La construction médiatique de l'islamophobie en France, 1975–2005*. Paris: La Découverte.

de Neuville, Héloïse. 2021. "La 'négrophobie,' un tabou dans la communauté franco-maghrébine." *La Croix*, June 11. https://www.la-croix.com/France/negrophobie-tabou-communaute-franco-maghrebine-2021-06-11-1201160669.

Déni, Flagrant. 2022. "Macron: l'escalade de la violence policière en chiffres." Media-part (blog), May 24. https://blogs.mediapart.fr/flagrant-deni/blog/240522/macron-l-escalade-de-la-violence-policiere-en-chiffres.

Fassatoui, Omar. 2021. "Tunisia's Law against Racial Discrimination: The Mixed Results of a Pioneering Legislation." *Arab Reform Initiative*, February 11. https://www.arab-reform.net/publication/tunisias-law-against-racial-discrimination-the-mixed-results-of-a-pioneering-legislation/.

Gauthier, Jérémie. 2015. "Origines contrôlées: Police et minorités en France et en Allemagne." *Sociétés contemporaines* 97: 101–27.

Hajjat, Abdellali, and Marwan Mohammed. 2016. *Islamophobie: Comment les élites françaises fabriquent le «problème musulman»*. Paris: La Découverte.

Hannoum, Abdelmajid. 2021. *The Invention of the Maghreb: Between Africa and the Middle East*. Cambridge: Cambridge University Press.

Jelassi, Mohamed Amine. 2020. *Rapport d'analyse des cas de discrimination récoltés par les points anti-discrimination*. Tunis: Points Anti-Discrimination.

Keaton, Trica Danielle, T. Denean Sharpley-Whiting, and Tyler Stovall, eds. 2012. *Black France / France Noire: The History and Politics of Blackness*. Durham, NC: Duke University Press.

King, Stephen J., and Zied Rouine. 2021. "Democracy and Progress towards Racial Equality in Tunisia: Interview with Zied Rouine." *Arab Reform Initiative*, March 26. https://www.arab-reform.net/publication/democracy-and-progress-towards-racial-equality-in-tunisia-interview-with-zied-rouine/.

Le monde. 1960. "Afrique noire et Afrique blanche." August 6. https://www.lemonde.fr/archives/article/1960/08/06/afrique-noire-et-afrique-blanche_2083242_1819218.html.

Ltifi, Afifa. 2020. "Black Tunisians and the Pitfalls of Bourguiba's Homogenization Project." *POMEPS Studies* 40 (Africa and the Middle East: Beyond the Divides). https://pomeps.org/black-tunisians-and-the-pitfalls-of-bourguibas-homogenization-project.

Maghraoui, Driss. 2011. "Constitutional Reforms in Morocco: Between Consensus and Subaltern Politics." *Journal of North African Studies* 16, no. 4: 679–99.

Mamdani, Mahmood. 2002. "Good Muslim, Bad Muslim: A Political Perspective on Culture and Terrorism." *American Anthropologist* 104: 766–75.

Montana, Ismael M. 2013. *The Abolition of Slavery in Ottoman Tunisia*. Gainesville: University Press of Florida.

Mrad Dali, Inès. 2009. "Identités multiples et multitudes d'histoires: Les «Noirs tunisiens» de 1846 à aujourd'hui." PhD diss., École des hautes études en sciences sociales, Paris.

Mrad Dali, Inès. 2015. "Les mobilisations des «Noirs tunisiens» au lendemain de la révolte de 2011: entre affirmation d'une identité historique et défense d'une «cause noire»." *Politique africaine* 140, no. 4: 61–81.

Oualdi, M'hamed. 2020. *A Slave between Empires: A Transimperial History of North Africa*. New York: Columbia University Press.

Parikh, Shreya. 2021. "The Limits of Confronting Racial Discrimination in Tunisia with Law 50." *MERIP Middle East Report* 299 (Summer). https://merip.org/2021/08/the-limits-of-confronting-racial-discrimination-in-tunisia-with-law-50/.

Parikh, Shreya. 2023a. "How Tunisia Produces 'Irregular' Migrants." Tahrir Institute for Middle East Policy, June 13. https://timep.org/2023/06/13/how-tunisia-produces-irregular-migrants/.

Parikh, Shreya. 2023b. "Making Tunisia Non-African Again—Saied's Anti-Black Campaign." *Review of African Political Economy.* https://roape.net/2023/03/01/making-tunisia-non-african-again-saieds-anti-black-campaign/.

Parikh, Shreya. 2023c. "Remembering Jamila Debbech Ksiksi—An Interview with the Late Tunisian Lawmaker and Anti-racist Activist." *Middle East Report Online.* https://merip.org/2023/05/remembering-jamila-debbech-ksiksi/.

Parikh, Shreya. 2023d. "Under Surveillance: Testimony from a Global South Migrant in Tunisia." *Nawaat,* January 25. https://nawaat.org/2023/01/25/under-surveillance-testimony-from-a-global-south-migrant-in-tunisia/.

Pouessel, Stéphanie. 2012. "Les marges renaissantes: Amazigh, Juif, Noir. Ce que la révolution a changé dans ce «petit pays homogène par excellence» qu'est la Tunisie." *L'année du Maghreb,* 8: 143–60.

Republic of Tunisia. 2014. *Tunisia's Constitution of 2014.* https://www.constituteproject.org/constitution/Tunisia_2014.pdf.

Sall, Aliou Moussa. 2022. *The Application of the 2015 Anti-slavery Law in Mauritania.* London: Minority Rights Group International (MRG).

Tayeb, Leila. 2021. "What Is Whiteness in North Africa?" *Lateral: Journal of the Cultural Studies Association* 10, no. 1: Spring. https://www.jstor.org/stable/48671628.

Terman, Rochelle. 2016. "Islamophobia, Feminism, and the Politics of Critique." *Theory, Culture, and Society* 33, no. 2: 77–102.

Tunisia Coup. 2022. "Translation of Kais Saied's proposed constitution." July 13. https://web.archive.org/web/20230622020316/https://tunisiacoup.com/2022/07/13/translation-of-kais-saieds-proposed-constitution/.

Walz, Terence, and Kenneth M. Cuno, eds. 2011. *Race and Slavery in the Middle East: Histories of Trans-Saharan Africans in Nineteenth-Century Egypt, Sudan, and the Ottoman Mediterranean.* Cairo: The American University in Cairo Press.

Zemmour, Eric (@ZemmourEric). 2023. "Les pays du Maghreb eux-mêmes commencent à sonner l'alarme." X (formerly Twitter), February 22. https://twitter.com/ZemmourEric/status/1628328739284176896?lang=en.

Lisa E. Wright

....

According to the Record

Abstract: In this piece Lisa E. Wright analyzes the penmanship on her grand-mother's birth certificate to question whether her great-grandmother gave birth to her Grandma Rickey in 1938 with a white doctor or with a midwife who may not have had a license. She explores if her grandmother's birth reflected changing attitudes toward Black midwives, her great-grandmother's choice, or a luxury afforded to her great-grandmother by her great-grandfather's status as a Black coal miner. To analyze the decisions of the next generation of women who gave birth in her family, in this piece Wright struggles with the reasons her grandmother looked outside their community of midwives for maternal care and gave birth in a Jim Crow hospital in Lynchburg, Virginia.

....

It was widely believed by whites that slave women gave birth more easily
and quickly than white women, and thus needed less attention during
pregnancy and labor.
—Deborah Gray White, *Ar'n't I a Woman?*
....

In May 1934 my maternal grandmother Grandma Rickey was delivered into
the world in the security of her parents' Alpoca, West Virginia, home. In
my late teens, to fill in a memory book, I once asked her if she knew any
details about her birth. She recalled the name, Dr. Penn. As an adult, once
I obtained a copy of Grandma Rickey's birth certificate I would find the
name Frank H. Penn, MD, inked onto the signature line.

Under his signature, on a dotted line labeled, "physician, midwife, par-
ent," Dr. Penn wrote *Covel, WVa*. The W and V, both uppercase, are connected

MERIDIANS · feminism, race, transnationalism   23:2 October 2024
DOI: 10.1215/15366936-11266356 © 2024 Smith College

and written in one stroke, while the *a* is lowercase. Both of my great grand-
parents' addresses are listed as *Alpoca, WVa.* The main body of her birth
certificate is completed in the same penmanship, which appears to be
Dr. Penn's.

My Aunt Diane, my grandmother's oldest daughter, asked her mother
her own set of questions regarding her birth. Aunt Diane always said there
were talks of a midwife being present at my grandmother's birth. I've never
been able to confirm if this was true. By the 1930s, West Virginia midwives
were required to be licensed to continue to practice. Though some midwives
continued to attend births without a license, others chose to become
licensed and were, therefore, able to register babies' births themselves.
During this transition in West Virginia, only 8 percent of births were handled
by midwives, and some coal-producing counties recorded the lowest number of midwife-assisted births (Bickley 1990). Alpoca was a coal mining town
located in Wyoming County, and so it's probable that my grandmother's
parents used their doctor through their medical assistance for childbirth,
which was available through my great-grandfather's coal mining company.

Mama Edna was listed as a sixteen-year-old *Col* (Colored) housewife at
the time of my grandmother's birth. Three years earlier she moved two
hundred miles away from her Appomattox, Virginia, hometown to Alpoca,
West Virginia, to make a home with her husband. Since white men had
begun to replace, degrade, and exclude Black midwives during childbirth
in the early 1800s after the passing of the Act Prohibiting Importation of
Slaves, and midwives handled fewer births in West Virginia in the 1930s, I
assume that Dr. Penn was a white male doctor, and the sole practitioner
present at Mama Edna's labor. Outside of other miners' wives, Mama Edna
may not have had much choice in who assisted her in labor. According to
Acella R. Bickley's (1990) "Midwifery in West Virginia," "Black and immigrant populations were heavily represented in the cities and the coal producing counties, which relied more on physicians than midwives by the
1930s." With Mama Edna being so young, and so far away from home, I
imagine her swathed in a community or female network similar to the
one the scholar Deborah Gray White discusses in her text *Ar'n't I a Woman?:
Female Slaves in the Plantation South.* Originally established by enslaved
Black females as a necessary tool to ensure "their own means of resistance
and survival" (White 1999: 119), the female network was maintained
in Black communities after slavery and included midwives and other
sisters involved in what Patricia Hill Collins termed *motherwork* (Collins

1990: 173–99). Collins defines motherwork as the everyday activities that
mothers participate in to ensure the survival of a community of women.
My grandmother was Mama Edna's second child. I imagine othermothers
(178), sister friends in her mining community, performed motherwork by
supporting her through her pregnancies, early stages of her delivery, and
kept her eldest daughter while she labored.

One of the women in the miners' female network may have served as the
community midwife. Her service, or *motherwork*, was as the woman who
ushered birthing mothers over the threshold into motherhood. Maybe her
name wasn't on my grandmother's birth certificate not because she wasn't
present but because she wasn't a registered midwife. I don't know if the
Covel, WVa written in the attending physician's space represents the location of Dr. Penn's office, which could mean that since Granddaddy Frank
was a miner his family was only served by the mining company doctor.
I don't know if the reason that Grandma Rickey didn't remember the name
of the midwife who attended her birth was because the midwife was
replaced by a white man or because the midwife's name was excluded and
replaced with her location. Or maybe Mama Edna and Granddaddy Frank
could have identified with Nikki Finney's family whom Finney describes in
the poem, "The Afterbirth, 1931." Perhaps my ancestors like Finney's family
members had "been caught / by tried and true Black grannies," before they
migrated to Alpoca. Possibly since "times had changed / and the midwife
wasn't safe anymore" (Finney 1931: 66), Mama Edna decided to only use
Dr. Penn. If this is the case, it would mean Grandma Rickey's birth initiated
the women in my most direct maternal line abandoning the use of midwives and preferring medical progress and the use of white medical institutions (66).

As a mining family, my Aunt Diane said Mama Edna and Granddaddy
Frank had a brick home, access to free schools, vouchers for food, and a
white picket fence. When telling me about them she'd always say, "They
had it good." In Finney's poem, readers are shocked by her retelling of the
violent childbirth of her father, who was delivered by a white physician. The
physician's lack of care leads to Finney's father's foot being snapped in half,
his collarbone shattered, and the neglect of Finney's grandmother, which
ultimately leads to her death. We leave the poem with a sense of a Black
family's desire to follow modern trends by hiring a white physician thinking they were doing "better" for the next generation. I've considered my
Aunt Diane's words. Maybe our family believed no longer having to give

birth at home with a midwife meant having it good, and I'll admit I know little about how my family defined progress. I do know that after Grand-daddy Frank was killed in the coal mine, Mama Edna would eventually migrate to Baltimore, Maryland, to find a better working and living environment. Maybe Mama Edna taught Grandma Rickey that being able to give birth in a hospital meant she and her children would have it good too.

Other 1953 RECORDS ARE NOT AVAILABLE
Sincerely, Centra Va Baptist Hospital

Grandma Rickey and I had very few conversations about pregnancy before I got pregnant in 2001. Every so often she'd inquire if my husband and I were planning to have children, how many, and when. About a year before I became pregnant, I began to engage in conversations about pregnancy and labor with my mother and sisters in my community. I accompanied two friends into labor and read a few books about pregnancy and labor like *What to Expect When You're Expecting*, and *Spiritual Midwifery*, but I hadn't felt the full measure of labor myself.

One of my sisters, who had given birth to a child around 2000, spoke of voicing her needs and feeling belittled and neglected during her first childbirth experience in a local hospital in Clarksville, Tennessee. Another, who labored around 2002, spoke of her not being given time or space to be in tune with her body during delivery and then being rushed into a decision to have a cesarean. Their experiences may reflect why "out-of-hospital births increased by 72 percent" in the United States during the years 2004 to 2017 (MacDorman and Declercq 2016: 117). When I became pregnant, I decided to give birth at Nashville's East End Women's Health and Birth Center, with only a Black midwife, my mother, and my husband, Ibrafall, present.

In 2004, when Grandma Rickey first shared the details of her first child-birth experience with me, I was twenty-six years old, thirty weeks pregnant, and had started preterm labor. Grandma Rickey was well into her sixties, and I imagine she was probably rolling her hair by this time on a July Sunday evening. She asked, "How far apart are your contractions?" I had avoided calling my tightenings "contractions," because I didn't think it was normal to have contractions at thirty weeks. I could hear her gum snap, so I knew she had pulled the phone closer to her mouth. I told her what I thought about the contractions. To mirror my movement into preterm labor with my first child, my grandmother recalled her first birth. She and I were suspended in time, our paths crossing only momentarily. The story of her first childbirth, her firstborn's death, and her survival rocked me while I rode contractions that came too early, too fast.

Four days later, my midwife's exam confirmed I was about one to two centimeters dilated and my cervix was thinning, effaced. She wrapped two big elastic belts around my abdomen and placed a clear glob of gel on the monitor. The nonstress test revealed that my contractions were twelve minutes apart. Patients at the birth center who had complications in their pregnancies were referred to a doctor at Centennial Medical Center. After my exam, I was sent to and then admitted to the hospital to be monitored.

Over the next few weeks, I would be put on bed rest, spend several nights in the hospital, undergo close observations by a white doctor, and have to take two prescriptions to ensure my first pregnancy went to full term. As years passed, me and Grandma Rickey's herstories became a blur for me in one particular detail. I thought Grandma Rickey shared her birth experience with me because her first birth began with preterm labor, or labor pains before thirty-seven weeks, but my aunts affirmed her pregnancy was full term and that only my mother and her last child were preemies. I also thought my grandmother *went to a hospital* for her first birth because she was in preterm labor, but I have learned this was not the case, and this fact has not been easy for me to accept. I believe my grandmother, like every birthing mother, has the right to give birth wherever and with whomever they choose. Naturally, though, I do wonder if Grandma Rickey's first child would have survived had she been under the care of a Black midwife. After all, I'm still not sure if Grandma Rickey's birth plans were firm.

Grandma Rickey drew her last breath in 2010. In the summer of 2021, I called her closest cousin, Harriet, who lived and gave birth at the same time as my grandmother, to help me understand my grandmother's decision to give birth in a hospital during Jim Crow. Cousin Harriet did not remember my grandmother's first pregnancy. Did the slow removal of the Black midwife from the Black female network usher in a disruption in communication between Black women about their reproductive lives?

About her own pregnancy, Harriet recalls she delivered all her children in her home with a Black midwife from Concord, Virginia, Essie Jones, except her last child. Harriet told me, "My feet were so swollen, the midwife was afraid to touch me." For generations, midwives cared for mothers during their pregnancies, through labor, and would visit them for several days after the baby was born to teach them how to care for their newborns.

During the early 1900s, several states required midwives to be registered. Once registered, they were not allowed to use the tinctures, teas, or many natural methods passed down to them for generations by the Granny midwives who trained them. Instead, their bags were regularly inspected by newly trained state medical officials who had less experience, and their practices replaced by Western medicine (Smith and Holmes 1996: 87).

Several years after the Emancipation Proclamation, some Black females defined progress as access to various birthing options. They struggled to maintain the autonomy of their reproductive health. This included not only access to care but with whom to entrust their reproductive care. When I told Cousin Harriet that my grandmother gave birth to her first child in the hospital, she speculated Grandma Rickey may have also had a medical emergency. I've wondered if Grandma Rickey contemplated working with Harriet's midwife, Essie. I imagine that in the 1950s, racial progress could have looked like turning toward white medical institutions and away from family traditions like using Black midwives and home births for maternal care.

Actual access to medical care was a right Grandma Rickey had been born with. Her decision to give birth in a hospital, despite Jim Crow restrictions, may have been her way of claiming and demanding access to the type of medical care she believed she and her unborn child rightfully deserved. Yet, Grandma Rickey's decision to give birth in a hospital during Jim Crow, despite long waiting times due to laws that guaranteed whites received care first, put her and her unborn child's life in danger.

When Grandma Rickey went into labor in June of 1953, she was nineteen years old, and there were no Black hospitals in Lynchburg, Virginia. In 1944 a group of Black doctors petitioned the city council to allow Blacks to practice at Lynchburg General Hospital, but this would not happen because the hospital was still under city ownership. In 1953, Lynchburg General Hospital was in the final stages of constructing and opening a new hospital. New buildings were being constructed (*OurHealth Magazine* 2013). New laws would have to wait. The 1954 *Brown vs. Board of Education* court decision only began the process of desegregation and thus Blacks would not work at Lynchburg General Hospital for another twenty years (*OurHealth Magazine* 2013).

I imagine Grandma Rickey wanted to be among the 88 percent of women who had begun to give birth in hospitals in the 1950s.[1] She must have had a shred of hope that she and her unborn child would receive equal treatment since Blacks were, at least, admitted to Lynchburg General. Grandma Rickey lived with Samuel Hubbard, the child's father, and his family in rural Concord, Virginia. Though they never married, the child's paternal grandmother and aunt along with Grandma Rickey's mother Mama Edna, were the closest members of her female network.

In the early mornings, Samuel could be found plowing Concord's red dirt as a construction worker. He may have been a part of the construction crew who built the Lynchburg General Hospital that would officially open in 1955. Grandma Rickey spent days with Samuel's mother and aunt, sharpening her skills as a homemaker. I wonder if the white women Grandma Rickey helped care for had shared their hospital birth experiences with her while she cleaned their silver or folded their laundry. As women who still used an outhouse, and had no electricity, I imagine Grandma Rickey's mother and othermothers encouraged her to travel the sixteen miles to Lynchburg General hospital to labor in a hospital instead of at home.

This could mean that Grandma Rickey's firstborn may have been one of the first children in our family to be born in an actual hospital. If access to medical care was a measure of progress, Mama Edna's birth with Dr. Penn at home, would mean that, despite segregation laws, and racism, the next generation of children should be born in a hospital, right? When my grandmother checked herself into Lynchburg General, no Black doctors greeted her in the lobby. She entered as an Other.

Other NO RECORDS HAVE BEEN FOUND FOR THESE PATIENTS. THE RECORDS MAY NO LONGER EXIST.
Sincerely,
Centra Va Baptist Hospital

If my grandmother were alive today, I'd ask her for more. She never put words to experiencing contractions as a first-time mother while simultaneously walking into the Colored Only entrance at Lynchburg General Hospital. I do wonder if my grandmother was inspired by various leaders of the civil rights movement who weren't afraid to demand equal treatment. For instance, close to where Grandma Rickey lived, Barbara Rose Johns demanded an equal learning environment from Prince Edward County, Virginia, schools in 1951 (SNCC *Digital Gateway* n.d). Johns eventually moved out of Virginia for her own safety, but not before leading her peers in a protest, and having her case included in the *Board of Education* court case. Could the rage of a sixteen-year-old—who galvanized her classmates to stand up against cold rain-filled classrooms and tar-paper shacks while their white counterparts enjoyed newly built buildings—have fueled Grandma Rickey to choose to give birth in a Jim Crow hospital?

I requested copies of my grandmother's hospital records. I had hoped to read the doctor's notes surrounding her treatment during her labor at Lynchburg General Hospital. I expected to transcribe timed stamped notes to decode the forms of violence and neglect my grandmother may have experienced. I wanted to search her records, and those of her firstborn child, to interpret how my grandmother's lawful right to equal medical treatment may have been denied due to her race. I wanted to read the archives for *her* fear, for the parts she chose not to recite. I wanted to connect her treatment and fear as a laboring Colored woman in a Jim Crow hospital with the fear I had felt as a Black woman in preterm labor. I was educated and aware of the history of America's violence upon the female laboring body, but I had no personal experiences. I wanted to use the archives to read, interpret, and transcribe the trauma that was my grandmother's initiation into motherhood.

I supposed her story would be similar to Toni Morrison's Pauline Breedlove, who went to the hospital to feel *easeful* (Morrison 2007). Who wouldn't want to feel at ease during labor? Yet, I've imagined my grandmother in a white room full of other Coloreds, some pregnant, others bloody, missing limbs, with scalding fevers. It was typical for Colored patients to all be placed in one location, despite their symptoms. If Mama Edna were by her side, she may have spoken for her daughter and hinted to the white doctors in her most respectful manner that her daughter was no different from their white mothers, wives, and daughters. She too was human.

Pauline Breedlove was alone and had no one to stop the doctors from ramming their fingers between her legs. No one to comfort her after overhearing an older doctor tell a younger doctor he was training, "These here women you don't have any trouble with. They deliver right away and with no pain. Just like horses" (Morrison 2007: 124–25). Despite what doctors may have thought about Black women's pain levels in the 1950s, maybe Grandma Rickey went to the hospital looking for medical treatments that might have eased her childbirth pains.

Other NO RECORDS HAVE BEEN FOUND FOR THESE PATIENTS. THE RECORDS MAY NO LONGER EXIST.
Sincerely,
CENTRA VA BAPTIST HOSPITAL
When the letters that labeled Grandma Rickey and Baby Girl Webb as Other arrived from Centra Va Baptist Hospital, I thought about Saidiyah Hartman's "Venus in Two Acts." Hartman (2008: 8) wrote, "The loss of stories

sharpens the hunger for them." For days I returned to those letters. I mourned what I could never know. The records may no longer exist, yet we are left with Grandma Rickey's words, the parts she chose to share. According to a birth certificate and Grandma Rickey Baby Girl Webb was named Edna Delores Webb.[2] Still, we don't have the whole story, and there is not much breath in the archives. Delores's birth certificate and death certificate only revealed so much. Reading that the hospital records were no longer available pinned me into a held space. I was denied access to archival data to amplify Grandma Rickey's experience, and yet I carried the awareness of countless Black mothers who leave hospitals empty-handed, or worse die themselves because of childbirth experiences gone wrong.

The enslaved girls Hartman wrote about in "Venus in Two Acts" left no verbal records of the violence they experienced on the slave boat, yet even without the records their lives are connected to my grandmother's birth experience and Delores's life. As Hartman writes, their lives reflect "the ongoing state of emergency in which Black life remains in peril" (13). Baby Girl Webb's death certificate states that the disease or condition directly leading to death is *asphyxia perinatal*. Without the hospital records, and with only Grandma Rickey's account of her labor, we can gather that Delores most likely suffered from a lack of oxygen during her delivery. On Delores's death certificate, John S. Morris, MD, certified that he attended the deceased from *24 june 53 to 24 June, 1953*, and that he *last saw the deceased alive on 24 June, 1953, and that death occurred at 820pm*. Jim Crow laws established that white doctors would see their white patients first.

In an article titled "Treatment of Prolonged Labor" Dr. Gerald W. Gustafson (1954) declared that nothing was more taxing for patients and physicians in the field of obstetrics than prolonged labor. Yet, doctors didn't agree on how to measure prolonged labor. At an American College of Surgeons December 1953 meeting, 25 out of 63 doctors voted that prolonged labor should be considered 24 hours (Gustafson 1954: 535). The Jim Crow laws and lack of consistency within the field of obstetrics cause me to question how often Dr. Morris checked on my grandmother.

Grandma Rickey didn't birth like a horse. She told us her labor lasted thirty hours, and that she was bound, hands tied to the hospital bed (Goer 2010: 33). When my grandmother began active labor, her white nurse may have been by her side. I want to believe my grandmother was comforted during her prolonged labor. Maybe Mama Edna rubbed her shoulders and pulled her hair from her face. Used her handkerchief to wipe the sweat and fear from her brow. Fed her ice chips. Maybe sips of water. Maybe once Delores's head finally began to crown Grandma Rickey began to crave holding her child. My grandmother never spoke of any interventions she was offered. It's feasible that the nurse untied her wrist so that my grandmother could use her hands freely to control her body and help push her daughter into the world. I wonder who caught Delores. I wonder if she were ever put in her mother's arms?

Dr. Morris wrote that one of the antecedent causes of Delores's death was long, hard labor. Another significant condition contributing to the death but not related to the disease or condition causing death was code 7610. Code 761 is listed as a birth injury. The zero signifies there was no immaturity. Maybe I should be thankful for the lack of medical records. If I had read that Grandma Rickey was neglected during her labor or even that she had refused certain technologies that may have ultimately saved her child's life, none of it would blow breath back into Delores. I would not have gotten to know my aunt, and reproducing my grandmother's trauma would never extend Delores's life. Just as knowing Grandma Rickey was allowed to labor for thirty hours and that Delores only lived for one hour and twenty-four minutes didn't provide Grandma Rickey with an extra minute with her child. Due to their race, I don't know how much time doctors spent trying to get Delores to breathe on her own, or how much time Grandma Rickey spent with her dying child. Both would have been historically unmeasurable, yet treasured, commodities denied to people of color.

When I asked Grandma Rickey what happened to Delores, she simply stated, "She was unable to breathe on her own." She did not mention any interventions done for her child, and she never said where she was buried. Dr. Morris signed Baby Girl Webb's (Delores's name isn't written on her death certificate) death certificate on June 30, 1953. By then he had rounded her interval between onset and death up to one and a half hours. This was after the autopsy and after the details of the death were collected in records no longer available to me. On June 25, Lynchburg General Hospital completed the cremation of Delores's remains. Remains that a funeral director assured me via a phone call through my tears, were yes, probably cremated like other hospital waste, like tumors, and then put in their own container, and laid to rest in a mass burial, if unclaimed.

Unclaimed. My grandmother took us to our family gravesite in Buckingham, Virginia, yearly when I was a child. Concord is the town she lived in when Delores was born. She made sure my brother and I knew who each person was and how we were related to them. I could not believe that her child's remains would have been put in a mass burial that now no longer exists. I asked my aunts if Grandma Rickey ever mentioned anything about Delores's remains. I was told, "Lisa, back then, they didn't tell you nothing. Or they may have told her that's what happens, and she may have felt like she had no choice, but to do what they told her to do." While my grandmother looked at the other graves, I now wonder if she silently yearned for her daughter's remains.

Grandma Rickey passed her birth story on to me because I called her utterly confused about the consistent sensations in my womb. As a first-time mom, I could barely recognize that I was starting preterm labor. After weeks of bedrest, when I reached thirty-six weeks, I was able to choose if I wanted to be released back into the care of my Black midwife. Grandma Rickey's first labor inspired me to ensure I maintained as much autonomy of my birth experience as possible. I was for the medications, machines, and even the care from a white male doctor that kept our baby in place until it was time for her to arrive. Yet, I still had faith in old technology, my body which was created to give birth. Also, I had faith in Black midwives.

At forty-one weeks pregnant, I labored for over six hours at the birthing center. With each contraction, I floated in a birthing pool of hot water and stared at walls painted with a blue calm ocean, brown sand, and palm trees. My mother rubbed my back, offered ice chips and water, and smiled. Ibrafall positioned himself behind me and led me to breathe, see light, feel pleasure, and seek happiness. I felt safe during my delivery and when there was a delay in our daughter descending my birth canal, I relied on the words of wisdom I had been given from an othermother in my circle of sisters, "Laugh, cry, embrace the new facet of yourself, the door has opened, welcome in the light and songs of motherhood." Her words encouraged me to affirm my body's ability to open up and birth naturally.

Even with me intentionally relaxing, my skin wasn't stretching enough to allow our baby's head to crown. Carlotta asked me if she could cut me. I said, "Yes!" I was ready to meet our baby girl. Carlotta used surgical scissors to cut about one eighth of an inch slit to allow our baby's head through. After I was slit, the baby's head came through smoothly, and to our surprise she was face up. The rest of her body slid into Carlotta's arms, but she was not breathing. Our daughter was Carlotta's one thousandth baby and her last delivery. She was determined not to lose her. She suctioned her nose, popped her tail, and the baby began to wail. Relieved and beaming with pride, my mother stepped into the hall to call her sisters and Grandma Rickey.

I want to believe there was nothing more the nurses or doctors could have done to help Delores breathe in her hour of life. Despite segregation laws, Grandma Rickey aspired to create more for her first child than her Jim Crow Virginian roots had offered her. I want to believe Delores received the same care a white infant who may have been born after prolonged labor in Lynchburg General Hospital would have received.

Grandma Rickey was an observer. Any minute spent with her firstborn was a minute spent drenched in love. Every spring she awaited and was fascinated with new blooms of azaleas, tulips, and cherry blossoms. I'm sure she watched Delores's pulse beat against her windpipe and inhaled her baby scent. I bet she smoothed her daughter's thick black curly hair, and inspected her pinky toes, for their family familiarity, just as she did when she met my firstborn. I've prayed that when Grandma Rickey left the hospital, she left with no impressions of cuffs on her wrists, and instead that she never forgot the feeling of Delores's tiny hand wrapped around her forefinger as her eyes performed their final bow.

. . . .

Lisa E. Wright is a lecturer in the University Writing Program at Johns Hopkins University. Her writing courses center on Black maternal health, with a particular focus on reproductive and birthing justice. Wright is working on a manuscript "The Ring of Fire: A Memoir," which chronicles her home births with her midhusband. It further examines Black women's birthing choices, with a particular focus on the delegitimation of Black midwives, and on creating safe birthing spaces inside and outside medical institutions. Her writing has appeared *College English*, *The Writing Center Journal*, *Praxis*, *Axis*, and *Hippocampus Magazine*.

Notes

1   Centers for Disease Control and Prevention, "NCHS—Natality Measures for Females by Race and Hispanic Origin: United States." https://data.cdc.gov /NCHS/NCHS-Natality-Measures-for-Females-by-Race-and-His/89yk-m38d /data (accessed January 15, 2023). "Nurse Practitioner," *Encyclopedia Britannica*, May 16, 2024, https://www.britannica.com/science/nurse-practitioner.

2   Though Edna Delores Webb was her full name, she was called Delores by Grandma Rickey and her siblings. I will refer to her as Baby Girl Webb and/or Delores in this essay.

Works Cited

Bickley, Ancella R. 1990. "Midwifery in West Virginia." *West Virginia Archives and History* 99: 55–68. http://129.71.204.160/history/journal_wvh/wvh49–5.html.

Collins, Patricia Hill. 2000. *Black Feminist Thought: Knowledge, Consciousness, and the Politics of Empowerment*. New York: Routledge.

Finney, Nikky. 2013. "The Afterbirth 1931." In *Rice*, 65–71. Evanston, IL: Northwestern University Press.

Goer, Henci. 2010. "Cruelty in Maternity Wards: Fifty Years Later." *Journal of Perinatal Education* 19, no. 3: 33–42. https://doi.org/10.1624/105812410X514413.

Gustafson, Gerald W. 1954. "Treatment of Prolonged Labor." *JAMA* 155, no. 6: 535–38. https://doi.org/10.1001/jama.1954.03690240001001.

Hartman, Saidiya. 2008. "Venus in Two Acts." *Small Axe* 12, no. 2: 1–14.

MacDorman, Marian F., and Eugene Declercq. 2016. "Trends and Characteristics of United States Out-of-Hospital Births 2004–2014: New Information on Risk Status and Access to Care." *Birth* 43, no. 2: 116–24. https://doi.org/10.1111/birt.12228.

Morrison, Toni. 2007. *The Bluest Eye*. New York: Vintage International.

OurHealth Magazine. 2013. "History of Healthcare in Lynchburg and Southside, Volume 3." issuu.com/ourhealthvirginia/docs/lbss_historyiii2013.

Smith, Margaret Charles, and Linda Janet Holmes. 1996. *Listen to Me Good: The Life Story of an Alabama Midwife*. Columbus: Ohio State University Press.

SNCC Digital Gateway. n.d. "Barbara Johns Leads Prince Edward County Student Walkout." 2020. snccdigital.org/events/barbara-johns-leads-prince-edward-county-student-walkout/ (accessed July 14, 2020).

White, Deborah Gray. 1985. *Ar'n't I a Woman?: Female Slaves in the Plantation South*. New York: W. W. Norton & Company, Inc.

Caroline M. Mar

. . . .

Catalog of Writings Left by Chinese Railroad Laborers of the CPRR and "唔 需 (No Need)"

```
[         ]
[                 ]
[     ]
[        ]
[          ]
[           ]
[     ]
[                  ]
[       ]
[          ]
[  ]
[             ]
[      ]
[        ]
[    ]
[          ]
```

唔 需

the not necessary, not needed, unrequired and
unrequited missing of your voice, your knotty hand
not near enough to mine, please pass the 清 蒸 魚,
no need to worry, no need, please pass back

MERIDIANS · feminism, race, transnationalism   23:2 October 2024
DOI: 10.1215/15366936-11266380 © 2024 Smith College

into this kitchen, this house, this life
that you left, don't bother, don't worry about it,
we say, you said, I say
to no one, I don't need it, I'm not hungry, but
I am always hungry, I do so need
you, and so much more

. . . .

Caroline M. Mar is the great-granddaughter of a railroad laborer and the author of *Water Guest* (forthcoming), *Special Education* (Texas Review Press), and the chapbook *Dream of the Lake* (Bull City Press). Carrie received her MFA from Warren Wilson, is a member of Rabble Collective, and teaches high school health education in her hometown of San Francisco. She has been granted residencies at Hedgebrook, Ragdale, and Storyknife, among others, and her writing has most recently appeared in *West Trade Review* and *Poetry Northwest*.

Ming Li (Ari) Wu

....

Maric***

¿Sabes cómo duele creer que tu lengua nunca te querrá?
No, hasta el punto de que nunca podrá quererte? Que tu corazón
se va a ahogar en tu propia sangre por no poder reconciliar
los latidos de sus dos mitades?
Creo que no sabes, otherwise alguien me habría llamado queride
mucho más temprano.

Cuando escribí que this non-binary mouth
will never be a home for this boricua tongue,
lo creía con todo mi cuerpo. Estaba equivocado,
pero lo creía. Cómo lo creía.

I've never been comfortable with the F-slur in English.
Es una de esas palabras que sabe a sangre ajena
even though the wound is in your own mouth,
que hace que no te reconozcas in the mirror
amidst the encroaching flames. Pero maricón
is a beautiful word, a word que te ruega que la mastiques.

It begins softly: mari. Mari takes your hand y te hace creer
que es una chica buena, the type you could bring home to
        introduce to your abuela,
y luego ese puñetazo: cón,

MERIDIANS · feminism, race, transnationalism   23:2 October 2024
DOI: 10.1215/15366936-11266388 © 2024 Smith College

an exclamation point que te quita el aliento con el frío de su
      pasión.
Yo jamás saldría con alguien como tú,
Mari tells you.

Tal vez me intriga porque es tan sencillo saltar a maricón
from Mariceli, my name del que me escondo. Mari
como mariposa, como las dragas que giran hasta que sus faldas las
      dejan volar.
Mari como Marielito, como les desterrades valientes que huyeron
      de Cuba
con solo sus sueños tentativos para cubrirse y que llegaron
a ser les primeres caribeñes cuir que conocí, mis madres
      espirituales.
Y sobre todo Mari como María, como la Biblia, como a name so
      sacred
que Dios te ordena que lo repitas over and over again tu vida
      entera.
Santa Maricón, amén.
Eso sí es un amor verdadero.

I would like to wear my name one day con orgullo, de una manera
that lets it underscore mi mariconeo. Mariceli me suena más dulce
cuando me lo imagino with the contrast of a freshly shaved face,
bien áspero debajo de pómulos afilados. Si yo luciera
más como lo que siento, my name would be a coat
of glitter, light on my shoulders. Claro que Mariceli is a boy's
      name
porque it's my name and I'm a boy. Mariceli te diría
que soy un maricón que juega con los ángeles.

Ahora veo que la posibilidad of this delicious contra-diction
ha estado conmigo desde el comienzo, desde mi nombramiento,
desde cuando mi papá misspelled Mariseli on my birth certificate.
Veo que poder confrontarte en español ahora
doesn't make me more latino than in tenth grade when we snuck
      out of class

to kiss as an experiment in the bathroom, no me hace más cuir que
  este verano
cuando pretendí ser esa chica llamada Mari para acomodar a mi
      abuela en Puerto Rico.
Siempre he sido un hijo de fruto y pecado.
Siempre he tenido una lengua que quiere enredarse con otra.

Mira que my blood glitters when I spit it from my mouth.
Mira que yo soy a quien le quieres rogar.
Que soy a quien le quieres rezar.
Y aunque no te perdono por hacerme creer
que no merecía abrazar cada parte de este cuerpo latinX,
todavía te voy a salvar.

Ming Li (Ari) Wu is a queer Chinese-Puerto Rican poet, teacher, and ethnic studies scholar from Huntsville, Alabama, by way of Reno, Nevada. Both their academic work and their poetry deal with themes such as queer and trans precarity, belonging, and futurity, especially in Latinx contexts. He is an alumnus of Harvard College and the Harvard Graduate School of Education and currently resides in Boston, Massachusetts.

Chamara Moore

....

Beyond Black Girlhood
An Underground Railroad to Nowhere

Abstract: How can Colson Whitehead's combining of the generic and the strange in his Pulitzer Prize–winning speculative text *The Underground Railroad* be read as Afro-Pessimist? This essay seeks to illuminate the ways in which Whitehead's novel provides narratives of self-making adjacent to coming of age while reinventing the historically white genre of the Bildungsroman for an intersectional identity in early America. Using Geta LeSeur's *The Black Bildungsroman* as a point of reference, the author argues that because the protagonist Cora is a Black girl born and raised under chattel slavery and thus forced to come of age before the bulk of the novel, her experience cannot be constrained to a genre defined primarily by Eurocentric traditions and frames of reference. In this way, "girlhood" has never been a possibility for her, making the novel's ambiguous ending a clearer Afro-Pessimist argument rather than any particular milestone of maturation we see in Bildungsroman. *The Underground Railroad* is a case study demonstrating how Black speculative fiction authors move through and beyond the Bildungsroman genre by imbuing their Black female subjects like Cora with the agency of self-making, while using speculative elements such as transforming into a railroad to demonstrate the intractable social death of enslavement.

In the 1992 documentary *Black Sci-Fi*, Octavia Butler describes the contrast between the freedom that speculative fiction allows and the constraints on genres more closely associated with canonicity: "Science fiction is a wonderful way to think about possibilities. . . . There are all sorts of walls around other genres. Romances, mysteries, westerns. There are no real

MERIDIANS · feminism, race, transnationalism   23:2 October 2024
DOI: 10.1215/15366936-11266364 © 2024 Smith College

walls around science fiction. We can build them, but they're not there naturally." Building from this contrast, this essay explores the ways Speculative fiction allows Black writers to inject narratives regarding allegories of freedom and liberation into more traditional genres like the Bildungsroman to blur and complicate their boundaries. Using Colson Whitehead's *The Underground Railroad* as an entry point, I will update Ramón Saldívar's (2011: 5) claim that Whitehead's work demonstrates how "Speculative Realism has become a mode of combining and reshaping the modern and postmodern versions of the historical novel and the *Bildungsroman*."

This essay builds on this point to suggest that the innovations Black Speculative writers have brought to the genre move us further away from a realist narrative tradition centered on Eurocentric subjectivities, making space for Black female characters at the intersection of race and gender oppression. By reading what I call speculative Black girl-centric narratives like *The Underground Railroad* through the lens of Afro-Pessimism, this essay seeks to bring us closer to defining what it means to "come of age" as a figure historically barred from both the categories of "girlhood" and human. While scholars like Geta LeSeur have notably suggested "The Black Bildungsroman" as an alternative, I argue that we should move away from Eurocentric genre categories altogether. I'd instead like to complicate LeSeur's argument by illustrating the ways in which contemporary Black Speculative narratives adjacent to our understanding of "Bildungsroman" are marked by moments of self-making that give their protagonists agentic experience. Thinking beyond the Bildungsroman as a concept allows us to better understand its adjacent forms in the speculative. *The Underground Railroad* is an example of a text utilizing this speculative form to play on safe staples of the white imaginary like slavery and utopic communes and subvert their meaning by adding weird elements like a literal subway in early America and a Black girl that chooses to *become* the railroad that allows readers to imagine Black girls defining themselves and reclaiming their agency.

Black "Girlhood"

Intersectional scholars often discuss girlhood and womanhood interchangeably in the context of Blackness, because the Black female subject exists under the simultaneity of racist and sexist oppression no matter her age. Many Black feminist scholars have focused their attention on the inescapability of marginalization within that double bind. In her memoir

Thick: And Other Essays, Tressie McMillan Cottom writes, "Black girls and Black women are problems . . . not the same thing as causing problems. We are social issues to be solved, economic problems to be balanced, and emotional baggage to be overcome" (Cottom 2019: 10). Cottom forces us to think about what it means to take up a racialized and gendered space that is ontologically considered a problem or a burden without the actual power to *cause* problems, specifically including both Black women *and* girls within that discussion to further illustrate her point. This move is mirrored within the field of girlhood studies, but this field specifies Black girlhood as a site of study *beyond* merely pain and suffering. In her seminal book *Black Girlhood Celebration: Toward a Hip-Hop Feminist Pedagogy*, Ruth Nicole Brown asserts that "Black girlhood Studies is about the representations, memories, and lived experiences of being and becoming in a body marked as youthful, Black, and female" (Brown 2009: 16). Since these perceptions can be ever changing, she does not consider Black girlhood as dependent on "age, physical maturity, or any essential category of identity" (16). While Brown defines it in the context of joy, celebration, and self-making, this lack of dependence on an "essential" category seems more due to the collapsing of age or maturation within the lived experience of Black girls. Defining Black girlhood and the narratives that center it requires a distillation of the ways in which the Black female body has been epistemologically considered *doubly* outside the human, beginning with the ways violence against her has not been historically considered a violent act.

While the rape and molestation of Black girls wasn't even defined as "rape" until our contemporary era, even now these instances are perpetually dismissed, rarely getting close to a discussion in the public eye until the recent wake of the 2018 Lifetime Series *Surviving R. Kelly*. In the series, clinical psychologist Dr. Candice Norcott refers frequently to the study conducted on poverty and inequality at the Georgetown University Law Center, citing the origins of its term "adultification." The full data and findings of the study were reported in "Girlhood Interrupted: The Erasure of Black Girls' Childhood," detailing how it expands on earlier research surrounding the adultification of Black boys. These results found that while Black boys are perceived as adults as early as ten, this starts as early as five for Black girls. Compared to white girls of the same age (five to fourteen), the survey participants perceived that Black girls needed less nurturing, less protection, and less comfort and support. They additionally assumed Black girls to be more independent, and to know more about sex and other adult topics. Thusly, *adultification* was coined to explain the "stark criminal justice and school discipline disparities between Black girls and their white counterparts" (Epstein, Blake, and Gonzalez 2017: 4). In the study, author Monique Morris explains how "the assignment of more adult-like characteristics to the expressions of young Black girls is a form of age compression" (6). This "truncated age continuum" is what makes "Black girls likened more so to adults than to children and treated as if they are willfully engaging in behaviors typically expected of Black women. . . . This compression then strips Black girls of their childhood freedom and renders Black Girlhood interchangeable with Black womanhood" (6).

Saidiya Hartman expands these sociological findings into a specific blend of the archival, literary, and speculative in her book *Wayward Lives, Beautiful Experiments*, in which she narrates erased personal stories of urban Black women and girls at the turn of the twentieth century. In the first chapter, titled "A Minor Figure," Hartman speculates about the life of a young girl who appears posed naked on a sofa in an archival photograph from the 1890s with no description. While the girl can be no older than ten, it is the lack of a narrative surrounding her staged nakedness that "details the violence to which the black female body can be subjected," which for Hartman makes it "impossible for her to be a child" (Hartman 2019: 27). She then uses historical context to explain the way Black girls "ripened too soon," like the girl from the photograph, already had their bodies "marked by a history of sexual defilement" and "branded as a commodity" in the "prevailing set of social arrangements, in which [they] were] formally free and vulnerable to the triple jeopardy of economic, racial, and sexual violence" (29):

> There was no statutory rape law to penalize what occurred in the studio, and had such law existed, a poor black girl would have fallen outside its reach. When a rape or assault was reported to the police or the Society for the Prevention of Cruelty to Children, the girl, seduced or raped, might be sentenced to the training school or the reformatory to protect her or punish her for being too fast, too mature, too knowing. . . . Innocence (that is, virginity) was the issue, not what age a girl was old enough for the taking. Previous immorality meant a man could do whatever he wanted. Colored girls were always presumed to be immoral. . . . Black girls came before the law, but were not protected by it. (28–29)

Here Hartman brings up the critical difference between the assumed space Black girls occupy and that of other girls—innocence. She reiterates that there is no age too old or young for Black girls to be preyed upon, since whether the legal protections exist for them or not, Black girlhood always exists on the outside of this. Understanding Black girlhood as Hartman does means coming to terms with the fact that "the entanglement of violence and sexuality, care and exploitation continues to define the meaning of being Black and female" (30). This suggests that Black girlhood is an arbitrary and ever-changing category marked by its marginalization and resulting "adultification," meaning a notable lack of "coming of age." If it is defined by this barring from the privilege of coming to age, then what does it mean to read Black girlhood through a narrative genre like the Bildungsroman? How do we map our understanding of a nonessential category like Black girlhood onto our understanding of a "coming of age" narrative? Can the Bildungsroman ever function for Black girls? Furthermore, how do speculative narratives move beyond the boundaries of the Bildungsroman to make room for Black girl protagonists to find themselves?

Afro-Pessimism Links Black and Female

This central question of what it means to build narratives that center characters ontologically barred from subjecthood is preceded by the legacy of Afro-Pessimist thought exemplified by scholars like Hartman, Frank Wilderson, and Hortense Spillers. *Afro-Pessimism: An Introduction* tells us that in the broadest sense, Afro-Pessimism is an understanding of Blackness predicated on the redefinition of the slave's being as object, commodity, and property. This understanding is built on the assumption that the slave is *socially* dead, meaning "they are 1) open to gratuitous violence, 2) natally alienated, their ties of birth not recognized and familial structures intentionally broken apart; and 3) generally dishonored or disgraced before any thought or action is considered" (8). This social death defines their ontology, meaning "the slave experiences their 'slaveness' ontologically, as a '*being for* the captor'" (*Afro-Pessimism* 2017: 8). Afro-Pessimist thought argues that though Blackness is no longer considered "slave" it still fits within the ontological enslavement that informs and motivates "anti-Black violence" which cannot exist simultaneously with "recognition and inclusion in society" without "result[ing] in social *and real* death" (*Afro-Pessimism* 2017: 10). This line of thinking deems that occupying the ontological space of the slave is a "loss of any self" regarding the slave as "the position of the unthought" outside of the subjectivity of thought and praxis (*Afro-Pessimism* 2017: 165).

This "unthought" is something that overlaps explicitly in Black female embodiment in that Black girls are an afterthought in addition to holding a liminal epistemological space. Hartman explains this in her 2003 interview with Frank Wilderson titled "The Position of the Unthought," using the example of Harriet Jacobs. She explains that the "paradox of agency" for Jacobs is in the tension between herself as "an agent versus the objective conditions in which she finds herself" (Hartman 2003: 187). This impossibility is dependent on "her position as a slave: her status as a thing and the negation of her will" (187). This negation is something centered in Afro-Pessimist methodology in the belief that since "Blackness is negated by the relations and structures of society . . . the only way out is to negate that negation" usually by removal from society altogether, which is often death (Wilderson 2010: 10). Hartman posits that the way in which Jacobs is forced to "efface her very condition in order to make [her] story intelligible to [white audiences]" is an example of this negation, a sort of social death: "This existence in the space of death, where negation is the captive's central possibility for action, whether we think of that as a radical refusal of the terms of the social order or these acts that are sometimes called suicide or self-destruction, but which are really an embrace of death" (187). Such negation appears by way of certain characters in Whitehead's work, but parts of Cora's narrative in *The Underground Railroad* seem to embody Harriet Jacobs's story and positionality directly. In the middle of the novel Cora spends months in North Carolina, hiding in the attic of Ethel and Martin Wells. This seems to be a direct reference to Jacobs's life hiding away in her master's attic. There are even similar moments of tension between Cora and Mrs. Wells and Jacobs and Mrs. Flint,[1] though ultimately Cora's story takes a new path and diverges from Jacobs's as the novel continues. This is a good example of how the Speculative makes room for exploration through historical slippage linked by way of the Black female body and its centricity in the narrative.

This narrative weaving is parallel to Hartman's methodology of "critical fabulation" regarding Black female narratives and the violence of the archive. In her seminal essay "Venus in Two Acts," Hartman describes her method of researching the lives of Black female slaves as "straining against the limits of the archive to write a cultural history of the captive, and, at the same time, enacting the impossibility of representing the lives of the captives precisely through the process of narration" (Hartman 2008: 11). This "fabulation" of what may have occurred within the space absent from the archive is a form of speculative writing that animates these historical "objects," acknowledging their existence as "commodity" in the space of the archive while still reckoning with "the precarious lives which are visible only in the moment of their disappearance" (11–12). In this sense, Black Speculative narratives like Whitehead's animate Black objects, while still emphasizing their objecthood and commodified existence forever tied to the overlap of their Blackness and femininity.

Hartman is not the only Afro-Pessimist to discuss the objecthood historically rooted in the Black female body in this way. Hortense Spillers (2003: 112) argues that the assumed slave captive is always "a female body" because it "locates precisely a moment of converging political and social vectors that mark the flesh as a prime commodity of exchange." She argues that this commodification is twofold when taking into account the reproductive potential of Black female bodies, sold for labor and breeding. She goes further to say that the Black female body specifically bridges the human and nonhuman: "[The Black American woman] became instead the principal point of passage between the human and non-human world. Her issue became the focus of a cunning difference—visually, psychologically, ontologically—as the route by which the dominant modes decide the distinction between humanity and 'other'" (207). With this quote Spillers lays out the stakes for centering the Black female subject. If she has been historically used in scaffolding the difference between human and other, then she will have a further journey toward "subjectivity." Perhaps it is Speculative fiction and fabulation that creatively imagine this journey Spillers describes.

Alexander Weheliye (2014: 42) explains this gendered posthuman relationship further in *Habeas Viscus: Racializing Assemblages, Biopolitics, and Black Feminist Theories of the Human* when he states, "The sociogenic anchoring of racial difference in physiology and the banning of black subjects from the domain of the human occur in and through gender and sexuality." Here he establishes the need to contextualize "girlhood" within the dehumanizing context of Blackness. He continues, "Gendered Blackness—though excluded from culture, and frequently violently so—is a passage to the human in western modernity because, in giving flesh to the word of Man, the flesh comes to define the phenomenology of Man, which is always already lived as unadulterated physiology" (43–44). If Black femininity is defined outside flesh, then Black Speculative writing may be the genre best equipped for depicting this through narrative metaphor. Is that why so many speculative narratives translate their Black protagonists into different physical forms? Building on these strands of Afro-Pessimist thought, what does it mean to have a speculative narrative like *The Underground Railroad* contextualized by the suffering of the Black female body without allowing this suffering to take center stage? Where does the Bildungsroman fall short regarding this history of suffering and imposed commodification? The Speculative has the potential to guide us in alternative directions that blur the firm genre boundaries historically associated with the Bildungsroman.

Resisting the Black Bildungsroman

The "Black Bildungsroman," as Geta LeSeur theorizes it, is defined by sorrow and suffering. She defines Black American Bildungsroman as "haunted by sorrow" and an "unrelenting awareness of the distinction between Black people and the traditional white ways of life" (LeSeur 1995: 17). LeSeur's coining of the "Black Bildungsroman" is essential in the conversation regarding alternatives to the Eurocentricity in the Bildungsroman genre, though her ideas about the novel remain centered in the realist tradition. In *Ten Is the Age of Darkness: The Black Bildungsroman*, she contrasts Black Bildungsroman by West Indian authors with that of white authors, illuminating the nuances of Black racial experience under the light of the European Bildungsroman structure. She posits Goethe's 1795 work, *Wilhelm Meisters Lehrjahre*, as a model of the form, defining the Bildungsroman as "the novel of development, the novel of education (the literal translation of Bildungsroman), an 'apprenticeship' novel, a novel of childhood and adolescence, and the novel of initiation" (3). The pitfalls of defining the genre in this way keep it aligned with particular structures of power that Black people have been historically barred from. Even the *Bildung* part of the genre's German title suggests a linkage between "knowledge" and institutional access like that of tutors, apprenticeship, and schooling rather than the lived experience and/or inherited knowledge that becomes central for survival under systemic oppression. In this way, LeSeur's definition of the "coming of age" genre remains not only tied to Eurocentric language, but also relatively limited when paired with her much wider critical race analysis of the protagonists of these Black novels.

In addition to the linkage to Eurocentric language, LeSeur's analysis fails to center the particularities of Black American girlhood in her conceptualization of the Black Bildungsroman. After describing the category of childhood in the African American Bildungsroman as "depressing, like America's history" earlier in her text, she gives very few details as to how these depressing challenges differ across gendered lines. Her introduction notes that "most protagonists of the Bildungsroman fall between the ages of 9&13 with 10 being a significant marker," which I would argue is due to the predominance of Black male characters in her texts of choice, as informed by the study I've already mentioned (LeSeur 1995: xii).[2] Nonetheless, she argues that the Black Bildungsroman as she defines it has few distinct age markers (13). She defines this genre of Black writing by its unique cultural characteristics, because the "Black experience in the United States or the West Indies cannot be limited or defined by parochial frames of reference and value that are derived from White and European traditions from which Black people have been largely excluded" (2). She concludes that contemporary Black writers have turned their attention inward to

> identify the traditions of their race by defining people individually, thus capturing a collective experience that is unique in terms of its circumstances of history and geography. They do not seek an entry into the mainstream of European or American writing, but wish to explore the indigenous currents of those experiences to communicate, often to educate, interpret, and reveal the varied experiences of four hundred years of suffering. (2)

Here we see LeSeur broaden her earlier definition of knowledge and education, making more space for narrative transformation, but this transformation still seems limited to the expectations of the Bildungsroman genre, not specifying the narrative innovation required to transform the narratives of Black American girls specifically. This is why I wish to take the heuristics that LeSeur has already provided further to rethink the breadth of nuances within the relationship between Black American girlhood and said narratives of transformation.

Nonetheless LeSeur provides the groundwork for this intervention in the way she embeds important notions of Bildungsroman in relation to Black girls and women in her chapter titled "Womanish Girls." The title alone is an important and impactful choice, as it functions in itself as an important reference to the adultification of Black girls in this "coming of age" context. She uses this chapter to examine Gwendolyn Brooks' *Maud Martha*, Toni Morrison's *The Bluest Eye*, and Ntozake Shange's two novels, *Sassafrass, Cypress, and Indigo* and *Betsey Brown*, as well as Paule Marshall's *Brown Girl, Brownstones*. The gendered distinction that she makes between Black male and female coming-of-age narratives in the American context seems minimal because it is wrapped up in a specific reference to Paule Marshall's words, stating that Black girls specifically "have a fear of growing up, and of other people, and of life, and ultimately retreat into their own worlds" (5). This moment of Black feminist citational strategy is important in its dual usage to simultaneously characterize the long historical relationship between Black American girls and the threat of violence from which they "fear" and "retreat," while also using the rich legacy of Paule Marshall to contextualize this history. Nonetheless wrapping this point up in the citation makes it feel minimized in some way, rather than taking more time to center the important specifics of Black girls and the way in which they face the hydra that is anti-Blackness and sexual violence in the historically fraught American context.

This lack of detail for all aspects of Black writing in relation to Black American girls, both joyful and "depressing," is what makes LeSeur's layout of the Black Bildungsroman too walled-in[3] to explore narrative nuance of Black American womanhood, which is defined by not only an untraceable history and the constant threat of violence, but also an indescribable joy in her triumph of survival (4). Narratives like those of Morrison, Shange, and Brooks are strong and inspiring, not just because they center Black women like LeSeur argues, but because they additionally nuance Black female subjects in narrative ways that demonstrate an awareness of the specific obstacles facing intersectional identity in America as well as the complex ways Black women and girls often transcend those obstacles. A Black coming-of-age narrative category without explicit discussion of the myriad of obstacles facing Black girls in America and the specific ways in which these Black women and girls persist under continental constructions of white supremacy feels too abridged. LeSeur's discussion does not include any Speculative fiction, which limits the possibility of both the Speculative and Bildungsroman genres, presuming little overlap. This adherence to the Eurocentric ideals of canonicity and textual value make her "Black Bildungsroman" arguably too limited for the additional narrative possibilities that Black girlhood offers.

Black Speculative fiction removes these limitations to expertly mingle the probable with the impossible in ways that distance them from the "haunt of sorrow" central to LeSeur's definition. Toni Morrison and Colson Whitehead both use images salient for audiences of any background that subvert their trauma-rooted meaning in the context of Black life (like blue eyes and underground railroads). I want to focus on Whitehead's work as an example of this, mostly because of his roots in the Speculative, but also because of the specific ways in which he plays on these historical concepts within the white imaginary for subversion. Many of the speculative elements in his novel create new meaning for conceptual staples of the white Bildungsroman genre while seemingly playing on the neo-slave narrative tradition. This proximity to the white imaginary is arguably what has brought Whitehead such wide success, since his narratives seem more legible to white audiences all the while subverting their meaning. Speculative narratives rooted in frequently taught Black histories like slavery are often more popular because of their presumed legibility. They are more easily read as being in conversation with the long history of the African American novel than more futuristically oriented speculative narratives of the likes of Nnedi Okorafor's Speculative Bildungsroman trilogy *Binti*. This would explain why speculative novels like *The Underground Railroad* have had wide enough appeal to win a Pulitzer Prize, while Whitehead's other speculative works like *The Intuitionist* are discussed differently. Scholars have similarly said that Octavia Butler's *Kindred* was more accessible for students because "contemporary Americans both white and African American . . . all want to imagine we would be the defiant and brave African American slave or Underground Railroad worker" (Long 2002: 463). This is why I'd like to unpack the subversive elements of Whitehead's text in particular.

Whitehead's Afro-Pessimist Novel

The Underground Railroad is a 2016 novel about a runaway slave named Cora who uses a complex underground railway system built by other escaped slaves to flee her Georgia plantation and travel state to state escaping capture from Ridgeway, an infamous slave-catcher, while painting a new American geography and thus a new image of freedom. While the speculative elements of Whitehead's texts are often read with comedic undertone, or even "speculative satire" as coined by Matthew Dischinger,[4] many of these elements in *The Underground Railroad* carry the weight of an Afro-Pessimistic leaning. Creating the Underground Railroad as a literal railway in a world in which enslaved people build railroads and skyscrapers in cities in the antebellum South makes freedom *seem* even more possible, but it doesn't take long for a reader to see the challenge of Blackness in the novel's America. While the enslaved people are not navigating a network of passageways and safe houses to reach the North, in the novel's reality the actual railroad is notably unreliable. The trains pass at unpredictable times and go to unpredictable places with "its secret trunk lines and mysterious routes" (Whitehead 2018: 88). The railroad stop that Cora encounters in Indiana is not even "made for a locomotive" and doesn't "connect to the rest of the line" (395). Cora discovers that the "station was not the start of the line but its terminus. Construction hadn't started beneath the house but at the other end of the black hole. As if in the world there were no places to escape to, only places to flee" (396). Here it becomes evident that the central speculative element of the novel that establishes the technological advancement of this version of America also establishes an underlying argument of the novel; there is no physical freedom. The railroad of freedom leads nowhere at all; the Black people in the novel are ontologically dead and only materials barred from adolescent freedom.

In addition to the railroad metaphor, the novel uses its Black female characters to illustrate this underlying point. While Cora is the text's protagonist, Whitehead actually introduces us to the narrative with a summative understanding of how Cora's grandmother Ajarry was brought to the US. Similar to how Afro-Pessimism discusses *the hold* as the inception of social death and the ontological negation associated with the racialization of the Black body, Whitehead centers the hold in both the beginning of Ajarry's story, her adultification, and the novel itself. Only a few pages into the novel we learn that Ajarry's captors "did not immediately force their urges upon her" because of her "tender age," but ultimately "some of the more seasoned mates dragged her from the hold six weeks into the passage" (11). Here we can read Ajarry alongside the Afro-Pessimist female figure of the Black Venus, as named by Saidiya Hartman. In her essay "Venus in Two Acts," Hartman (2008: 1) describes the Black Venus as "an emblematic figure of the enslaved woman in the Atlantic world" that "makes plain the convergence of terror and pleasure in the libidinal economy of slavery." She continues, "Variously named Harriot, Phibba, Sara, Joanna, Rachel, Linda, and Sally, she is found everywhere in the Atlantic world. The barracoon, the hollow of the slave ship, the pest-house, the brothel, the cage, the surgeon's laboratory, the prison, the cane-field, the kitchen, the master's bedroom—turn out to be exactly the same place and in all of them she is called Venus" (1). Ajarry is named for us but takes up the same meaning and space as Hartman's Venus, starting with the hollow of the slave ship and eventually moving through some of the other spaces Hartman listed. In addition to being adultified into slavery, Ajarry is forced into sexual maturity in the Middle Passage, ontologically transformed before even reaching America's shores. The novel also offers descriptions of her changing price as she was "sold and swapped and resold over the next few years," deemed another "asset liquidated by order of the magistrate" (Whitehead 2018: 14). In this way, Whitehead establishes Ajarry's Black womanhood as objecthood at the very start of the novel, emphasizing her position as an "asset" to the state (14). She maintains this object-oriented relationship with her own body, learning quickly "that the white man's scientists peered beneath things to understand how they worked" so that she later "ma[kes] a science of her own black body and accumulated observations" (15). The narrative suggests that her only understanding of her own value is as a "thing" since "each thing had value and as the value changed, everything else changes also" (15). Ajarry is the first Black female character we get to know in the novel, more easily read as an object, while the narrator follows an entire journey for the protagonist Cora. This is one of many ways the novel doesn't fit firmly within the Bildungsroman.

Our traditional understanding of the Bildungsroman assumes this text as a classic coming-of-age narrative since Cora is sixteen (though she's unsure of her exact birthdate) and gains sexual maturity and autonomy by the end of the novel. She technically "comes of age" prior to the start of the novel, as we are told "her womanhood had come into flower" and that she was dragged behind the smokehouse and raped by four white men after her "chest started to sprout" (21). Here Whitehead shows us how her story is immediately complicated by her embodiment of Black girlhood, her assumed sexual maturity and "adultification." The only way she keeps track of her own development is by tracking the benchmarks of her own trauma: "Sixteen or Seventeen. That's where Cora put her age. One year since Connelly ordered her to take a husband. Two years since Pot and his friends had seasoned her. They had not repeated their violation, and no worthy man paid her notice after that day, given the cabin she called home and the stories of her lunacy. Six years since her mother left" (25). We learn that Cora is so mature in her body that she is always aware of it, an awareness that most Bildungsroman protagonists don't gain until the narrative progresses. Cora has already made this progression, always aware of her body's proximity to the dangers associated with men. When the other enslaved people have a birthday party for Jockey she refuses to dance because she is wary of how "sometimes when the music tugged, you might suddenly be next to a man and you didn't know what he might do. All the bodies in motion, given

license" (28). Her Blackness and her girlhood is predicated on her knowledge of how best to police her body's movement in ways that protect her
from unwanted advances, from men who give themselves license to her
body and the space it occupies even with the good intention and "nice
thought" (28).

Even after Cora is supposedly free when she and Caesar escape to South
Carolina, the white railroad station agent embraces them to say goodbye
and "Cora couldn't help but shrink away. Two white men in two days had
their hands around her. Was this the condition of her freedom?" (66). The
inquiry baked into this question is, What is expected of her body in exchange
for this "freedom"? Is it presumed to be touched by strange men with the
power and privilege to get away with the violence against it? Even these
well-intentioned abolitionists took "license to her body" with embraces
she hadn't asked for, something we already know she fears. This awareness
of her own body and skepticism toward people with "nice" intentions at
the start of the novel establishes Cora's adultification. There is no transition from childhood to adolescence because the factors she has to be aware
of for her own survival are adult in nature. These factors, most notably the
"violence that structures black subjectivity itself" (L. 2013), overlap with
those governing Black life altogether in ways that Afro-Pessimists claim
affirm Blackness. This negation as affirmation is where the "pessimist"
part of the theory is incorporated, but it is something that is so integral to
Cora's understanding of herself that the novel doesn't cast it as negative
or otherworldly. It instead builds off of that objecthood established with
Cora's grandmother earlier in the narrative.

Imbuing this into the narrative seems to be the crux of what it means to
create something narratively beyond the Bildungsroman if in fact there's
no such thing as a "coming of age narrative" as we understand it for Black
girls. Whitehead leans into this Afro-Pessimistic lens of Black bodies incapable of existing as "subjects" in Eurocentric society by removing his characters from it altogether, either by way of physical death, or an alteration of
physical being. This changing of physicality makes these Black women characters something other than "embodied," which in turn makes them free of
the white ideological limits of the physical world—outside of the Bildungsroman and out of reach of a Eurocentric "coming of age" framework.

At every turn, Whitehead's novel only offers us the inescapability of
social death rather than any elements of LeSeur's definition of the Black
Bildungsroman or any sign post of transition from childhood to adolescence. This is predicated on Cora being marked as both Black and female,

and additionally a "slave," all contributing to the threat of danger and capture even when she's supposedly free. Frantz Fanon tells us "the position of the slave" leaves existence by the wayside (qtd. in Spillers 2003: 110), while Hortense Spillers (2003: 215) tells us "the quintessential [African] 'slave'" as object "is *not* male, but a female." In this narrative, Blackness is *never* associated with true freedom because even when Black people are born free men (outside of slavery), they inevitably face death, as Royal's character does in the massacre of Valentine's farm. Whitehead more often connects this ontological death to Black female embodiment with Ajarry, Cora, and eventually with the example of her mother Mabel. In the second to last chapter of the book we finally learn what's become of Cora's mother, which Whitehead frames narratively with the beginning of the chapter: "The first and last things she gave to her daughter were apologies. Cora slept in her stomach, the size of a fist, when Mabel apologized for what she was bringing her into" (291). This is then followed up at the end of the chapter: "The snake found her not long into her return . . . She could have made it farther—working Randall land had made her strong, strong in body if nothing else—but she stumbled onto a bed of soft moss and it felt right. She said, Here, and the swamp swallowed her up" (294–95). Here Whitehead plays on our assumption that Mabel was free the entire novel, only to reveal to us at the end that her freedom was found only in death. This reifies the social death associated with Black womanhood while translating the Afro-Pessimist belief that "the attempts at recognition and inclusion in society will only ever result in further social *and real* death" into narrative form (*Afro-Pessimism* 2017: 10). Mabel's only real escape was from the living world, a society structured by anti-Blackness and misogyny that she feared to bring her own child into.

Whitehead's placement of Mabel's death at the end of the novel also adds to the legacy of defining Black girl fictional narratives outside of the Western linearity of time. There is much alluded to in the novel that doesn't happen for us in the narrative until later, if at all. Whitehead thus builds on the history of re-memory that we associate with Black girl narratives like Toni Morrison's *Beloved* or Julie Dash's *Daughters of the Dust*. Emphasizing that cyclical nature of time also leans into this Afro-Pessimist tradition that doesn't define death as a single specific moment because the Black subject is always already dead.

Ultimately, the novel's ambiguous ending exemplifies how Speculative fiction can allow us to get closer to defining a narrative of Black girlhood, which Whitehead tells us is really Black "objecthood." At the end of the novel, Cora is distraught and panicked, escaping from Ridgeway in a railcar on the underground railroad; but Whitehead uses language that melds Cora with the Railroad: "She pumped and pumped and rolled out of the light. Into the tunnel that no one had made, that led nowhere. She discovered a rhythm, pumping her arms, throwing all of herself into the movement. Into northness. Was she traveling through the tunnel or digging it, becoming it?" (Whitehead 2018: 303). It's after this that she dreams of having sex with Royal (who's dead), the only time we hear of her sexual agency. So Whitehead seems to suggest that coming of age for a Black girl, coming into her own sexual agency and discovering herself and her own freedom means embracing her objecthood. This means the only fictional narrative of maturation from Black girlhood into Black womanhood shows us Black women moving beyond human subjectivity.

In his book, *In the Break*, Fred Moten pressures the assumption of the equivalence between personhood and subjectivity, suggesting Blackness as an object, polarized with "subject" as an entity defined by possession of itself and its objects (Moten 2003: 131). In this sense, Cora doesn't have access to the subjectivity of girlhood, she has only objecthood from the beginning of the narrative on her Georgia plantation, to the end where she becomes the railroad. The only transition that happens for her is what Hortense Spillers charts as transitioning from "a being into becoming being *for* captor . . . giving birth to the commodity and to the Human, yet" having no subjectivity to show for it, which she argues specifically for the Black female body (Spillers 2003: 95). This centers the Black female subject in the posthuman as a way for us to better understand the boundaries of Black girlhood, more specifically its lack of a bounded nature. Marrying this specific thread of "unthought" with these other ideas associated with Black girlhood demonstrates what it means to narratively center a positionality that has been barred from girlhood.

The Self-Making Alternative to the Bildungsroman
While Afro-Pessimism defined Blackness as a lack of agency, speculative narratives like Whitehead's redefine their Black characters as outside of subjectivity to allow them to reclaim agentic expression. They claim their agency by leaning into objecthood and away from constructions like childhood and girlhood that are centered on subjectivity. Tressie McMillan Cottom says in *Thick* that a Black girl "does not need the protection of childhood, for she has never been a child" (Cottom 2019: 187). If Black girls don't exist within such a paradigm, then it makes sense that the

Speculative creates space for new paradigms that stretch beyond the Bildungsroman, moving beyond previously limited constructions of childhood, girlhood, and even home. Cora creates a new home *on* and *as* the
railroad, and the speculative nature of Whitehead's text allows us to
imagine beyond that, whereas through memoir Cottom tells us "for Black
girls, home is both refuge and where your most intimate betrayals happen . . . home is where they love you until you're a ho" (2019: 194). If being
Black and a girl means being a problem, an object, and a ho, then Cora's
narrative is only the beginning of imagining beyond that condition.

Black women and girls have long centered their identities on self-
making as an alternative to home as a grounding space and concept.
Actress Viola Davis has been vocal about the pain and trauma she associates with the home through her work with the MeToo movement, but she
has also become famous for being a champion of individual self-making.
When asked to give young female viewers one piece of advice on the 2015
Oscars red carpet, Viola said, "Do not live someone else's life, and someone else's idea of what womanhood is. Womanhood is you, womanhood
is everything that's inside of you." Here, as in many of her acceptance
speeches, she defines womanhood as something made, something defined
from within with an emphasis on one's agency. It is through this agency
that Black girls as "objects" may act as subjects, though they do not themselves possess subjectivity.

Speculative writers have used tales of self-making to reclaim this agency
and help us imagine futures for Black girls that have never been allowed
access more than commodity or objecthood. It is this self-making that
allows Black girls to progress in ways that mirror "coming of age" for historically white characters. In *The Underground Railroad*, Cora's self-making
allows her access to freedom. When she uses the railway to escape Ridgeway, she *decides* to pick up the pick-ax and dig the tunnel herself, to use her
body as a tool to physically free herself. These events in the final chapter are
preceded by a final runaway ad, but the text this time reads, "RAN AWAY
from her legal but not rightful master fifteen months past, a slave girl called
CORA . . . She has stopped running. Reward remains unclaimed. SHE
WAS NEVER PROPERTY" (Whitehead 2018: 275). This announcement that
Cora has stopped running functions to emphasize the fact that it was her
choice. She chose to defend herself and kill Ridgeway just like her choice to
become the railway. The monetized reward is unclaimed and thus she has
freed herself from the confines of commodification and the very condition

of enslavement. She is literally no longer property. This choice is an agentic act predicated only by her decision to do so, rather than being asked by Caesar or Royal or anyone else in her life. It is an act that is primarily for herself, a brief act of *making* herself into a subject with the capacity to be free.

While Whitehead's use of the Speculative in this way has allowed him awards and wide approval such as inclusion in Oprah's book club, it's important to note that other writers, particularly within the long legacy of Black women in speculative fiction have made similar arguments outside of the neo-slave narrative genre. While Cora is an agent of self-making, so is Lilith from Octavia Butler's (2014) *Dawn*, Syenite from N. K. Jemisin's (2016) *The Fifth Season*, and Binti from Nnedi Okorafor's (2015) novel of the same name. In *Dawn*, Lilith gains agency by both choosing to lead a team of humans to resettle the ravaged earth and choosing to give birth to a human-oankali (alien) hybrid child. In Okorafor's novel, the Himba girl, Binti, becomes part Meduse (the alien conquerors that kidnapped her and killed her classmates) and chooses to become a peace ambassador between the humans and Meduse in order to end the war. This allows her to make herself into something more than human, doing so to reclaim the agency lost in her capture. By the end of the novel, Binti has tentacles for hair, her flesh part human and part Meduse, which allows her to communicate with both races in her ambassadorial role. Arguably the most complex of the three texts, N. K. Jemisin's Hugo award–winning novel *The Fifth Season* expertly weaves together three different narratives of self-making to subvert the "coming of age" structure and make room for both Black women and girls in these narratives. The five-hundred-page novel is split into three sections with Black women of different ages, the young Damaya, middle-aged Syenite, and older woman Essun, all processing their traumas of abuse and enslavement in different ways. At the end of the novel we learn that all three are the same woman at different times in her life. In this way Jemisin shrewdly blurs the temporality we associate with Black girlhood in that each character is always *all* of the characters, just like Black girls are always already women, already grown. These examples of self-making are modes of resistance because these characters do not ask for permission, but instead resist the permission that their racialized and gendered bodies assume. This is arguably just a speculative and genre-bending version of the way Valerie Smith has described Black protagonists "affirming and legitimizing their psychological autonomy in nineteenth-century slave narratives" and contemporary Black historical novels (Smith 1987: 2). In this way, contemporary Black speculative narratives merely update this self-making and push it further.

Tressie McMillan Cottom (2019: 184) says, "Black Girlhood ends whenever a man says it ends. Two Sides to every story. Almost ready. She a ho . . . Puberty becomes permission." This brings us back to the initial idea that Black girls are not allowed to be girls, but instead women—"hoes," which as a colloquialism sufficiently represents their objecthood. Speculative fiction uses that objecthood for liberation, shifting the permission from other subject positions to the Black women themselves. This freedom the Speculative offers allows these writers like Whitehead and Jemisin to sketch narratives of self-making around women previously relegated as objects in the Bildungsroman. Speculative narratives of self-making allow us to envision stories of Black futures for girls that weren't supposed to have access to them, bringing critical fabulation to the world of the speculative and fantastical.

....

Chamara Moore (they/them) is an assistant professor in the English Department at Queens College CUNY. Their multidisciplinary research reads various constructions of Blackness, womanhood, and otherness through the Speculative in all its forms, primarily by way of a Black feminist cultural lens. Their work appears or is forthcoming in the *Black Scholar*, *ImageText*, *Transition* magazine, *Studies in the Fantastic*, and more.

Notes

1   In *The Underground Railroad* when Cora is bedbound with sickness while hiding in North Carolina, there is a moment of sexual exploitation, coercion, and tension when Ethel "kisse[s] the girl" with "two kinds of feeling mixed up in those kisses" (303). This tension is similar to the moment in Jacobs's narrative in which Mrs. Flint tries to sexually exploit her in order to determine if she's slept with her husband.

2   The study from the Georgetown University Law Center noted that boys were perceived as adults as early as ten, while girls were adultified much earlier at age five.

3   "Walled" in this sense, referring to the "walls" Octavia Butler mentioned speculative fiction being free of at the start of this essay.

4   Dischinger's (2017) essay in the *Global South* "States of Possibility in Colson Whitehead's *The Underground Railroad*" defines "speculative satire" as "a term that names the practice of using speculative premises to realign through satire our understanding of national and regional histories (84).

Works Cited

Afro-Pessimism: An Introduction. 2017. Minneapolis. https://libcom.org/files/Afro Pessimismread_Afro-pessimism-AnIntroduction.epub.

Brown, Ruth Nicole. 2009. *Black Girlhood Celebration Toward a Hip-Hop Feminist Pedagogy.* New York: Peter Lang.

Butler, Octavia E. *Dawn.* 2014. London, UK: Headline.

Cottom, Tressie McMillan. 2019. *Thick: And Other Essays.* New York: New Press.

Dischinger, Matthew. 2017. "States of Possibility in Colson Whitehead's *The Underground Railroad.*" *Global South* 11, no. 1. https://doi.org/10.2979/globalsouth .11.1.05.

Epstein, Rebecca, Jamilia Blake, and Thalia Gonzalez. 2017. "Girlhood Interrupted: The Erasure of Black Girls' Childhood." *SSRN Electronic Journal,* June 27. https://doi .org/10.2139/ssrn.3000695.

Francis, Terrence, dir. 1992. *Black Sci-Fi.* Indiana: Moonlight Films. DVD.

Hartman, Saidiya. 2003. "The Position of the Unthought." Interview by Frank Wilderson. *Qui Parle* 13, no. 2: 183–201.

Hartman, Saidiya. 2008. "Venus in Two Acts." *Small Axe: A Caribbean Journal of Criticism* 12, no. 2: 1–14. https://doi.org/10.1215/-12-2-1.

Hartman, Saidiya. 2019. *Wayward Lives, Beautiful Experiments.* New York: W. W. Norton.

Jemisin, N. K. 2016. *The Fifth Season: The Broken Earth.* New York: Orbit.

L., R. 2013. "Wanderings of the Slave: Black Life and Social Death." *Metamute,* June 13. Rifams Distro. https://www.metamute.org/editorial/articles/wanderings -slave-black-life-and-social-death.

LeSeur, Geta. 1995. *Ten Is the Age of Darkness: The Black Bildungsroman.* Columbia: University of Missouri Press.

Long, Lisa A. 2002. "A Relative Pain: The Rape of History in Octavia Butler's 'Kindred' and Phyllis Alesia Perry's 'Stigmata.'" *College English* 64, no. 4: 459–83. https://doi.org.10.2307/3250747.

Moten, Fred. 2003. *In the Break: The Aesthetics of the Black Radical Tradition.* Minneapolis: University of Minnesota Press.

Okorafor, Nnedi. 2015. *Binti.* New York: Tom Doherty Associates.

Saldivar, Ramón. 2011. "Historical Fantasy, Speculative Realism, and Postrace Aesthetics in Contemporary American Fiction." *American Literary History* 23, no. 3: 574–99. https://doi.org/10.1093/alh/ajr026.

Smith, Valerie. 1987. *Self-Discovery and Authority in Afro-American Narrative.* Cambridge, MA: Harvard University Press.

Spillers, Hortense J. 2003. *Black, White, and in Color: Essays on American Literature and Culture.* Chicago: University of Chicago Press.

Weheliye, Alexander G. 2014. *Habeas Viscus: Racializing Assemblages, Biopolitics, and Black Feminist Theories of the Human.* Durham, NC: Duke University Press.

Whitehead, Colson. 2018. *The Underground Railroad: A Novel.* New York: Vintage Books.

Wilderson, Frank B. 2010. *Red, White, and Black: Cinema and the Structure of U.S. Antagonisms.* Durham, NC: Duke University Press.

Maryam Ala Amjadi

. . . .

The Ice Seller of Hell

"Now, girls, pay attention!" Mrs. Vafai tapped twice on the whiteboard with her forefinger knuckle, protruding and plump in her long carbon cotton glove that ebbed into her soot-colored manteau sleeves. "When you get married, you are wedded to the entire family. Remember, the man you love today may be educated in Europe, but his mother, his sister, could be the ruin of you at some point. Even an *intellectuel* man is an instinctive being. So, get that certificate before anything, even if the groom's family doesn't demand it. Get it. Fold it or frame it. Trust me, it will do you a lot of good."

It was one of those early morning sessions, 7:30 sharp to 9. No one should have to put up with such an upbeat timbre and witness the innards the instructor squiggled on the board before letting caffeine settle into one's veins and the day fully crack open its eyelids.

"Family Planning course, my ass!" Gelareh blurted under her breath as she doodled a brown toothbrush mustache in the groove between Mrs. Vafai's nose and upper lip and changed pencils to sketch a green distorted male anatomical figure over her head. "Have they no shame? My great-grandmother had a better sense of *liberté* than this excuse for a woman."

I had to nudge her twice to let her know that Mrs. Vafai had narrowed her eyes and was now looking in our direction. I sat up straight and raised my hand.

"But how do we know if *the man* is a virgin?"

The thing is, I didn't have a question in me. I had long learned, however, that questions are the best way to deflect and distract. Mrs. Vafai raised one

MERIDIANS · feminism, race, transnationalism · 23:2 October 2024
DOI: 10.1215/15366936-11266348 © 2024 Smith College

of her disproportionately tattooed eyebrows and parted her vermillion border filler-injected lips, the tip of her tongue on the verge of slithering out, but instead, she walked back to the podium and put down the red marker without capping it. The black pen in her hand went up and down the roll book. She looked up at me again before the left corners of her mouth flinched upward, and her pen dashed left and right. I felt my face thicken from the stares and whispers around me.

"Now, I get your point . . . Ms. Derakhshan, is it?" Mrs. Vafai returned to the whiteboard. "But you must understand where you live . . . it's not always about what you want. It's also about your circumstances."

"We are the circumstances! We are the ones who assign meaning to it!"

Ugh, there she goes again. That's great! Bravo, Mrs. Mary Alltalk-nocraft! That's another three hours of spiritual banter with the moral committee. Or maybe they'll ask us to sit out the semester exam since this is strike two. Should I intervene with yet another question, or maybe if I keep mum, I could come out untainted from this fecal detonation of words? This is what I find hard to believe about evolution. How did we ever relinquish the impulse to lick our wounds? And for what? To fling words at each other and do harm that cannot be undone, if ever, but by words? What wound did ever heal but by the dab of the tongue?

Gelareh's eyes stared into Mrs. Vafai's, like two colonial-knotted hazel buttons in the hoop of her short olive-green maghnaeh that she had changed into just before class. After crossing the main gate and somehow making it past the security guards, who would sometimes stop us for violating the "dress code," and before going to class, Gelareh would stand in front of the restroom mirrors and pull out two inches worth of her new pink highlights over her forehead and then a few strands from behind her ears to arrange them as sideburns poking out of her headgear. She would run to the mirrors right before every class to ensure everything was still in place for the rest of the day. I tucked all my hair at once under my headgear before setting foot out of the house. Living in this hair purgatory of showing and not-showing, of mane-being and unbeing, could whittle down one's wits and lock in one's world into a tapered game of duality. I wanted whatever was left of my mind to myself to do as I please. No, I could not become the regulator of my transgressions to serve, and free of cost too, the gamemasters. That would be a disservice to me, to bear the titles they had carefully carved: "rebel," "oppositionist," "agitator." I wanted to bake my titles and rake my own life. So, hair better fully in than half out, I had decided. For now.

"All right. Explain this to me, Ms. Montazeri," Mrs. Vafai sighed as she pulled at the fabric that encased her bulbous chin, "Suppose a nice young man asks for your hand. You are sitting there with his family and yours in the introduction session . . . would it be easy for you to tell him your past in front of everyone? And even if, say, you do have an understanding with him in private . . . what if you argue one day or he decides to leave you, you don't think word gets out? If you do not consider your reputation, imagine what shame it could bring to your family . . . to your father?"

We could hear students pouring out of the classrooms. Mrs. Vafai pursed her lips. "That's it for today! Please read the chapter on the advantages of university marriages for next week," she declared as she pulled off her licorice-black chador from the chair, and save for her nasal bone and left eye cloaked her entire face before dashing out.

"Batwoman has left the building," someone from the back announced, same as last week. And the week before that. And the week before that week. No one laughed anymore.

I went to the desk and capped the red marker.

"Look at us!" Gelareh waved her hand left and right as though brandishing an imaginary staff, "All girls! This should be the one course where boys and girls learn together."

I sank back into my seat. A few students still in the classroom gave us concerned looks as they gathered their things. I looked through the window at the boys and girls walking or sitting in groups, in twos and threes, across the campus, always mindful of the prescribed distance between them. Lately, everything had taken the morbid shape of an argument. Everyone was a whiny critic. In the classroom, in the taxi, in the shops. Everyone seemed to know how things should not be done. I wanted to talk less and understand more, or I thought I did. It was the last few weeks of the winter semester, and we only had a late afternoon class for the day. So, I convinced Gelareh to stroll with me in Laleh Park, hoping it would wash away that daybreak dirt.

Soon Noruz, the Persian New Year, would arrive with its dances and songs, knocking on everyone's door to woo them away from winter's lullaby. The slopes of Damavand were still inundated with snow. You could even see its proud peak once or twice a year on those rare smog-free holidays when three-fourths of Tehranis deserted the city for towns along the Caspian Sea. We walked through the heavier-than-usual traffic jams to the southern gates of the park. "Purchasing power be damned," my father used to say, "It's hard to kill the Iranian spirit. It's Noruz. Do you know what that means, my love? It means a new day, new beginnings. And new beginnings we shall celebrate. Come what may!"

We ambled through the park's entrance, scatting in a low voice the tune of Rammstein's "Du Hast," which I'd had on replay since we first heard it at our monthly political poetry meet. A few men in t-shirts and shorts jogged past us. As we milled about the park's main square, we came across the usual large circle of middle-aged women doing jumping jacks. A large boombox blaring an instrumental version of Kanye's "Gold Digger" was perched on the rim of the marble stone ring surrounding the water fountains. Their full-body tracksuits and the headscarves they had either tucked into their jackets or ribboned behind their heads seemed a face shield short of a Hazmat suit. It reminded me of last month's Channel 2 interview with a niqab-wearing woman who, holding a swaddled baby in her arms, claimed scientists had discovered the reason behind women's premature aging: radiation of rays from men's eyes. One woman had an orange bobble hat, and every time she wiped the sweat drops off her forehead, she stopped to tuck in her ash-blonde bangs that fell out now and then. Another wore a yellow hoodie, the drawstrings pulled tight around her face like she was in a sunflower costume that had lost its petals. A man with salt-and-pepper hair scurried by, and before he disappeared into another pathway, raised his fist and cheered, "Bravo! Bravo!" Only a few women looked up while the rest carried on unperturbed. A potbellied man in navy blue suspender pants curled his lips and angled his head toward the young lady who roofed and floored her swollen belly between her hands as she waddled beside him. "And women keep saying they have no freedom! What more do they want?"

We giggled and, holding each other's hand, paced away until we found our way behind the Cypresses and into the clearing with the rectangular wooden tables and benches, where we could sit across from each other and lay out our books and snacks. As of last month, we had agreed that we would no longer converse about the disturbing assortment of men with whom we periodically fell in and out of love. Our dialogue had suffered enough; we both conceded. Hadn't we scrutinized ad nauseam every single detail of our love interests? How they looked at us. How we looked when they looked at us. Did we give away too much too soon? At first, our menstrual cycles synced, and then gradually, our stories about the men we were interested in developed disturbingly similar patterns. We would point out these synchronicities and laugh about their absurd connections but never spoke of what was eating us.

The day we liberated our words from the tyranny of amor's verbosity cannot be marked on the calendar, but I believe it was after one of our meetings at the Rhino Café. It was one of those hipster places where nobody goes for an Americano or crème brûlée, but to engage in people watching, taste in vignettes the latest trends of *les arts*, and most importantly, pursue new lovers. The owner was a budding theatre director who staged a domesticated version of Ionesco's *Rhinocéros* for the first time in the country. He mandated that all spectators wear a rhino costume that was handed to them at the door. It created a media craze in the capital. Six months later, he opened the café on ValiAsr Avenue and, a year later, a Rhino Supermarket. It was a small up-and-coming joint modeled after early twentieth-century French cafés with vintage Polish chairs carved out of beech and walnut wood from Tabriz. The owner could neither convince nor bribe the city council to permit the chairs to face the street. Instead, he laid out the furniture so that, except for a few blind spots, you could see all the patrons at once regardless of where you sat in the café. At the center of every table was a small plastic rhino head with "*I'm just as good as you are* . . . " printed in white calligraphy on its grey horn. In the beginning, the one-page penny university menu was easy on the pocket, but as the cafe's reputation as a nexus for the world of eggheads and highbrow glitterati soared, so did the prices. Here, people could order a cup of coffee and jaw for hours, pretend to read a book, or write one as they longed for their next hunt or waited to be ensnared. Cliques, friendships, and coteries formed over coffee and fume. And so did the circle of "bitter bobs" who boycotted the café in defense of artistic integrity (because at the end of the day, they contended, do you count words or coins? Low-hanging fruit could break your neck. Remember Tantalus?) and were socially shunned by those who didn't, particularly after the *salonnier* added a new item to the menu, *Not a Dicky Bird (15 mins max): 10,000 tomans.*

How dare you declare the place insufferable? Men with high ponytails, buns, and, ah, that meticulously planned, effortless look! Men in Panama hats, blonde and blue highlighted goatees, Chekov and Turgenev beards, and Dali, Trotsky, and Gorky mustaches brooding over books they had probably perused for café repartee. Women with bob cuts, red, blue, and green highlighted fringes sticking out of their headscarves. Women in large-brimmed bohos, and backward baseball caps that they would flip with the headscarves around their necks the second someone suspicious walked in. The in-betweeners with shaved heads, buzz cuts, pixies, wedge cuts, eyebrow piercings, and cargo pants, all dressed down to ragamuffins and up to the nines, leafing through books and eyeing each other in between long and slow sips from their cups, rolling and lighting cigarettes amid egg-cracking laughter. The now-and-then casual glance. The deliberate look-away. The trading of the glimpse before the return of the glance. Rinse and repeat. The stink of perpetual vapor floating to Edith Piaf, Matt Monro, Banan, and Delkash from the gramophone in the face of the signs on the wall: "Women smoking is strictly prohibited in this café" and "We apologize we are unable to serve ladies with improper hijab."

For two months since the opening of Rhino, we would head there straight from the university almost every other day. I must have drunk half a month's worth of rent money in coffee and puffed out the rest in cigarettes, one of those dolorimetric estimates that you can reflect on only years later when you have mastered the art of surrogating "the order of events" with the "why-ness" of them, when it finally dawns on you that maybe, just maybe crying over spilt milk is the one true pacifier after all. At first, I was intrigued by the idea of coffee with a side of literary flirtations that did not have to escalate into anything else. By the end of the second week, I had yawned out all I had, and that's when someone who couldn't care less for clever comebacks caught my eye.

He had a messy pineapple ponytail, the most pretty bloody perfect day-old Gordon Comstock stubble, a pretty bloody tiny Marx monocle hung around his neck, and a son overseas that he referred to as the "residue" of a torrid and brief marriage to a Greek woman. While others sat around the table sweating quotes and aphorisms, he stretched out his legs with a look of perpetual content, as though he were in a massaging recliner puffing on his slender cigarette holder, and uttering "please" and "thank you" through his teeth to the waiters or nodding in agreement to ongoing conversations.

In hindsight, letting his subpar coquetry skills slide was a mistake as I soon learned that the stillness he sported came at the labor of those who interacted with him. The silence that engulfed him could make just about anyone seem like a garrulous duck, at the rate of one word per minute. Left with no other recourse, I borrowed books from him that I had already read. The third time I went to his house to return the books and nothing happened, I was baffled.

"I don't understand it either . . . ," Gelareh consoled me, "Sanaz would know."

Sanaz was a senior in French literature and seasoned in the art of sex sans courtship. A few days later, we sat on the asphalt behind the university's main building, our secret spot, smoking and eating tangerines, while Gelareh kept an eye out for the security guards and the campus morality force.

"How old is he?" Sanaz asked as she rolled her second cigarette for the day.

"Late thirties . . . I think."

She nodded. "I know you said he doesn't look like one . . . but it takes longer with older guys. You should give it some time."

I did not wait around to find out.

"For some reason, I can't maintain a one-sided attraction for very long," I confessed to Gelareh on one of our walks. "I need to know that I'm desired."

"But why abandon Rhino?" she asked, trying to cloak the plea in her voice. I shook my head and gingerly removed my hand from hers, which only resulted in her tugging at my manteau sleeve. "Oh, come on! The entirety of this life is a one-sided love!"

Not that I wished to keep things under wraps, but for reasons still unknown to myself, I could not tell Gelareh why I had grown out of going to Rhino. Just how many threads of meaning can one salvage through the maze of run-of-the-mill conversations and garden-variety conquests?

○ ○ ○

That late February morning in the park, we had just left the benches and were lying on the grass next to each other under the immersive silence of the weeping willows, sharing a carpel from a large blood orange and laughing at something one of us had just said when I heard a twig snap. We were in our usual hideout, a sequestered area hedged by long boxwood shrubs that twenty-something canoodling couples and drug addicts frequented, immune to the prying eyes of the morality police who patrolled the park on their motorbikes at random hours. I sat up startled, folding my knees to my chest, and turned my head to see a pair of black oxford shoes approaching, hands in pockets before a slick grey-bearded smile towered over us. That was as far as I could see, the sun being in my eye. For once, I wished Gelareh would just cover up her hair. What in the world possessed me to wear this rather short red manteau today? I imagined my mother receiving the call to go down to the police station to bring me a chador and the sermon I would have to endure on the drive back home.

"Babes, fancy a little chat?" the smile splintered in different directions. Ah, okay. So, he's just a dick with a line. What next?

"Fuck off!" Gelareh groaned, laying there without shooting so much as a glance at him while I turned my head away, clenching my teeth.

"Aw, don't be a pisser now . . . God's pleasant day!"

"It was!" Gelareh's brow furrowed as she got up, dusted herself, and gathered her books. She must have seen my hands tremble.

"Uni bitches! Where do you think you're headed, eh? Sleeping under a man and washing baby bottoms. Who do the fuck you think you are, eh?" We could still hear him yelling after us as we scampered through an opening in the shrubs and ran until we reached the safety of the main footpaths. We stopped to catch our breath as soon as we saw the first group of people, some elderly chess players and a peddler who was serving them saffron-coated sugar sticks and hot tea in paper cups from the large flasks he carried over his shoulders. We walked for a while without saying a word. What could we say or do that would unburden us from the weight of the moment that was no longer there?

I slowed down as I tried to suppress what seemed like another coughing bout when a looming darkness abruptly flickered before my eyes, forcing me to a standstill. For a moment, I thought I was blacking out. When I looked up again, there it was, some ten to twelve feet away, a wavering throng of blackness on a forlorn tree as though it were ablaze with the densest darkness in the middle of the day. As if two hundred and thirty spotless starlings hanging from its every branch suddenly decided to swing in the direction of the wind choreographically, or was it three hundred ravens who, negotiating the dearth of space, hung upside down, aggressively flapping their wings to ward off newcomers after each perching?

"What . . . what is that?" Gelareh muttered by my side.

I quickened my pace and did not look back to check on her until I found myself standing beneath the lofty Persian Oak. As I neared, the dark legion of moving grove dissolved into a quivering of long black leaves, a bewitched tree that had come to life right off the labyrinthine pages of *Samak-e Ayyar*—where female guerrilla warriors often swore, "Though a woman, I am in the battlefield a thousand men"—gracefully biding its time for a hero or heroine to blow away the spell so it could churn into yet another element that would perpetuate the story.

When I was finally under her, long narrow pieces of evenly spaced plastic strips stringed to every branch that had no foliage fluttered above my eyes. I stood on my toes, held the ends of a few between my fingers, and noticed the tiny intricate knots that had made this stuporous assemblage possible. For a while, we both stood there in silence, overstretching our necks, touching, and slightly tugging at the strips. This garbage bag-streaked tree had made even a chatterbox like Gelareh shut up shop, a miracle as far as wish-granting trees go.

I looked around. We were once again off the main footpath and in the middle of one of the most expansive lawns of the park with no visible desire paths in sight. A man in a teal-green uniform was walking away from the lawn. I raised my hand, and he turned his empty wheelbarrow toward us.

"Excuse me, sir?" I asked, looking at the blue municipality logo on his shirt pocket, "Why is this tree covered in . . . what are these black ribbons?"

"Ah, this one," he replied, baring his upper silver-capped fangs, "this one did not bloom last year."

I waited for him to explain, but he started taking things out of his pockets and queued them up on his left hand: a few coins, some crumpled receipts, a long piece of floss thread, and a lighter.

"So, why does it have . . . these garbage bag strips?" I persisted, trying not to look at the yellow floss strand.

"Ah! See, we tie them to encourage the spirit of the tree."

"The spirit?"

"Maybe it can grow its own leaves this year."

I wanted to know how they had managed to tie so many strips to the highest branches but refrained when I saw his hungry metallic smirk.

"You look like puffing girls," he said as he sized me up. "Can I bum one?"

He turned to Gelareh, who instantly held out a pack before him. He patted his hand on his pants as if to dry it from the spittle on the floss and looked to the left and right before fishing out three cigarettes.

"Good girls," he crooned as he picked up his wheelbarrow. "Yep, such good girls you are!" and walked away after giving us the two-finger salute.

Gelareh knuckled the trunk that seemed to have sloughed off most of its brittle bark. "You think it's fair to . . . you think she'll be tricked into hope?"

"It's getting late," I pleaded, "Should we head back?"

○ ○ ○

Professor Almasi was already in session by the time we returned to campus.
That his classes were a literary rehab for the wounded and stray, those
depleted and repelled by the conspicuous complacency of other professors,
was an open secret. Unlike others, he refused to merely stand in front of the
class to deliver soliloquies. He would often sit among us, which he
admitted was, more often than not, absurd and a pain in the neck (nothing
Kafkaesque about it, he deliberated, though it's hard to tell what we're
missing without a beetle-strong peripheral vision), given that all the chairs
were welded together and screwed into the floor to face the whiteboard.
Almasi was the first teacher to assert there is no such thing as a trivial
question, only tired takes. In his spare time, he voluntarily taught a select
few of us the comparative study of Rumi's *Masnavi* and the Quran. You
could probably cut out a cantaloupe with the pointed iron-set crease in his
pants, and much like J. Alfred Prufrock, he concealed the frugal economy of
hair on his dome-shaped head by parting it behind. "You can talk about
anything in my class . . . anything really. Futsal, your mouse pad, or even
toilets, as long as . . . " he told us on the first day as we watched out for the
descending intonation that he had so eagerly made us anticipate, "as long
as you can relate it to literature." I knew he would not last long.

"So, before you two came in, we were reading this section from Sanai's
The Garden of Truth," Almasi said as he handed us a copy before he sat down
in the third row between two male students. Then he asked someone to
take it from the top.

> *Your place in the Abode of Vanity's allure*
> *Is the Ice Seller's likeness in Neyshapur*
> *He set up his pile of ice trade in July*
> *Not a coin in his pocket, none came to buy*

"Sanai adapts the account of a dervish in Neyshapur who is said to have
walked around the city begging for alms every morning," he explained,
glancing at the students to his right before he rotated his neck to the left,
"He would then buy ice with the money he had scoured in the hope of selling it to the denizens of Neyshapur who wouldn't buy any from him. So,
he was left with nothing but melted ice by evening. Come morning, he did
the same thing again and again and again. All right," he beamed, turning
his torso to face the students in the back and slapping the tablet arm of his

chair, "Let's dig into the symbolism at work here and just get that out of the way, shall we?"

"Isn't it obvious? Ice represents the transience of the materialistic world," Azizi, a Basiji-bearded guy in a buttoned-up white shirt who always sat by the window in the second row, replied, "How the charms of our materialistic approach to life make us vain and how instead we should make worthwhile investments that will help us prepare for the other world . . . this is what the poet advises."

There was a moment of silence before a female student in the last row gasped, and we all turned toward her. "Um, the ice imagery reminded me of Dante's *Inferno*?" she faltered for a few seconds, "Like how Satan is punished like by being frozen at the bottom pit of like hell? I don't know . . . but like I thought it was like interesting that like hell is freezing in Dante's account, which is not like the image of hell we are like used to? . . . and like here you have the ice as like a symbol too? It's . . . "

"The idea of hell as a frozen place existed long before Dante," Mohseni, another male student who sat next to Azizi in the second row, the Brethren Corner, scoffed. "It's in the scriptures. You'd know if you'd read them."

"Thank you all," Almasi said, uncrossing his legs and shifting in his chair before he looked in our direction, which made my stomach summersault. "Anyone else cares to share a different viewpoint? Ms. Montazeri, I see by your facial expressions you disapprove?"

"I don't understand these dichotomies that Mr. Azizi refers to," I heard Gelareh saying with a hint of scorn in her voice that I only hoped Azizi was not shrewd enough to detect, "Heaven! Hell! This world! That world! . . . I mean, what does materialistic even mean? Isn't the right to food and shelter . . . "

"What commie claptrap!" Azizi fidgeted in his chair at the opposite end of the classroom without looking in our direction, "You don't understand the concept of this world and that world? The Great Hereafter? The entire scriptures are based on this premise," Azizi concluded as he raised his voice. We were always wary when he and his sidekicks didn't make a sound and were ill at ease when they did.

"Well, I'm glad . . . " Almasi interjected, "Glad we have different opinions in this class and the maturity to share our discomforts. Why else would we read literature? Ms. Montazeri, what makes you uncomfortable with this poem?"

"I think the ice seller is a screwed-up version of Sisyphus."

"Ah. That's a good start for a comparative approach," Almasi nodded. "What do you suppose our next question should be?"

"The question I would ask is the question I have been asking myself lately. What is a worse metaphor, ice or stone? The ice is a block of nonsense that disappears. The stone is somewhat eternal," Gelareh drawled in a distant voice, "Between nonsense that melts and one that remains, I prefer the latter. At least it's . . . it's consistent and dependable in its drivel."

"It is not drivel! Too many martyrs . . . too many great honorable men have dedicated their lives . . . their sweat, and blood so that you know . . . so we know . . . and there is the Truth," Azizi's face turned into the color of an eggplant as he kept his eyes on the mosaic tiles. "How can you . . . you deny the existence of the Truth?"

"A lie gets halfway around the world before the truth has a chance to get its pants on," this was Mahshid, the goddess of axioms, the deity of platitudes. She had one up her sleeve for every occasion.

"Ever wonder what the truth was busy doing that it had no pants on?" Gelareh leaned further back into her chair, looking pleased with herself.

"Defecating! Sunbathing! Coupling!" someone cried from the back, and the room erupted into one laughing face. We could be this carefree only in Almasi's class.

"Are you suggesting that truth, by definition, should not make us hesitate or linger?" Almasi asked as he walked back to the whiteboard.

"Well . . . " Gelareh said, sitting up again, "I guess I'm saying maybe there is no such thing as the Truth and . . . and it's vanity that makes us think there is."

"That's because Western philosophy has clouded your judgment!" Azizi looked up to Almasi, who followed our words with his eyes like a ball boy following a tennis match. "God's Truth is always alert and prepared. It can never be without pants!" he seethed, shaking his right hand at Almasi.

"So, what are you going to say next? That pants are Western? Is that what you are going to say?"

"Why? So you can then ask me why wear them if I think they are? FYI, they're not!" Azizi snapped while he continued to keep his eyes on Almasi, like Cassio imploring Desdemona to intercede and erase that polite distance.

Before Gelareh could open her mouth, Almasi raised his hand. "We can study the fascinating genealogy of pants later . . . what I want you to take away from this discussion is the diversity of approaches to reading a classical text from a contemporary perspective . . . for the semester assignment, those interested can also hand in a short essay on a comparative study of Camus's *Sisyphus* and Sanai's Ice Seller."

On our way out, we passed by Azizi, who was moseying down the hallway with two other guys. As soon as we were behind them, Gelerah quickly pulled a long tress from under her headgear. As she neared him, she flicked back her hair in Azizi's face, who walked away without batting an eye. A warm cloud of aromata flared up in my face that by now I knew to be a layered ritualized concoction of her strawberry-chocolate shampoo, vanilla-honey conditioner, lemon-ambergris hair perfume followed by a few spritzes of musk, then towel-dried by a cloth wrapped overnight around a wet sandalwood stick and styled with carrot-cake-banana-bread hair cream.

"I've got to go home. Got a headache," was all I managed to say before I sneezed into my palms.

∘ ∘ ∘

Once off the main street to campus, I flipped my black maghnaeh for a cobalt blue shawl I carried in my bag and felt my cold fingertips go down my throat. Parting is such sweet sorrow. Free from the tight grip of the fabric that had pushed against it all day, my neck skin now found room to itch and burn. In the shared taxi, the radio regurgitated the news.

"The US House of Representatives has passed a new bill of sanctions against Iran today. We are joined by the celebrated economist Professor Yasamin Nazarian from Tehran University, who is here to tell us about the impact of these sanctions on oil export and the current economy's . . . "

The driver spluttered some profane words that were lost in the intermittent honking of the sea of cars that surrounded us and turned off the radio. Black smoke sputtered from the exhaust of an idling BRT to my right. I quickly rolled up the window as I and the other passengers started coughing. The refined-gasoline shortage, the import of second-hand buses from East Europe that were decades beyond their useful life, and a pollution-choked Tehran were some of the perks of the sanctions.

"Bastards!" the man sitting behind me snarled between coughs. I searched for his mouth in the sideview mirror but looked down when he returned my gaze. Good thing I could snatch the less-eventful front seat today.

"God damn them!" the driver chimed in.

"What can one say?" the man flanked by the other two passengers, ruminated. "What kind of a life they've made for people, so close to Noruz? Still, I thank God I have my health," he said as I heard him sigh and slap his thigh.

"God forbid you're a father and embarrassed to go home empty-handed. It's never been like this," the driver said, shaking his head.

That cued the old man behind the driver to reminisce. "When we were kids, we couldn't wait for Noruz to come. This was Shah Reza Street, and that was Mojassameh Square," he said as he stretched out his hand past the driver's face to point out the locations. "All I ever wanted to do with my Noruz money was to buy striped candy from a shop that used to be there." I dodged toward the window as his hand went past my face this time.

"It's still Shah Reza Street to me. It'll always be," I heard the guy in the middle slap his thigh again.

"Could have saved us decades of misery if he'd opened fire on these fools. But he just wasn't man enough," the driver said, rolling down the window and lighting up a cigarette.

"He was a kind soul. Left because he didn't want to massacre his people!" the man behind me retorted.

The driver blew a raspberry. "Even his father knew that he didn't have it in him. Regretted that Ashraf was a daughter and not a son . . . one look from his eyes, a twist of his mustache, and all the crooked and corrupted shit their pants. That was the Great Reza Khan for you."

"His son did a lot of good, too. What a forgetful and ungrateful nation we are! He modernized Iran too quickly . . . now, that was his mistake," the man behind me said. "We were progressing rapidly, but the cross-eyed British and the CIA just wouldn't have it . . . Sir, you forgot about the Coup?" The two men next to him concurred with grunts.

The traffic hadn't budged much for the last seven minutes. "How much do I owe you?" I asked before the driver could respond to the man, ready to whisk out the notes I had placed in the outer compartment of my wallet.

"It is not worth your trouble, Miss," the driver said as he turned toward me. "8,000 tomans."

"8,000 tomans?! I always pay 6,000."

"That was last week's rate. A medium can of tomato paste was 9,000 tomans last month," he lifted his forefinger as he machine-gunned the prices at me. "Now it is 12,000 tomans. Half a dozen eggs were 3,000 tomans three weeks ago. Now it's 6,000. Don't you live here, Miss?" he grumbled as I gave him a ten-thousand note and got down at the Revolution Square, where a new message on the huge billboard in red calligraphy against the backdrop of the flag was the first thing I saw: *An Iran for All Iranians.*

From Revolution Avenue toward Dec7–1953 Street, I walked past the small cafés, liver Kabab, Falafel, and Aush eateries, the long line of bookstores that stretched to the ValiAsr intersection, forty-percent-off boutiques, stationery, and Anything10000Tomans shops. A young woman in a knitted pink manteau, white headscarf, and black woolen trapper hat sat on a flattened cardboard box playing "Nothing Else Matters" on the santoor as pedestrians, who mostly wore masks to protect themselves from the air pollution, threw money in the wooden case before her. Hawkers had spread piles of used uncensored books published before the Revolution and offset editions of books published abroad by writers who had fled the country. When I reached the Book Mall, I saw the two men glued to their everyday spots holding up the usual signs: "Master's and PhD Theses, ISI Articles, University Projects at a reasonable rate. Office Upstairs." I passed the second man who yelled at me in a singsong tone, "Thesis? Articles? Papers? Upstairs! Upstairs!" with the same swiftness that his forebearers had hissed, "Foreign Music? Porn? DVD? CD?" at me a decade ago.

As I turned into Apr1–1979 Street, a longer walk home, I put on my headphones to listen to *Tazkerat al-Awliya*, my new favorite audiobook interspersed with tanbur capriccios.

And he buried all the seven bookcases of the Hadith in the ground and did not speak a word of them. "The reason I do not speak," he explained, "is that I perceive in myself a lust to do so. If I perceive in my heart a lust to keep silent, then I shall speak.

I was about to replay that part when I saw a matronly woman in a green headscarf and black manteau who had her back to the wall of a narrow lane wave at me. A young boy stood by her side, who couldn't have been over ten years old. They looked like they were on a stakeout that they knew would end badly. I took off my headphones and threw my chin up to indicate a response.

"Excuse me, Miss?" she half-whispered without stepping forward. "Please come here for a minute?"

She didn't look like one of those people who asked for money by holding up their medical bills to pedestrians. I hesitated for a bit before going into the lane.

"Be a dear and go to this shop," she pointed toward the main street behind her and unfolded a 10,000 toman note from her other hand, "and buy me three packs of sanitary napkins, please?"

Seeing my face, she explained, "He won't sell me . . . the shopkeeper."

"What? Why?"

"I asked him for seven packs," she said, pointing at the black plastic bag in the boy's hand, "and he sold me only four. Just refused to give me more."

"Why don't you just buy the rest from that shop across the street?" I asked, looking at the boy who followed our conversation with his eyes.

"These are the cheapest ones. They're only 3,000 tomans," she sighed. "And he is the only one selling them at a price I can afford. I'm buying them for my granddaughters; God bless them . . . got four in the house."

I took the note from the woman and heard her thank me as I marched into the shop without a greeting and put my hand on the glass counter, "Three packs of sanitary napkins, please."

"Why do you need three packs?" The middle-aged man behind the counter asked, scratching his balbo beard. "I can sell you only two."

"How dare you ask me how many packs I need? Do I have to explain simple female physiology to you?" I snapped, a little shaken by how militant I sounded.

The shopkeeper bit his lips. "I'm . . . I'm so sorry, Miss. Didn't mean to offend. I've daughters at home. Sisters too."

"Then you do know that sometimes a woman needs more than one pack during her cycle?" I heard myself demand. The lady doth protest too, too much.

"I certainly do," he bit his lips again and lowered his gaze.

"Then . . . why?"

"Look here," he pointed with his head, "there are no more goods!"

My heart sank as I saw the barren shelves behind him. I had read in the news that people were hoarding bulk diapers and sanitary napkins because of the sudden jump in the prices due to biting hyperinflation and a shortage of raw materials, another outcome of the renewed back-breaking sanctions and the state's financial mismanagement. To bleed or not to bleed. That is the question.

"Since this morning, at least fifty people have come in for sanitary napkins. The uptowners come here because they know it's a steal. They all want boxes of 100, 60, 30," he said, lifting his forefinger in the air, "I refuse to sell that many, and I refuse to raise the prices. I sell a few, but I want to sell to everyone."

He then stuffed two packs in a black plastic bag.

"I didn't know that," I heard myself stutter as my eyes burned.

"I have been in this neighborhood for forty years. Even during the War, people didn't have these kinds of problems . . . May God strike them down!"

I heard my voice soften. "Look, these are not even for me . . . they are for the woman who just came in, and you refused to sell. I hope it's okay. She has four granddaughters at home . . . you know how it is."

"It's okay. I don't mind. But how do we know she has four grand-daughters?"

Seeing my puzzled look, he nodded. "See? This is how it is. We start mistrusting each other . . . Go in peace, daughter. I wish you well, like a father . . . May God strike them down!" he said, looking to the ceiling.

The woman and the boy now stood a few feet from the shop's entrance.

"I'm sorry. He only sold me two," I said as I handed her the black plastic bag and the remainder of the cash and walked away before she could thank me.

I gulped down the ball of fire in my throat and fought back tears by keeping my eyes on the consistent disappearance and reemergence of my red sneakers till I was about to bump into two women who stood in the long queue outside the Sangak bread shop. I felt a breathy string of apologetic words come tumbling out of my lips. The meaty odor of the head-and-feet soup eatery from across the street and the smell of freshly baked burnt-sugar glazed donuts converging in the air made me queasy. A chilly strip of sweat climbed down my spine as I wrapped my arms around myself.

A few feet ahead, a young man held up a cat-sized sewer rat he had just whisked off from the now-dry garbage-strewn concrete water channels that flanked both sides of the street.

"Yup, it's a man all right," he announced. "Just look at those balls!"

At this, the group of young men reclining on their motorcycles roared with laughter. I crossed the street to avoid them and with mine eyes looking right on, with mine eyelids looking straight before me I hurried past the fruit and vegetable vendor just before the lane to our house, knowing that his son would be on the lookout to ogle me again.

When I reached my room, I made a ball out of my shawl and hurled it into a corner. From my backpack, I took out a small twig that forked into three small branches, each breaching into two or three prongs with at least ten black plastic strips knotted to them. I carefully put the twig on my pillow and turned up the heater. I stripped off all my clothes, laid down my body on the bed, and pulled up the quilt over myself and her. I caressed her cold, unyielding wood with my fingertips. The branches curled upward like raised hands that had once upon a time gestured "why" only to be frozen mid-air, as though they had never bloomed and lost, as if they were born with rigor mortis.

A new message from a social media channel I followed popped up on my phone.

"Did ancient Iranian women cover their hair? Don't be fooled. The chador is not originally Iranian. The myth was popularized by the reg . . . "

I turned off my phone, held on to the black strips between my fingers, and closed my eyes.

....

Maryam Ala Amjadi is an Iranian writer, translator, researcher, and a City of Asylum fellow at the Black Mountain Institute (UNLV). She is the author of two poetry collections and a poetry chapbook, and the translator of a selection of Raymond Carver's poems into Persian. Ala Amjadi holds a joint PhD in interdisciplinary literary studies as an Erasmus Mundus fellow from Kent (UK) and Porto (Portugal) universities. She was previously a writer for the *Tehran Times Daily* and a writer-in-residence at the International Writing Program at the University of Iowa. Ala Amjadi's poems and translations of contemporary Iranian poets have been published and anthologized internationally. Her poetry has been translated into multiple languages, including Italian, Spanish, Hindi, and Chinese. Her latest poetry collection, *Where Is the Mouth of That Word? (Selected Poems)* was published in November 2022 by Poetrywala.

La Vaughn Belle

For Those of Us Who Live at the Shoreline

Taking the first line of Audre Lorde's poem, "A Litany for Survival," this work explores the relationship between the body, landscape, history, and memory. The topography is constructed by blending plant species that grow specifically at the coastline and function to both hold in and feed the soil. Species such as sea purslane, sea grape, manchineel, and mangroves are the keepers of boundary, constructing a kind of living archive as the root systems hold in the erosion of memory and time. They also protect, filter, and some even poison as they are a part of dynamic marginal ecosystems. For those of us who live at the shoreline, at the liminal spaces between subject and citizen, our survival is based on the crucial decisions of what we remain rooted in and what we know must wash away.

La Vaughn Belle makes visible the unremembered. Through exploring the material culture of coloniality Belle creates narratives from fragments and silences. Working in a variety of disciplines, her practice includes painting, installation, photography, writing, video, and public interventions. Her work with colonial-era pottery led to a commission with the renowned brand of porcelain products, the Royal Copenhagen. She has exhibited her work in the Caribbean, the US, and Europe in institutions such as the Museo del Barrio (New York), Casa de las Americas (Cuba), the Museum of the African Diaspora (California), and Kunsthal Charlottenborg (Denmark), with large solo exhibitions at the Halsey Institute of Contemporary Art (South Carolina) and the National Nordic Museum (Washington State). Her art is in the collections of the National Photography Museum and the Vestsjælland Museum in Denmark and the National Gallery of Art and the Virgina Fine Art Museum in the US. She is the

MERIDIANS · feminism, race, transnationalism   23:2 October 2024
DOI: 10.1215/15366936-11534698 © 2024 Smith College

cocreator of I Am Queen Mary, the artist-led groundbreaking monument that confronted the Danish colonial amnesia while commemorating the legacies of resistance of the African people who were brought to the former Danish West Indies. The project was featured in over one hundred media outlets around the world including the *New York Times*, *Politiken*, VICE, the BBC, and *Le monde*. Her work has also been written about in *Hyperallergic*, *Artforum*, *Small Axe*, and numerous other journals and books.

Belle holds an MFA from the Instituto Superior de Arte in Havana, Cuba, and an MA and BA from Columbia University in New York City. She was a finalist for the She Built NYC project to develop a monument to memorialize the legacy of Shirley Chisholm, and for the Inequality in Bronze project in Philadelphia to redesign one of the first monuments to an enslaved woman at the Stenton historic house museum. As a 2018–20 fellow at the Social Justice Institute at the Barnard Research Center for Women at Columbia University, she researched the citizenless Virgin Islanders in the Harlem Renaissance. She is a founding member of the Virgin Islands Studies Collective (VISCO). Her studio is based in the Virgin Islands.

Erratum for Dia Da Costa, who respectfully declined the 2024 Paula J. Gidding Award Honorable Mention. However, despite her declination, Dr. Da Costa was erroneously included in the announcement page published in *Meridians* 23, no. 1 (2024). The online version of the Paula J. Gidding awardees announcement in volume 23, no. 1 has been updated.

Erratum for Elena Ruiz, "Structural Trauma," *Meridians* 23, no. 1 (2024): 29–50. Due to a publisher error, proof corrections to this article missed the duplicated sentence on page 34: "Today, while trauma can be used to refer equally well to physical or mental injury, accounts of trauma's cause, duration, and function diverge." The online version of this article has been updated.

https://doi.org/10.1215/15366936-10926944

MERIDIANS · feminism, race, transnationalism   23:2 October 2024
DOI: 10.1215/15366936-11614745 © 2024 Smith College

TULSA STUDIES IN WOMEN'S LITERATURE

FALL 2024, VOL. 43, NO. 2

@TSWLJOURNAL   //   UTULSA.EDU/TSWL // LIKE US ON FACEBOOK

Keep up to date on new scholarship

Issue alerts are a great way to stay current on all the cutting-edge scholarship from your favorite Duke University Press journals. This free service delivers tables of contents directly to your inbox, informing you of the latest groundbreaking work as soon as it is published.

To sign up for issue alerts:

1. Visit **dukeu.press/register** and register for an account. You do not need to provide a customer number.

2. After registering, visit **dukeu.press/alerts**.

3. Go to "Latest Issue Alerts" and click on "Add Alerts."

4. Select as many publications as you would like from the pop-up window and click "Add Alerts."